Nietzsche's *Unfashionable Observations*

Edinburgh Critical Guides to Nietzsche
Series editors: Keith Ansell-Pearson and Daniel Conway

Guides you through the writings of Friedrich Nietzsche (1844–1900), one of modernity's most independent, original and seminal minds

The Edinburgh Critical Guides to Nietzsche series brings Nietzsche's writings to life for students, teachers and scholars alike, with each text benefitting from its own dedicated book. Every guide features new research and reflects the most recent developments in Nietzsche scholarship. The authors unlock each work's intricate structure, explore its specific mode of presentation and explain its seminal importance. Whether you are working in contemporary philosophy, political theory, religious studies, psychology, psychoanalysis or literary theory, these guides will help you to fully appreciate Nietzsche's enduring significance for contemporary thought.

Books in the series

Nietzsche's *Unfashionable Observations*

A Critical Introduction and Guide

Jeffrey Church

EDINBURGH
University Press

Edinburgh University Press is one of the leading university presses in the UK. We publish academic books and journals in our selected subject areas across the humanities and social sciences, combining cutting-edge scholarship with high editorial and production values to produce academic works of lasting importance. For more information visit our website: edinburghuniversitypress.com

Edinburgh University Press Ltd
The Tun – Holyrood Road
12(2f) Jackson's Entry
Edinburgh EH8 8PJ

Typeset in 11/13 Bembo by
IDSUK (DataConnection) Ltd, and
printed and bound in Great Britain.

A CIP record for this book is available from the British Library

ISBN 978 1 4744 2827 9 (hardback)
ISBN 978 1 4744 2829 3 (webready PDF)
ISBN 978 1 4744 2828 6 (paperback)
ISBN 978 1 4744 2830 9 (epub)

Contents

For Catherine and Michael,
who taught me the art of close reading

Chronology

1844	Nietzsche is born on 15 October in the small village of Röcken in the Prussian province of Saxony, the son and grandson of Protestant clergymen.
1849	Nietzsche's father dies.
1858–64	He attends the Gymnasium Schlpforta, one of the most famous boarding schools in Germany.
1864	Begins study at the University of Bonn in theology and classical philology.
1865	Transfers to Leipzig University, following his philology professor F. W. Ritschl. He first reads Schopenhauer's *The World as Will and Representation*.
1866	First reads Lange's *History of Materialism*.
1868	Meets Richard Wagner for the first time.
1869	With the support of Ritschl, Nietzsche appointed Extraordinary Professor of Classical Philology at the University of Basel without yet earning his doctorate. Begins frequent visits to the Wagners at Tribschen, on Lake Lucerne.
1870	Volunteers as a medical orderly in the Franco-Prussian War, but contracts severe illnesses and returns to Basel within two months.
1872	Publishes his first book, *The Birth of Tragedy Out of the Spirit of Music*, which is sharply criticised by other philologists.

1873–74   Publishes the first three *Unfashionable Observations*, which mark Nietzsche's increased movement away from his philological training. Relationship with Wagner begins to sour.

1876   Publication of the final *Observation*, 'Richard Wagner in Bayreuth', timed to coincide with the Bayreuth Festival. Nietzsche attends the Festival and is disgusted by it.

1878   Volume 1 of *Human, All Too Human* appears, beginning what scholars consider to be Nietzsche's middle period, influenced by Voltaire. Friendship with Wagner ends.

1879   Publishes volume 2, part 1 of *Human, All Too Human: Assorted Opinions and Maxims*. Health problems force Nietzsche to resign from Basel (with a pension), and he spends the next ten years in Swiss and Italian boarding houses.

1880   Volume 2, part 2 of *Human, All Too Human: The Wanderer and his Shadow* appears.

1881   Publication of *Dawn: Thoughts on the Presumptions of Morality*.

1882   Publishes *The Gay Science*, books 1–4. In April travels to Rome, meets Lou Salomé, and proposes marriage to her. She declines and the relationship ends badly.

1883   Writes and publishes the first and second parts of *Thus Spoke Zarathustra: A Book for All and None*. Wagner dies.

1884   Completion of third part of *Zarathustra*. Breaks with his sister Elizabeth over her fiancé's anti-Semitism.

1885   Final part of *Zarathustra* circulated privately.

1886   Publishes *Beyond Good and Evil: Prelude to a Philosophy of the Future*. New publisher reissues *Birth of Tragedy* and *Human, All Too Human*, with new prefaces by Nietzsche.

1887   Publishes *On the Genealogy of Morality: A Polemic*. Also reissues *Daybreak* and publishes expanded edition of *The Gay Science*.

1888   Publishes *The Case of Wagner* and writes his final four short books: *Twilight of the Idols*, *The Antichrist*, *Ecce Homo* and *Nietzsche contra Wagner*.

1889   Suffers a physical and mental collapse in Turin and never recovers. After being briefly institutionalised, he spends the remaining years of his life in his mother's and sister's care.

1894   Elizabeth founds the Nietzsche Archive, which is eventually moved to Weimar.

1900   Dies on 25 August in Weimar.

Abbreviations

Kant
CJ   *Critique of Judgment*, Kant 2000
I   'Idea for a Universal History with a Cosmopolitan
            Aim', in Kant 2007
WIE   'What is Enlightenment?', in Kant 1996

Nietzsche
BGE   *Beyond Good and Evil*, Nietzsche 2002
BT   *The Birth of Tragedy*, Nietzsche 1999a
EH   *Ecce Homo*, in Nietzsche 2005
GM   *On the Genealogy of Morality*, Nietzsche 1994
HAH2   Unpublished fragments from *Human All Too Human II*,
            in Nietzsche 2013
KGB   *Sämtliche Briefe*, Nietzsche 1986
KSA   *Kritische Studienausgabe*, Nietzsche 1999b
PPP   *The Pre-Platonic Philosophers*, Nietzsche 2001a
TL   'On Truth and Lies in an Extra-Moral Sense', in
            Nietzsche 2009
UW   *Unpublished Writings from the Period of Unfashionable
            Observations*, Nietzsche 1995b
WC   'We Classicists', in Nietzsche 1990
WEN   *Writings from the Early Notebooks*, Nietzsche 2009

Introduction

Unfashionable Observations was Nietzsche's second published work of philosophy, written in four 'pieces' [*Stücke*] between 1873 and 1876 as he was struggling as a university professor and as a friend to Richard Wagner. Scholars classify it as an early period work, coming after his first book, *The Birth of Tragedy*, and just before the beginning of his middle period with *Human, All Too Human*. As a work of Nietzsche's youth, it is one of his most under-studied books.[1] The essay 'On the Utility and Liability of History for Life' has received a great deal of scholarly attention, but the other essays that comprise the book have been widely neglected. Most importantly, readers have tended not to treat the book as a unified whole, neither identifying the overall argument nor detailing how the different parts execute that argument.[2] This Guide aims to rectify this neglect by discerning the unifying structure of the *Observations* and by offering a section-by-section commentary on each essay.

The *Observations'* overall argument is that modern life is dehumanising, and that we must create a new form of culture that will foster the best or most exemplary life for human beings. The argument is reflected in the book's structure, the two halves of which mirror one another. In the first, critical half of the book, Nietzsche decries the dehumanised individual in his first essay on David Strauss, and then the corrupting modern culture in the

---

[1] I discuss much of the literature on the particular essays below. The most important work on the *Observations* is Zuckert 1976, to which this book is heavily indebted.

[2] For an important exception, see Brooks 2018. In his 'Translator's Afterword', Gray enumerates several common themes that tie the essays together (1995: 410–11).

second essay on history. In the second, positive half, Nietzsche sketches a plan for a healthy, productive modern culture in his third essay on Schopenhauer, and presents an exemplary individual in his fourth essay on Wagner.[3] Or, more straightforwardly, the book moves from the dehumanised individual to the corrupt culture that gave rise to him. It then shifts to a healthy culture and then finally to an exemplary individual who could be the fruit of that community.

This early work is significant for two reasons. First, it is an important work for understanding Nietzsche's development. It introduces two positive ideals that would animate his philosophical project for the rest of his career: the exemplary individual and culture. In his major mature works, Nietzsche celebrates a variety of higher individuals: the *Übermensch* (*Thus Spoke Zarathustra*), the philosopher of the future (*Beyond Good and Evil*) and the sovereign individual (*The Genealogy of Morality*).[4] In many ways, these exemplars of humanity represent the ultimate aim of his philosophy. Accordingly, attending to their first appearance in his corpus can shed light on Nietzsche's view of human excellence. Throughout his career, Nietzsche also examines the cultural preconditions for the emergence of genius. Although he famously lauds Apollinian and Dionysian Greek culture and castigates modern culture in *The Birth of Tragedy*, the *Observations* develops a theory of culture and extends his cultural critique of modernity to its economic and political conditions. The critique of the scholar and the state in this work, for instance, remain important in Nietzsche's late reflections on the preconditions for the higher human being.

The *Observations* is significant for a second reason: it is itself an important, under-appreciated work of philosophy, particularly in its ethics. Nietzsche's ethics of the *Übermensch* is often regarded as a philosophical embarrassment.[5] It is regarded in this way because

---

[3] See Nietzsche's own gloss on the structure of the book in *Ecce Homo* – he groups the first two *Observations* as critical, while the latter two 'point to a higher concept of culture, to reestablish the concept of "culture"' (EH 'Why I Write', 'The Untimely Ones', 1).

[4] There is an ongoing scholarly debate about whether the sovereign individual is in fact a Nietzschean ideal. See, for instance, Janaway 2006; Leiter 2010; Acampora 2006.

[5] See Detwiler on its 'odious' character (1990: 5).

many readers understand it to be a form of social Darwinism. Yet the *Observations* offers a considerably more sophisticated account of the nature and justification of the exemplary human being. For Nietzsche, following Schopenhauer, natural existence is irrational and valueless. Unlike Schopenhauer and like Kant, however, Nietzsche argues that we can confer value on our existence by realising our distinctively human freedom. Unlike Kant, Nietzsche holds that the achievement of freedom comes not at the end of history, but in the peaks of human excellence. This excellence is spiritual in nature and so takes cultural form in art, religion and philosophy. Culture shapes the life of a community, giving it a meaning and purpose it otherwise lacks.

This work, then, reveals Nietzsche at his most idealistic, in contrast to the naturalism often attributed to him in the works of his later period.[6] Idealism and naturalism are complicated and contested terms in the history of philosophy, and especially so in the context of Nietzsche scholarship. By *naturalism*, Nietzsche scholars generally mean the position or belief that our biology does and should determine and guide our lives. By *idealism*, I mean to invoke the philosophical tradition inspired by Kant and followed by Schopenhauer and Lange, among others. Again, in broad strokes, this view holds that our self-determined ideals and identities should determine and guide our lives.[7] The *Observations* also highlights Nietzsche's fundamental commitment to freedom. In this early work, natural inequalities do not determine our fate and our moral status; rather, Nietzsche insists that we are able to shape our life in our own image.[8] This work uncovers the basic communal nature of his ethics: individuals do not gain value by themselves, at the expense of others, but only in concert with others for the benefit of all.[9] All these philosophical claims are to my mind quite compelling. They reveal that Nietzsche had a deeper and more complicated relationship with his philosophical

---

[6] On Nietzsche's mature period naturalism, see Emden 2014; Leiter 2013.
[7] See recent work on Nietzsche's early idealism: Havas 2000; Church 2016.
[8] A good deal of recent work on Nietzsche's view of freedom has been published. See, for instance, the essays collected in Gemes and May 2009.
[9] See recent work on Nietzsche's valuing of community, for instance Young 2006; 2014.

predecessors than previously considered. As such, they portray a Nietzsche unfamiliar to many readers, casual and scholarly alike. The aim of this book, then, is to reconstruct the overall argument of *Unfashionable Observations*. To do so, I will discuss in the remainder of this Introduction the genesis and composition of this work in the context of Nietzsche's life. In the first chapter, I will then situate the overall argument of the work in the debates of late modern philosophy, in particular comparing and contrasting Nietzsche with Kant and Schopenhauer. Chapters 2–5 then present Nietzsche's argument through an introductory section that discusses the argument as a whole, a structural overview, and then a section-by-section commentary on the essays. Chapter 6 concludes with a brief discussion of Nietzsche's own mature views of this early work.

This book is intended as a guide for students reading the *Observations*. It is most profitably read all the way through, alongside Nietzsche's text, since later essays refer back to claims in earlier essays. However, readers interested in only one essay, or even a few paragraphs of one essay, may benefit from consulting my running commentary on these portions of the text. This book also aims to contribute to Nietzsche scholarship, both on the *Observations* – in my interpretation of the whole and its parts – and on Nietzsche's early practical philosophy.

Chronology of life and work

In April 1873, when Nietzsche began work on the *Observations*, he was still lecturing at the University of Basel as a professor of philology. He maintained a close relationship with Cosima and Richard Wagner, and still saw Wagner as the last living hope for the renewal of German culture. In the previous few years he had written a number of works that departed strikingly from his philological training, works that dealt with grand philosophical and cultural themes. He had published *The Birth of Tragedy* (January 1872), held a popular lecture series *On the Future of Our Educational Institutions* (January–March 1872) and composed an unpublished essay on *Philosophy in the Tragic Age of the Greeks* (April 1873). After the classicist Ulrich von Wilamowitz-Möllendorf published his scathing review

of *The Birth of Tragedy* in 1873 – and Wagner and Nietzsche's friend
Erwin Rohde launched counter-attacks – Nietzsche delved further into philosophy and culture, penning a series of notes on the
nature and significance of the philosopher (sometimes referred to
as Nietzsche's *Philosophenbuch*).

What motivated him to write the *Observations* in particular? Nietzsche himself offers an answer in an unpublished note
from 1875, which was intended to contribute to an envisioned
introduction to a collected edition of all the 'Unfashionables'
[*Unzeitgemässen*]. The 'genesis' [*Entstehung*] of the work was due
to three causes: first, his 'desperation' at seeing Wagner's project
in Bayreuth decline into debt in 1873, after the auspicious cultural event a year before at the groundbreaking ceremony for
Wagner's opera house (KSA 8.5[98]). In the first appearances of
the *Observations* in Nietzsche's notebooks, he originally entitled
the book 'Bayreuth Horizon Observations' (KSA 7.19[303]), in
an effort to provide philosophical support for the endeavour.

Second, Nietzsche 'discovered' in his own 'deep reflections'
the 'most fundamental problem of all culture' (KSA 8.5[98]). His
lectures on educational institutions and his *Philosophenbuch* were
concerned deeply with the decline of culture in modernity, and
how to arrest or reverse this trend. In 1872 Nietzsche even went
so far as to compose a memo 'to submit as a question to the
Reichsrat', purporting to demonstrate that it had 'missed a gigan-
tic opportunity of founding an authentic German educational
establishment for the regeneration of … "culture"' (Hayman
1980: 152). The *Observations*, then, is devoted to identifying this
fundamental problem of culture – as well as a distinctive solution
to it – which we will explore in the next chapter.

Finally, Nietzsche traced the triggering cause of the work to a
conversation with Wagner in April 1873, in which Wagner com-
plained to him about David Strauss's recently published book, *The
Old Faith and the New*. Nietzsche read Strauss's book, and he began
work immediately on his first *Observation*, which was a vicious critique of the work. He completed it on 25 June 1873, a mere two
months after his conversation with Wagner, despite being nearly
blind for several weeks because of treatment with 'atropine (deadly
nightshade)' (Hayman 1980: 162).

The four essays composing the *Observations* were published separately as free-standing essays from 1873 to 1876. As a result, scholars have tended to treat the essays separately, that is, as stand-alone works. From the very inception of the project, however, Nietzsche conceived of the essays not as free-standing, but as parts of a unified whole. Each essay was published as part of a whole work that Nietzsche entitled *Unfashionable Observations*. Although, as we will see, he sketched many different plans for the series, the *Observations* were unified by their respective treatments of the thematic concerns discussed above: the notion of the exemplar and the political and cultural preconditions for its genesis. One of the main aims of this Guide is to counter the tendency of the scholarship and to disclose the overall argument that animates and structures the work's different parts. By understanding the *Observations* as a whole book, we can profitably compare its overall argument to that of *The Birth of Tragedy* before it, and the 'Free Spirit Trilogy' (*Human, All Too Human, Daybreak* and *The Gay Science*) that follows it.

The book's title in German is *Unzeitgemässe Betrachtungen*, which is difficult to translate into English, and has led to a wide variety of translations. *Unzeitgemäss* means literally *not [un] in accordance [gemäss] with the times [zeit]*. This could mean 'old-fashioned' or 'unmodern', as one translation has it. As we will see, however, Nietzsche does not aim to turn back the clock to pre-modern culture, but rather to improve the corrupt conditions of modern culture for a better future. The term has been most commonly translated as 'untimely', which renders the German with a literal English analogue. Yet the English word presupposes that there is an appropriate time that Nietzsche has failed to find. A more positive term – though less literal – is 'unfashionable', which is preferred in the Stanford University Press translation that I cite throughout this book. This translation captures Nietzsche's insistence throughout the work that he fights against the superficial fashions of the times in an effort to improve culture.[10] However, even this translation misses some of the subtlety in the German. Most importantly, *gemäss* is related to *Mass* in German, which refers to a standard or measure for evaluation.

---

[10] See Schaberg (1995: 31n) and Arrowsmith (1990: xi) for more support on this point.

The title, then, announces this dual project of the book: Nietzsche develops a standard (*Mass*) from within and against the age, but also aspires for that standard to be timeless (*unzeit*).

The word *Betrachtung* means an 'observation' or an 'examination' – that is, a concrete activity of regarding or looking closely at something. However, the word also can mean a (metaphorical) 'reconsideration' or 'reflection' or 'meditation', in the sense that we observe or examine the contents of our own minds. A popular translation has been 'meditation', which connects Nietzsche's work to that of Descartes, but, as several commentators have remarked, there is little evidence that Nietzsche intended this connection.[11] More likely, Nietzsche employed the term because of its scientific connotations, since he was steeped in reading neo-Kantian scientific treatises, beginning in the early 1870s.[12] As such, 'observations' seems the better translation.

The style of the work marks a departure from the dense Schopenhauerian philosophical prose of *The Birth of Tragedy*, and it anticipates the light, aphoristic style that Nietzsche would develop just after the *Observations*. Nietzsche's style is 'timelier' inasmuch as he adopts the traditional essay genre in an attempt to reach a broader public audience. In contrast to his works before and after, Nietzsche develops a sustained line of argument across the 40–50 pages of each essay, although with many digressions and repetitions. As others have noted, the influence of Ralph Waldo Emerson's essays is evident here.[13] The essay form allows us to discern the structure of argument in each, which I outline at the beginning of each chapter.

The first *Unfashionable Observation*, his critique of David Strauss and of the 'philistine' culture he represented, was published in August 1873. Due to its polemical broadside against contemporary writers, it received a great deal of attention and critical scrutiny, with over nineteen reviews in just a year after publication (Reich 2012: 276–412). In a letter to Wagner in September 1873, Nietzsche brags that his essay has had an 'indescribable effect',

---

[11] Gray 1995: 396; Zuckert 1976.

[12] See *Nietzsche Wörterbuch* entry on *Betrachtung* (Nietzsche Research Group 2004: esp. 294, 312f.).

[13] See Cavell 1990; Stack 1993.

and that a 'tremendously hostile literature has emerged against [him]' (Reich 2012: 311). The elderly Strauss was puzzled that a young academic would attack him so vociferously. Unrelated to Nietzsche's essay, Strauss died not long after its publication. Nietzsche reported feeling guilty, thinking he was partly responsible for Strauss's death (Young 2010: 171).

In July 1873 Nietzsche proceeded to dictate an essay that he would not bring to publication, 'On Truth and Lies in an Extra-Moral Sense'. However, the themes and concepts of this important work reappear in the *Observations* in ways that we will examine below. In the second half of 1873 Nietzsche sketched several plans for the *Observations*. Initially, and indeed through 1876, he conceived of the book as comprising twelve or thirteen essays, an ambitious project that would have required him to adhere to a 'publishing schedule of one *Observation* every six months' (Schaberg 1995: 40). The proposed topics included art, religion, science, philosophy, the university, scholars, journalists, history, the military, nationalism and language, all of which were to be discussed in the context of the corruption of modern culture and the possibilities for its renewal (Reich 2012: 311; KSA 7.19[255], 19[274], 19[330], 29[163–4], 30[38], 32[4]; KSA 8.1[3–4], 16[10]).

After composing an 'Exhortation to the German People' in the autumn of 1873, in support of Wagner's Bayreuth project, Nietzsche continued to work on the second *Observation* in November and December of that year. The essay 'On the Utility and Liability of History for Life' has been the most important of all the *Observations* for later critics, but it was received rather unfavourably by his friends, most notably the Wagners, but also Erwin Rohde (Reich 2012: 457).[14] Cosima Wagner described it as 'very unripe', criticising Nietzsche for failing to use examples and for not providing a clear structure for his discussion (Reich 2012: 458). The immediate critical reception of this essay was also quite muted, as it garnered only four reviews (Reich 2012: 458–79). The 'David Strauss' essay sold poorly – just over 500 copies out of the

---

[14] See Jensen (2016: ch. 1) for a wealth of information on the title and genesis of this work.

original 1,000 printed – but the 'History' essay fared even worse. Just over 200 copies were sold (Schaberg 1995: 205–6). The third *Observation*, 'Schopenhauer as Educator', took Nietzsche a bit longer to write than the previous two. He sent his completed draft to his new publisher in August 1874, and it appeared in print on his thirtieth birthday, 15 October 1874 (Young 2010: 195). This essay begins the positive or constructive task of the *Observations*, as Nietzsche himself 'promised' in a letter to Emma Guerrieri-Gonzaga, an admirer who was enthralled with Nietzsche's criticisms of culture but who also longed for his vision of the 'future religion' (KGB 4.370). The Wagners' reception of this essay was warmer, with Cosima writing, 'This is my Unfashionable [*Unzeitgemässe*]', in part because it reminded her of the 'Birth of Tragedy' (Reich 2012: 482). As Julian Young reports, one of the more amusing reactions to the work was an anonymous telegram that read, 'You are like the spirit that you can understand, but you are not like me. [Signed] Schopenhauer' (Young 2010: 199). Schopenhauer had died in 1860.

In the first half of 1875 Nietzsche began work on a fourth *Observation*, 'We Philologists', but abandoned it in its early stages. The notes for this essay are collected in KSA 8, notebooks 1–5. In these notes, Nietzsche continues his examination of the 'meaning of life' [*Sinne des Lebens*] and the 'vale of life' [*Wert des Lebens*]. He argues that the modern philologist 'kills off his own existence' by making himself 'wholly the product of preceding generations', and by generating labour 'exclusively with a view to posterity'. The philologist does not live for himself, but in his 'ant-like labor' he lives for others (KSA 8.3[63], WC 340). He does not have a 'calling' to exist for himself, but always for others (KSA 8.3[64], WC 341). The Greeks, by contrast, provide an alternative model of living in naïve freedom for themselves (KSA 8.3[55], WC 338), a model that is misunderstood and distorted by modern philologists. At the same time, Nietzsche does not advocate a simple return to the ancients, but sees in the universality and self-reflection of the modern age an opportunity to 'educate the great individual in a wholly different and better way than by leaving his education to chance, which has been the case until now' (KSA 8.5[11], WC 348).

The next – and ultimately last – *Observation*, 'Richard Wagner in Bayreuth', took Nietzsche the longest to compose and publish. The most important reason is that his relationship with Wagner had begun to deteriorate, beginning in 1874, when Nietzsche deigned to leave on Wagner's grand piano a copy of Brahms's *Triumphlied*, a work that Wagner detested (Young 2010: 193–4). The story of the rise and fall of their friendship has been told and retold by many scholars, and these interesting biographical details need not detain us here. Nietzsche's ambivalence to Wagner initially prevented him from publishing this essay (Hayman 1980: 185; Young 2010: 218). Although the essay continues the positive task of the *Observations*, pointing to Wagner as the hope for a renewal of culture in Germany, Nietzsche's faith in Wagner had clearly been shaken. In April 1876, just four months before the Bayreuth Festival, his new friend Heinrich Köselitz convinced him to complete the essay and publish it. Nietzsche was concerned that his ambivalence had seeped into the essay, as he 'made at least four attempts to draft the letter to the Wagners that would accompany their complimentary copies'. Nevertheless, Wagner loved the essay, exclaiming, 'Friend! Your book is terrific! – Where did you get such knowledge of me?' (Young 2010: 222).

Although Nietzsche projected twelve or thirteen *Observations*, 'Richard Wagner' would be the last to appear. He began a new essay, 'The Ploughshare', which instead became the basis for his next book, *Human, All Too Human*. In a response to his publisher's request for the next instalment, Nietzsche states, 'Shouldn't we consider the "Unfashionable Observations" finished?' (qtd Schaberg 1995: 53–4). Scholars have offered various explanations for Nietzsche's decision to abandon the project: his disillusionment with Wagner (Kaufmann 1978: 36f.); his personal sense of the failure of the Bayreuth Festival (Safranski 2002: 139); and his growing friendship with Paul Rée, who may have pushed Nietzsche away from his early concerns with Schopenhauer and metaphysics (Young 2010: 212f.).

Although Nietzsche abandoned the *Observations* before its projected completion, we should not consider it a failed or incomplete book. First of all, from the very beginning Nietzsche conceived of these essays as part of a larger, unified whole. The title page for each essay places *Unzeitgemässe Betrachtungen* in large type at the top of the page, and the title of each individual essay is printed near the bottom. They are numbered as consecutive '*Stücke*' or parts. Second, after abandoning the project, Nietzsche himself still regarded the book as a whole. In an 1887 advertisement for Nietzsche's earlier works, for example, the *Observations* is included alongside his other books, with the four parts of the book listed as well (see Jensen 2016: 12).

Nietzsche indicates in the title of the work, and in his notebooks, that we should treat this book as a unified whole. More importantly, however, he also suggests in the course of the book that we treat it as a whole, beginning, of course, with its intentionally mirrored structure: corrupted individual ('David Strauss') to corrupt culture ('History') to redemptive culture ('Schopenhauer') to redemptive individual ('Wagner'). In addition, many of the arguments he makes in early parts of the work are taken up again later. In order to treat the work as a whole, then, it is best to begin with the overall context and problem that motivates it. This is the task of Chapter 1.

1
Philosophical Background

Unfashionable Observations is a difficult book. In the course of the text, Nietzsche responds to several philosophical problems raised in the nineteenth century, and he employs many concepts developed by previous philosophers. Unfortunately, much of this background remains unstated, because it would have been implicitly understood by the philosophical audience of the time. As a result, for contemporary readers, it is not always clear why Nietzsche uses the terms that he does and what his overall philosophical aim might be. This chapter discusses the most important nineteenth-century philosophical problems and arguments that are necessary for a proper understanding of the *Observations*.

Nietzsche, neo-Kantian

For many years, scholars interpreted Nietzsche as a 'post-modern' thinker. Based on the powerful, influential readings developed by Jacques Derrida, Michel Foucault, Paul de Man and many others, scholars argued that Nietzsche broke with his 'modernist' predecessors on fundamental issues pertaining to metaphysics, epistemology and ethics. To simplify quite a bit, the post-modern Nietzsche was understood to have delivered a devastating challenge to the notion of a unified subjectivity and universal truth, arguing instead that all knowledge is relative to (or dependent upon) particular perspectives. Scholars grounded this interpretation largely on the works of Nietzsche's later period, but also drew on 'On Truth and Lies in an Extra-Moral Sense', an important unpublished essay written contemporaneously with the *Observations*.

Recently, however, scholars have challenged the 'post-modern' interpretation on several fronts. They have done so in part by examining more closely the philosophical texts and problems that influenced the young Nietzsche. Far from making a clean break with his predecessors, Nietzsche in his early works demonstrates a sustained engagement with them. Schopenhauer is, of course, the best-known influence on Nietzsche, with *The Birth of Tragedy* the text that most clearly demonstrates his debts. However, scholars have also detailed a much more extensive list of influences on the young Nietzsche, the most important including Kant, F. A. Lange, Kuno Fischer, Afrikan Spir and Herman Helmholz.[1]

In the 1860s and then especially in the early 1870s, Nietzsche read extensively in what can be broadly described as the neo-Kantian movement.[2] At this point in the nineteenth century, the neo-Kantian movement was indeed broad and diffuse, well before its institutionalisation into different schools near the end of the century. In the middle of the century, the grand project of Hegelian Idealism was in decline, and materialism – the view that everything, including human beings, is matter – was on the rise. However, many philosophers rejected the materialism of Büchner or Feuerbach on the grounds that materialism fails to capture and explain what distinguishes humanity from the rest of the matter in the cosmos. These same philosophers were similarly dissatisfied with the elaborate Hegelian system of metaphysics, as armchair *Naturphilosophie* of that great Idealist tradition was growing increasingly implausible due to the advances of modern natural science.[3]

As such, in the 1860s these philosophers began to call for a return to Kant, that towering critic of metaphysics who neverthe-less sought to vouchsafe our humanity against the encroachments

---

[1] See, for instance, Hill 2003 on Kant; Stack 1983 on Lange; and Green 2002 on Spir.

[2] For Nietzsche's reading on neo-Kantianism and nineteenth-century science, see Emden 2005; Moore 2002; Hussain 2004; Brobjer 2008: ch. 4.

[3] This paragraph and the next relies on the excellent research on neo-Kantianism by Köhnke (1991) and Beiser (2014).

of materialism. Despite their many differences, Lange and Schopenhauer, for instance, both criticised materialism and sought to
mount a defence of freedom on Kantian grounds. Lange's final
chapter in *The History of Materialism*, the 'Standpoint of the Ideal',
which was very influential on the young Nietzsche, argues that
the creative freedom distinctive of humanity can protect and
redeem us from the dehumanising tendencies of materialism.
Although Schopenhauer criticised many neo-Kantians, he nevertheless relied on and transformed Kantian idealism in his theory of
the will and his call for humanity to liberate itself from the will.[4]
Finally, much of the effort among neo-Kantian philosophers, most
prominently Helmholz, involved marshalling the findings of modern natural science to support Kant's views.

Nietzsche's early work reflects these very concerns. In an
1867–68 note entitled 'On Schopenhauer', he criticises Schopenhauer for failing to adhere to Kant's restrictions on metaphysics.
According to Nietzsche, here echoing Kant, Schopenhauer 'puts'
the will 'in place of the Kantian X', but only 'with the help of
a poetic intuition', which cannot be a claim to knowledge
(WEN 3). In his lectures on 'Pre-Platonic Philosophy' from the
early 1870s, Nietzsche argues that 'materialism has always been of
the greatest utility' as a 'rigorous, scientifically useful hypothesis',
and he cites Kant's *Natural History of the Heavens* in support of his
claim (PPP 126). However, he insists, we cannot prove materialism true – that everything is matter – because we only have an
'extremely mediated' access to the 'immediate given' and so cannot decisively determine what is in itself. The materialist dogmati-
cally 'proceeds from objectivity', whereas Nietzsche, like a good
Kantian, argues that 'everything objective is conditioned by the
knowing subject in multifarious ways' (PPP 130). Finally, like the
scientifically minded neo-Kantians, Nietzsche appeals to scientific
evidence to make the case that our understanding of time is mediated by our 'pulse rate, rate of sensation'. On Nietzsche's view, the
faster our pulse, the faster time seems to move (PPP 61).

---

[4] As Beiser (2014) points out, Schopenhauer's own neo-Kantian philosophy was published long before the 1860s, but only gained popularity during the mid-century rise
of neo-Kantianism.

Nietzsche's most extensive early employment of neo-Kantian epistemology is found in his unpublished essay 'On Truth and Lies in an Extra-Moral Sense' (1873). In this essay, he traces the origin of our truth-claims back to the basic needs of human beings in the process of forming the earliest communities. Much of the essay examines the subjective mental apparatus that generates our standards of truth. Like Kant, Nietzsche claims that independent of our cognitive apparatus, there is 'only an X which, for us, is inaccessible and undefinable' (WEN 257). Our cognitive judgements do not, then, refer to things in themselves, but rather to the categories and standards that we posit for ourselves. Thus, he concludes, 'all we really know about' the world 'is what we add to' it (WEN 261). Undoubtedly, Nietzsche innovates on Kant's view, synthesising Schopenhauer and Gustav Gerber, and positing an 'artistically creative subject' in contrast to Kant's rigid, universal table of categories (WEN 259).[5] Nevertheless, Nietzsche's early work is best seen not as a repudiation of the neo-Kantian project, but as an extension of it.

Schopenhauer and the fundamental problem

Much more can be said about Nietzsche's early contributions to epistemology, philosophy of language and mind, and other topics in theoretical philosophy.[6] However, *Unfashionable Observations* is not intended as a work of theoretical philosophy, but as a contribution to practical philosophy in the distinctly Kantian sense – that is, it is concerned not primarily with the nature of knowledge, but rather the nature of the good life. What is the fundamental problem in practical philosophy that the *Observations* sets out to solve?

From the 1860s through the 1890s, the dominant question in practical philosophy was that of the value of human existence. As Beiser (2016) has documented, the *Pessimusstreit* involved all the major philosophers of the late nineteenth century. Schopenhauer's pessimistic philosophy, which held that human life was not worth living, expressed the problem that all other philosophers of the age

---

[5] See Scheibenberger (2016) for excellent background on 'Truth and Lies'.
[6] See, for instance, Clark 1990: ch. 3; Crawford 1988.

set out to answer. For Schopenhauer, all human beings live in the grip of the will to life that drives us in an unfulfillable quest to satisfy our desires. This quest must always end in failure and suffering. Human existence can be redeemed, however, by liberating oneself from the grip of the will to life, either through artistic contemplation, moral compassion or asceticism. In the years after Schopenhauer's death, followers such as Julius Frauenstädt, Eduard von Hartmann and Julius Bahnsen modified and deepened his argument. On the other hand, philosophers such as Eugen Dühring sought to defend the intrinsic value of human life, arguing that Schopenhauer's vision of human existence was far too bleak.

The pessimism controversy was in full swing in Nietzsche's early period, and it decisively shaped his basic philosophical motivation. Siding squarely with Schopenhauer, Nietzsche insists that human existence is naturally without value. In a note from 1873 he states that Schopenhauer 'discloses once again the profound foundations of existence' (KSA 7.28[6], UW 187). In *The Birth of Tragedy*, Nietzsche voices Schopenhauer's pessimistic challenge to the value of existence in the story of Silenus. When King Midas comes upon the 'wise Silenus, companion of Dionysos', he asks him, 'what is the best and most excellent thing for human beings?' Silenus answers, 'the very best thing is utterly beyond your reach, not to have been born, not to be, to be nothing. However, the second best thing for you is: to die soon' (BT 3, 22–3).

While Nietzsche agrees with Schopenhauer's assessment of human existence, he disagrees with his response to it. Already one can see Nietzsche's disagreement with Schopenhauer in *The Birth of Tragedy*, since in that work he does not embrace aesthetic contemplation but rather combines Apollinian individual agency with Dionysian self-denial. However, in the *Observations*, Nietzsche begins to develop an alternative response to Schopenhauer's challenge, a response that he would refine and deepen throughout his life. Instead of relying on artistic works to redeem humanity, Nietzsche turns to the beautiful lives of exemplary individuals. The *Observations* is the first place where these 'higher individuals' appear in Nietzsche's corpus, and they subsequently pervade his later work. For Nietzsche, exemplars play a fundamental role in solving the problem of existence by living a free or self-determined life.

Kant, exemplarity and the value of freedom

What are the intellectual influences on this notion of the exemplar? Where does it come from? Few of Nietzsche's contemporaries look to the idea of genius to overcome the challenge of pessimism – many instead invoke friendship, love, art or religion.[7] However, like his contemporaries, Nietzsche turned back to Kant – as well as to Kant's Romantic critics – for inspiration. As is often remarked, Nietzsche seems to have read few of Kant's primary critical texts. Nevertheless, he became quite familiar with Kant's arguments in the 1860s by reading many secondary works on Kant or by neo-Kantians such as Lange and Kuno Fischer. He even sketches a plan for a study of 'Teleology after Kant', and most likely studied the third *Critique* (Hill 2003).

Kant employs the notion of the 'exemplar' [*Exemplar*] in his third *Critique*, but it plays a narrowly aesthetic role for him. For Kant, art, unlike physics and morality, is not governed by objective rules. Aesthetic judgement is guided instead by subjective affect and the free play of our cognitive faculties. However, in order to be able to argue about art – and to develop genres and aesthetic criticism – there must be certain general rules that are recognised by aesthetic admirers. Kant thus looks to 'genius' as that 'inborn predisposition of the mind through which nature gives the rule to art' (CJ 5:307). The genius is in this sense the legislator of an aesthetic community, giving a rule to himself and others. However, this genius cannot produce objective rules that the audience simply applies to aesthetic phenomena, since to do so would undermine the free play distinctive to the aesthetic experience. Instead, the genius 'models' excellent art and is in this sense 'exemplary'. The genius does not produce a 'determinate rule' for an artwork, but the work as a whole nevertheless serves 'as a standard or a rule for judging' (CJ 5:308). The audience can thereby preserve its aesthetic autonomy by engaging in free play with the work of the genius, while still employing that work as a standard to evaluate other works.

---

[7] See Beiser's 2016 survey of the variety of responses to pessimism.

Nietzsche appropriates Kant's concept and builds on it by dissolving the latter's distinction between morality and art.[8] For Nietzsche, there are no determinate ethical rules that we can establish through reason, just as Kant thought that there are no determinate aesthetic rules that we can deduce through reason. This is not to say that 'anything goes', because a genius must model a form of human excellence that is recognised and championed by a cultural community. In other words, the genius cannot be 'original nonsense', as Kant argued (CJ 5:308). As such, in Nietzsche's early writings he speaks repeatedly of the role of the philosopher in 'legislating greatness' for a community (Nietzsche 1962: 43). In 'Schopenhauer as Educator', for instance, the true philosopher 'is capable of setting an example' (183).[9] These 'great thinkers' are the 'legislators of the measure, mint, and weight of things' (193).

More importantly, however, Nietzsche marries the concept of the exemplar with a Kantian notion of autonomy. As we will see below in our discussion of the essay on 'Schopenhauer as Educator', Nietzsche draws a sharp distinction between animality [*Tierheit*] and humanity [*Menschlichkeit*]. According to him, animality is characterised by heteronomy, that is, being determined by external forces. Humanity, by contrast, is capable of aspiring to autonomy, whereby one determines the character of one's life in accordance with principles that one legislates to oneself. For Kant and Nietzsche, the vocation of human existence involves living up to what is distinctive to our humanity. However, Nietzsche differs from Kant in holding that pure reason cannot guide human beings to autonomy. Although he acknowledges no objective principles that human beings may apprehend, he nevertheless insists that exemplary individuals – 'those true human beings, those no-longer-animals' (211) – model to others a life predicated on self-determination. The lives of these exemplars thus serve to illuminate the standard for a truly human life.

---

[8] See also Conant's 2001 helpful discussion of Nietzsche's appropriation of Kant's notion of exemplarity.

[9] Throughout, citations from *Unfashionable Observations* are given by page references in parentheses to Nietzsche 1995a.

How does this appropriation of Kantian freedom and exemplarity help Nietzsche respond to Schopenhauer's problem? Once again, Kant provides a model for Nietzsche in his account of the value of freedom as sketched in an appendix to the third *Critique*. There, Kant argues that nature is without intrinsic value, and that human freedom alone confers value on it. We thus read, for example, that bare natural existence – that of 'lifeless beings or . . . living but nonrational beings' – possesses 'no value at all', since value is a 'concept' legislated by 'rational beings' (CJ 5:449). Nature itself is subject to 'all the evils of poverty, illnesses, and untimely death, just like all the other animals on earth, and will always remain thus until one wide grave engulfs them all together . . . and flings them . . . back into the abyss of the purposeless chaos of matter from which they were drawn' (CJ 5:452). Kant strikingly concludes that 'it is easy to decide what sort of value life has for us if it is assessed merely by what one enjoys', that is, by one's submission to heteronomous impulses: 'Less than zero'. No one would choose life again if the value of life were bound up exclusively with 'enjoyment' (CJ 5:434n).

The 'value of [a human] existence' lies instead, Kant argues, in the 'freedom of his faculty of desire' (CJ 5:443). This freedom lifts us out of the purposeless causal order of nature and allows us to give ourselves our own purpose. We can make our own distinctively human freedom our highest value. We thus introduce into an otherwise indifferent world something that is of infinite and unconditional value. Kant then envisions the aim of history, as of culture and politics, to be devoted towards making freedom the ultimate end of our collective lives. Only by devoting ourselves to this end can we confer value on our existence. Kant thereby anticipates Schopenhauer's condemnation of natural existence, while suggesting a positive path for human redemption, namely, the moral perfection of the human race.

Nietzsche similarly understands nature and natural existence to hold no intrinsic value, yet he argues that our lives can 'obtain the highest value' if we contribute to the twin causes of creating and preserving exemplary individuals (216). These individuals bring unconditional value into the world by creating for themselves a free or self-determining life. In doing so, the exemplary individual extends 'the concept of "the human being" and giv[es] it a more beautiful substance', thereby making it 'eternally present' (97). As such, this activity amounts to a 'protest against the change of generations and against [the] transitoriness' of nature (98). The purpose of 'every culture', Nietzsche claims, is to 'lift the individual human being out of the pushing, shoving, and crushing of the historical stream and make him understand that he is not merely a historically limited being, but also an absolutely extrahistorical and infinite being with whom all existence began and will end' (KSA 7.35[12], UW 367). Nietzsche shares with Kant, then, the claim that human freedom confers unconditional value on existence by transcending the meaningless becoming of nature. At the same time, Nietzsche differs from Kant in his understanding of the nature of freedom. Like Kant's Romantic critics, Nietzsche thinks that Kant underestimates the concrete, embodied, individual way of life expressed by the exemplar.

This connection to Kant places Nietzsche's celebration of the exemplar in its proper philosophical context. In particular, it challenges a standard reading of Nietzsche, according to which the exemplary genius coerces or manipulates the mass of human beings for his own benefit.[10] On the contrary, the exemplary individual serves to liberate humanity from the becoming of nature by establishing a rule for human excellence, a model that we can follow in our efforts to transcend the heteronomy imposed on us by our natural impulses. As we will see below, human beings do not serve as tools for the exemplar so much as participate in the freedom of his personality. For instance, Nietzsche sees Goethe and Schiller as constituting the common substance of the cultural life of Germany. Their personalities enrich the lives of all Germans, providing them with a model of a free life and a justification for the value of their existence.[11]

---

[10] See, for instance, Appel 1999; Detwiler 1990.
[11] See Yack (1992) for a discussion of Nietzsche on redemption and his connection to the Kantian tradition.

Schiller and the artistic life

The exemplar is not the only aesthetic concept that Nietzsche adopts and broadens for ethical purposes. Throughout the works of his early period, he employs aesthetic categories in many contexts. In his epistemology in 'On Truth and Lies in an Extra-Moral Sense', he eschews the rationalistic subjectivity of Kant in favour of the 'artistically creative subject' (WEN 259). In his metaphysics, Nietzsche famously envisions two aesthetic 'drives' – the Apollinian and Dionysian – as shaping human thought and action (BT 1, 14). In his ethical thought, he holds that only as 'an aesthetic phenomenon' can 'existence and the world [be] eternally justified' (BT 5, 33). These aesthetic categories pervade the *Observations* as well, most prominently in his theory of culture as a 'unity of artistic style that manifests itself throughout all the vital self-expressions of a people' (9).

As Nietzsche himself remarks in his 1886 preface to *The Birth of Tragedy*, the comprehensiveness of the aesthetic in his early thought owes quite a bit to the broad movement of German Romanticism. The influential 1796 Romantic tract 'Oldest Programme for a System of German Idealism' illustrates the pan-aestheticism of the Romantics. In this work, the author argues that the 'highest act of reason, by encompassing all ideas, is an aesthetic act, and that truth and goodness are only siblings in beauty'. As such, the 'philosopher must possess as much aesthetic power as the poet', and the 'philosophy of spirit is an aesthetic philosophy' (Bernstein 2003: 186).

As is often discussed, this Romantic embrace of the aesthetic grew out of the perceived failures of Kant's critical philosophy.[12] In particular, Romantic philosophers argued that Kant failed to identify the unity of reason that would encompass the divergent cognitive capacities and inclinations that Kant analyses. For these philosophers, Kant articulates the correct principle of morality that would perfect our highest capacities. However, the sharp distinction between practical reason and inclination in Kant's thought renders humanity incomplete. The longing for wholeness – which Kant understands as a longing of reason but one that goes unfulfilled – drives the

---

[12] See, for instance, Pinkard 2002; Smith 1989.

Romantic thinkers to develop aesthetic categories that unify our cognitive and affective natures. Accordingly, they rely heavily on Kant's third *Critique*.

Friedrich Schiller nicely illustrates this Romantic reaction against Kant. The young Nietzsche read and admired Schiller, who was likely one of the main Romantic influences on him.[13] In his *Letters on the Aesthetic Education of Humanity*, Schiller argues that Kant's separation of reason and natural desires leaves human beings internally divided, which in turn generates social and political problems. Later in the *Letters*, however, Schiller further argues that Kant's moral law, in its unconditional necessity, renders human beings unfree. He turns instead to our capacity for 'play' to redeem our freedom and reconcile our divided nature (2004: 74). Kant theorised this free play as characteristic of the aesthetic experience, but here Schiller broadens the notion. Through play, we are free from the necessitating drives of reason and of natural desires, since we can transcend both (2004: 75). Yet in addition, play also reconciles our cognitive and affective natures through the formation of a unified character. In his essay 'On Grace and Dignity', Schiller further explores the way in which character can unify our rational and affective natures. Character does so by shaping our affective natures such that they become more responsive to the call of our moral conscience. When our character becomes unified, we appear graceful or beautiful in our moral actions, since the aims of reason and desire work in harmony. As such, as Schiller argues in his *Kallias* letters, beauty is a form of 'autonomy', as our actions are the outcome of a character we ourselves have created (2003: 159).

As we will see, in the *Observations* Nietzsche is influenced by Schiller's views of the unifying role of art, the free, creative function of aesthetic play, and, finally, the deep connection between artistic beauty and freedom. Nietzsche's main contribution once again is to synthesise these insights in his theory of the exemplary individual. For Nietzsche, the exemplar forges a character for himself in which his principles are expressed 'in his visible life, and not merely in his books' (183). His actions are not the result of natural desire or social convention, but emerge from internal self-determination.

---

[13] See Martin 1996.

All of Wagner's actions, even the most 'quixotic trajectory of his plans', are 'governed by a single inner law' (263). Nietzsche also uses Goethe throughout his career as the best example of a genius whose life resembles a work of art – that 'epic poet' whose life has 'something of an epic quality' (263) – that is, whose life itself reflects and expresses the principles he espouses.

To appreciate further the early Nietzsche's debt to Kant and Schiller, consider the contrast between Schopenhauer and Schiller on the function of art. For Schopenhauer, art aims to express the archetypes or ideas that exist in nature. He cleaves in this way to a Platonic conception of art. By contrast, for Schiller, art does not describe something pre-existing in nature, but rather creates something new and self-determining, what he calls an 'appearance' or 'semblance' [*Schein*] (Schiller 2003: 151; cf. KSA 7.29[17], UW 198). Nietzsche announces his debt to Schiller in a note, claiming that his philosophy is an 'inverted Platonism: the further something is from true being, the purer, more beautiful, the better it is. Living in illusion as the goal [*Das Leben im Schein als Ziel*]' (WEN 52). Nature does not supply us with a worthwhile existence, so instead of escaping from life (as Schopenhauer suggests), we must create an artificial ideal that is self-determining and redemptive.

Culture in Kant and Schiller

Nietzsche's response to Schopenhauer's problem consists in the exemplary individual. However, the answer is not a secret held solely by exemplars themselves. On the contrary, the exemplar's life redeems human existence more broadly. Other human beings participate in the exemplar's freedom, by maintaining the memory of the exemplar in their own lives. Nietzsche's answer to Schopenhauer has an inescapably communal component to it, in order for the exemplar to redeem all of humanity. Indeed, an early note describes as the main purpose of the *Observations* to 'collect what makes individuals great and self-sufficient, and also the standpoint from which they can be bound together', namely, in 'culture' (KSA 8.17[22]). The question then arises, what is the nature and structure of such a community, devoted to humanity's redemption? For Nietzsche, culture is that community, and the *Observations* has as one of its central concerns the analysis of the nature of culture, as well as those forces that help and hinder it.

This notion of *Kultur* was a recent development in Nietzsche's day, and can be traced back to Kant and Schiller.[14] It emerged in response to concerns about the hollowness of modern civilisation. By civilisation, philosophers meant the institutions and processes that in the modern age have led to an unparalleled explosion in material wealth and prosperity, advances in technology, protections of liberty and property, as well as the softening of manners and morals. However, this modern transformation in our external lives tended to undermine pre-modern communities which cared for our inner life. As religion declines in the modern world, these philosophers worried, our inner lives become colonised by civilisation's purposes, making us more materialistic, governed by our appetites, and less human. Schiller speaks of 'utility' being the 'great idol of the age' (2004: 26), and that under these conditions, 'man himself grew to be only a fragment', and 'instead of imprinting humanity upon his nature he becomes merely the imprint of his occupation, of his science' (2004: 40).

However, a return to the traditional religious institutions of the past was regarded as both undesirable and impossible. The task, then, was to create a new form of community founded on modern freedom that would tend to our souls, just as civilisation cared for our bodies. *Kultur* is that new form of community. Kant distinguishes it from 'civilisation' by indicating its function as cultivating 'art and science' and indeed the 'inner formation [*Bildung*]' of our moral character and 'mode of thought' (I 8:26). Without the 'morally good disposition' cultivated by culture, civilisation 'is nothing but mere semblance and glittering misery' (I 8:26). Schiller further argues that the purpose of 'culture' is to foster our 'autonomy' as well as the 'intensity' of natural 'feeling' (2004: 68–9). Culture would thus unify our cognitive and affective nature in an 'aesthetic' community, that is, one devoted to the production of great works of art, philosophy and science (2004: 110).

Nietzsche follows Kant and Schiller in his critique of civilisation and his quest to create this new form of community. On

---

[14] See Church 2015a.

the one hand, he identifies many more problems with civilisation. Throughout the *Observations*, he discusses four main institutions of modern civilisation that displace culture and corrupt our humanity: the modern state, commercial society, mass society and modern scholarship. He thus offers a decidedly gloomier assessment of the spiritual state of modern humanity. On the other hand, the *Observations* as a whole is an attempt to create a new German culture, one that is unified by the great works of exemplary individuals in art, religion and philosophy.

There are many other influences on the young Nietzsche in general and *Unfashionable Observations* in particular, including, for instance, Goethe and Richard Wagner. I will discuss these thinkers and several more in the chapters that follow. In this chapter, I have provided what I take to be an overview of the decisive philosophical problem animating the book – the value of existence – and the background to Nietzsche's solution – namely, the Kantian notions of freedom and exemplarity, and Romantic notions of art and culture, which Nietzsche synthesises in his theory of the exemplary individual. As we now turn to the text of the *Observations* itself, it is important to recognise that Nietzsche himself presents this argument in reverse order – he begins with culture before moving to the fundamental problem of the value of existence and then to the exemplary individual.

2
David Strauss the Confessor
and the Writer

Nietzsche's first *Unfashionable Observation* is often dismissed as a polemical work (Johnson 2001), one that is least 'philosophically interesting' (Brobjer 2008: 58), one that 'pales into insignificance in Nietzsche's oeuvre' (Pletsch 1991: 166). Alternatively, scholars have read it in the biographical context of Nietzsche's relationship with Richard Wagner. In the 1860s Wagner and the famous left-Hegelian philosopher David Strauss had a personal feud. When Strauss's *The Old Faith and the New* was published in 1872, Wagner enlisted Nietzsche to demolish the book publicly (Magnus and Higgins 1996: 25). Nietzsche was all too happy to do so as a way to 'please Wagner' (Young 2010: 168).

In this chapter, I will argue by contrast that the essay develops a deep philosophical argument about the nature of culture.[1] Nietzsche does this particularly by expounding on what I will call the 'anti-culture' represented by contemporary German culture. In addition, by attending to the philosophical significance of the essay, we can begin to grasp the structure of *Unfashionable Observations*. I will suggest that this essay comes first in the *Observations* because Strauss represents the 'anti-genius', the highest expression of corrupt contemporary cultural leadership, and hence the model that Nietzsche seeks to displace in the course of the *Observations*.

---

[1] There are a few good discussions of the philosophical content of the David Strauss essay – see Ansell-Pearson 2013; Large 2012; Johnson 2001. My contribution to this discussion is to identify the notion of the 'anti-culture' as central to the essay.

Structural overview

1 The political corruption of German culture

The first section reveals that there is more to this essay than Wagner's row with Strauss. Indeed, Nietzsche worries that German 'culture' [*Kultur*], and the related notions of German 'spirit' [*Geist*] and 'cultivation' [*Bildung*], are in jeopardy (5–6). These concepts have a long tradition in classical German thought from Kant, Herder, Schiller, Goethe and others. As we saw in our discussion of culture in the last chapter, Kant and others celebrated the emerging freedoms of individuals in the modern age, embodied in the political and economic institutions of modern civilisation.[2] However, they worried that the decline of religion and the growing fragmentation and materialism of modern societies would leave us spiritually impoverished. Accordingly, they envisioned a new form of community modelled on the unity of the ancient Greek polis, yet based on the modern aspiration for human freedom. This type of community they called culture, devoted to the cultivation of our mental or spiritual capacities, pre-eminently expressed in art and philosophy.

The task of *Unfashionable Observations* as a whole is to retrieve and transform the classical notion of culture, a task that Nietzsche begins here in the first section of the book.[3] He offers an important first pass at defining the notion of culture: 'Above all else,

---

[2] Nietzsche distinguishes between culture and civilisation in a note to this essay: 'we have no culture, but only civilization with a few cultural fashions; however, even more barbarism' (KSA 7.27[66], UW 176).

[3] See Taylor (1997: part 2) and Church (2015a: chs 4–6) on the notion of culture in Nietzsche's early period.

culture is a unity of artistic style that manifests itself throughout all the vital self-expressions of a people [*Lebensäusserungen eines Volkes*]' (9). This definition is extremely elliptical, and will be amplified throughout the *Observations*. Yet we can see in it the classical commitment to a unity of national character, expressed clearly in Goethe's sentiment that Nietzsche cites to close section 1. We also find the influence here of F. A. Lange and Richard Wagner in emphasising the artistic or creative character of culture (Nietzsche speaks in section 1 of 'delusions' [*Wahn*] as sometimes 'most salutary', referring back to his *Birth of Tragedy* and before that to Wagner's view of the benefits of artistic 'delusion'). Finally, Nietzsche offers his own contribution in seeing culture as manifest in the 'life' of a people, the *Leben* in their *Lebensäusserungen*. He would return to the notion of 'life', beginning with the title of the second *Observation*, 'On the Utility and Liability of History for Life'.

Even if Nietzsche's discussion of these issues is elliptical, we can grasp the core of his point through his examples. For Nietzsche, the Germans exemplify the lack of culture – 'barbarism' – that results from the condition of modern fragmentation. Germans live in a 'chaotic hodgepodge of all styles', and he observes that 'every glance at his clothes, his room, and his house; every walk through the streets of his cities; every visit he pays to the shops of the fashion mongers' leads to the conclusion that Germany is 'that modern carnival motley' of 'stylistic tumult'. Only the German language, Nietzsche argues in a draft of this section, 'has been spared all the intermingling of nationalities', and can provide hope of engendering 'unities out of diversities' (KSA 7.26[16], UW 153–4). By contrast, Nietzsche sees in the French the model of a 'genuine, productive culture', in which everything about French life, intellect and manners issues from its own distinctive identity (9). German life is dependent on external sources – Nietzsche singles out Paris – to shape its moral and intellectual life, whereas the French draw their cultural expressions from themselves (10). In this way, the French are self-determining and so free, whereas the Germans are determined by others and so unfree, not yet 'liberated' [*befreit*] from their influences (9).

Germany once embraced the 'pure concept of culture' in its classical, Goethean period, but this 'has been lost' in his time (8). It is lost because two forces – politics and the intellectual class – both serve to 'delude' German 'public opinion' into a self-satisfied spiritual stupor (5). Nietzsche discusses the first force in this section and the second in the next section.

Nietzsche begins his essay and the *Observations* as a whole with untimely reflections about the tension between politics and culture. Prussia, under Otto von Bismarck, had in early 1871 achieved a great military victory against France, extending its territory into Alsace-Lorraine and unifying the varied small German states into a single 'Reich'. 'Public opinion' [*öffentliche Meinung*] exulted in Germany's success, and many popular writers, journalists and scholars celebrated the victory (5). However, Nietzsche notes, though the Germans may have proved their military and political superiority, they did not prove their cultural superiority. In fact, they defeated the French because of 'strict military discipline, natural courage and perseverance, superiority of leadership, unity and obedience among the led', which are 'qualities that have nothing at all to do with culture' (6). Nietzsche draws a parallel with the Macedonians who had 'discipline' and 'silent obedience' and who bested the 'incomparably more cultivated Greek armies' (8). Superiority in politics consists in discipline and authority, qualities distinct from and indeed in tension with the self-determining freedom of culture.

However, Nietzsche notes, the public is of the contrary opinion. For it, superiority in war proves superiority in 'morality, culture, and art' (5) – it is the 'measure of value' (6). Germany was long dependent on France, but now it expresses its independence by subjugating it politically. For Nietzsche, the Germans display here a feature of 'human nature' that makes it 'more difficult … to endure victory than to endure defeat' (5). By achieving military victory and political rule, the Germans indeed extended their influence over external or physical bodies. However, they did not extend their influence over the inner life of spirit, which remains 'just as dependent on' France 'as we were heretofore' (6). They do not bother to extend this influence, because physical superiority is easier to see and understand than spiritual subservience. Physical superiority thereby lends itself to a 'delusion' of spiritual superiority (5). By contrast, enduring defeat is paradoxically easier because defeat forces the loser to turn inward. The loser must submit physically, but can find independence in the inner development of spirit. Indeed, Nietzsche wishes but doubts that the Germans would do just this, 'mobilize that calm and tenacious courage . . . against their own inner enemy', so that 'all hope for a truly genuine German cultivation . . . would not be in vain' (6–7).

For Nietzsche, this delusion has very deleterious consequences, leading to the 'defeat – indeed, the extirpation – of the German spirit for the sake of the "German Reich"' (5). The delusion leads not only to 'complacency, but even joy and delirium', and 'joy, dignity, and self-assurance'. Since the war, German culture has become 'confirmed and sanctioned . . . even ordained almost sacrosanct' (7). Judging themselves to have achieved the pinnacle of cultural excellence in the form of the political state, Germans will no longer seek an artistic unity of style. Rather, they will replace cultural aims with the further development of their political capacities, obedience and discipline. In demonstrating 'subservience to these [political] principles', they will obliterate the freedom and artistic creativity that are preconditions for any genuine culture (6). With the destruction of the inner 'German spirit', we will be left only with the outer 'German body' of the Reich. Nietzsche here offers the first of many examples throughout the *Observations* of the conflict between modern politics and culture and between the related concepts of the external and internal, subservience and freedom, and animal and human.

2 The democratic corruption of German culture

In addition to modern politics, Nietzsche identifies a second force that debases culture, what he calls 'cultivated philistines' [*Bildungsphilister*] (10). In the first section, Nietzsche introduces this group as 'those writers who know of no opinion that is more important than public opinion', those who promote the delusion of German superiority in culture (5). They are the elite literati of German society, those 'journalists' and 'fabricators of novels, tragedies, poems, and histories', the chattering classes emerging from a new middle class and enlightened public sphere in Germany in the nineteenth century (7). These writers do not possess 'genuine German cultivation' [*Bildung*], but rather 'nonnative "cultivatedness"' [*Gebildetheit*] – that is, the literati do not form or shape [*bildet*] their own style, but rather it is formed or shaped [*gebildet*] by other cultures. They draw from other cultures, not from within.

As such, they are philistines, the 'opposite of the son of the muses, the artist, the genuinely cultured person' (11). Yet they are distinctive in holding a 'single superstition', the delusion that they have produced a worthy culture – thus, *Bildungsphilister*, an amusingly paradoxical term. Indeed, the illusion of culture has become powerfully reinforced in each philistine, 'since he everywhere encounters cultured people of this same type, and since all public institutions, all institutes of schooling, education, and art, are organized along the lines of his cultivatedness and according to his needs' (11). The philistine sees everywhere philistines, and the main institutions of public life continue to churn out new philistines. So he 'infers from this uniformity' the unity characteristic of culture (11).

As such, the totalising of philistinism goes beyond barbarism. Barbarism is merely lack of coherence, which is actually an opportunity for those true productive geniuses who could synthesise a whole out of the barbaric aggregate. Cultivated philistinism is more dangerous because it is not lack of culture, but anti-culture. It shares with culture a 'unity' but this unity derives from 'the conscious or unconscious exclusion and negation of all the artistically productive forms and demands of a true style'. Philistinism is a chaos of cultural influences, yet it uniformly resists any imposition of order characteristic of genuine artistic culture. Accordingly, it perversely demonstrates a negative 'stylistic unity', in which 'all [the philistine's] actions bear a negatively uniform stamp'. When the philistine encounters a rare genuine genius, he 'wards off, negates, withdraws, plugs his ears, looks away' (12).

This anti-culture helps us understand through its negative characteristics what, for Nietzsche, the genuine positive end or purpose of culture is. The word 'culture' has etymological roots in the cultivation of the land, and so Nietzsche employs an agricultural metaphor throughout the *Observations* to explain the development and end of culture. Culture needs good 'soil' and the 'finest seeds' to grow a productive and beautiful harvest (13, 7). The harvest is the reaping of 'all who are powerful and creative', those geniuses 'pursuing higher aims' (12). The problem with the anti-culture is that it is an 'impediment' to such figures, a 'labyrinth to all who are circumspect and lost, a morass to all who are weary, leg irons to all those pursuing higher aims, a poisonous cloud to all fresh seeds, a parching desert to the German spirit' (12). The entire system of public institutions and public opinion conspires to thwart the development of creative geniuses, and instead encourages the production of chaotic and small souls, the very opposite of what culture ought to do. Finally, as we will see, the anti-culture perversely resembles culture as well in producing its own anti-genius, that figure who embodies the anti-culture in a perfected or exemplary form, David Strauss.

After analysing the nature of the cultivated philistine and its anti-culture, Nietzsche proceeds to explain its emergence in German history. He does so in part to underscore the gulf between the heights of the classical German period and his contemporaries, but also, more importantly, to trace the weaknesses of this seemingly all-powerful anti-culture so as to provide hope for destroying it.

Nietzsche carves up recent German history into three periods – the 'classical' period, the 'Romantic' era, and finally the 'philistine' epoch – spanning roughly 1770–1872. The classical period comprises, for Nietzsche as for many Germans, the period of partnership between Goethe and Schiller in Weimar in the 1780s and 1790s. In this time, a 'series of great heroic figures passed before us' (12–13). However, for Nietzsche, his contemporaries overlook that these writers were not complacent with their artistic success, but on the contrary 'were seekers', and 'fervently and with earnest perseverance' sought to found and build a 'genuine originary German culture' (13). In the 'classical' period, the 'German spirit' was suffused with longing and self-transcendence (12). Now, Nietzsche bemoans, philistines 'dedicate statues and initiate festivals and societies in their names', but fail to 'seek in their spirit' (13).

However, Nietzsche proceeds to argue, the Romantic period that followed upon the classical involved too much striving – some complacency here, he suggests, 'made a certain sense'. He identifies the 'first decade of this century' – 1800–10 – as the period of 'confused seeking, experimenting, destroying, promising, surmising, hoping', which all 'got so muddled that the intellectual middle class was justified in fearing for itself' (14). Contrary to some impressions, Nietzsche shows here that he does not license unbridled creativity and self-overcoming. Longing and artistic creation must take place within existing conventional norms and standards, in which the genius shapes and transforms them, rather than destroying them utterly. The revolutionary destruction of conventional orders leaves no standard of judgement by which to render what is new intelligible.[4] What is new instead becomes nonsense – 'that brew of fantastic and language-perverting philosophies' of the German Idealism of Fichte, Schelling and Hegel; 'that fanatical-purposive view of history' of Hegel; 'that carnival of all gods and myths that the Romantics put together' of Schelling and Friedrich Schlegel; 'as well as those poetic fashions and insanities born out of intoxication' of Novalis, Schlegel and others (14).

However, instead of responsibly curbing the excesses of Romantic longing, the philistine 'exploited the opportunity to throw suspicion on the act of seeking as such and to promote instead the comfort of finding'. The emerging philistines thus lauded the 'idyllic' in artwork, and their artists 'portrayed the bliss, the coziness, the triviality, the peasantlike healthfulness and all that contentedness that the rooms of children, scholars, and peasants exude' (14). This 'Biedermeier' period in German history, as it has come to be called, celebrated the simple middle-class life which was in danger of cultural destruction in the wake of the Revolutionary period. Nietzsche here offers a cultural explanation of German history that complements the usual political history after the Napoleonic Wars and preceding the Revolutions of 1848.

After the Biedermeier period, Nietzsche sees philistinism consolidating its ideological power. It does so particularly, he suggests, by taking 'control over the discipline of history in order to guarantee that they would have peace'. As we will see in Nietzsche's second *Observation*, he has in mind here figures such as Leopold von Ranke (1795–1886), who developed a scientific approach to the study of history.[5] These philistines 'rescued themselves from fanaticism by means of historical consciousness' [*historische Bewusstsein*].

---

[4] See Zuckert (1976), who traces this theme in the *Observations*.
[5] See Beiser (2011) for further discussion of Ranke and his significance.

What they did was expose the myths that ground every historical movement and motivate fanaticism and great deeds in service to it. They 'understand everything historically', grasping the efficient causes of all historical deeds, observing them from an objective or third-person perspective, and thereby having 'nil admirari', no wonder, at the subjective, inner life of the German spirit. Soon, Nietzsche recounts, this historicism extended to 'philosophy and classical philology'. Under the philistines, philosophy ceased to evaluate arguments, and instead sought a historical account of why philosophers held this or that view in a particular time period. This historicising of all things had the effect of 'crippling, numbing, or dissolving . . . freshness and powerful movements', as these movements themselves become subject to the endless self-reflection of the historical consciousness (15).

These philistines were not content with simply historicising all human things, because such an effort would eventually turn back upon themselves. As such, they drew on a lingering Hegelian view, namely, the 'rationality of all that is real'. Famously, Hegel defended a philosophy of history according to which reason and freedom develop towards their full actualisation in the modern state. Thus, in the Preface to the *Philosophy of Right*, Hegel argued that what is 'rational is actual, and what is actual is rational' (1991a: 20). Later thinkers understood Hegel's comment to mean that 'whatever is "real"' – any work of art or philosophy, any activity by government – is rational, the culmination of humanity's historical development. Hegel himself would have disagreed with this interpretation (1991b: 29–30). However, it had the effect of providing the philistines with a powerful ideological self-confidence that their 'own reality' is the 'measure of reason in the world' and could not be challenged nor transcended (15).

After examining the philistines' strategy at length, Nietzsche identifies what he thinks is the motivation for philistinism at bottom: 'what they really hated was domineering genius and the tyranny of true cultural demands'. As we have seen, the philistine movement comes from the emerging middle class in Germany, and is threatened by the disruption and power of the Romantic cultural elites. The philistines seek freedom and hate tyranny, and thereby want to make it 'permissible for anyone . . . to reflect a little, to do research, to wax aesthetic, and above all to compose literature and music' (15). Although Nietzsche does not call it by this name, this is the democratic movement in culture that he had begun to examine the year before this essay in his lectures on education.[6] The philistines eschew the 'aristocratic nature of the intellect as such', according to which the standard of creative excellence is legislated by the best, not the many (43). Yet this democratisation of culture means that philistines require a 'universally effective formula' and standard for evaluating cultural products, something intelligible and achievable for all human beings. Unfortunately, such a standard does not thereby enjoin participants towards self-transcendence and higher states of the soul, but rather expresses something within reach – in this case, 'healthiness' becomes the index for good cultural work (16).[7]

Nietzsche concludes the section by observing that, despite their formidable ideological control, philistines will occasionally reveal their own weakness. These 'confessions' provide Nietzsche with an opportunity to shine a light on the fundamental contradiction of philistinism. Nietzsche here discusses a revealing comment from the critic Friedrich Vischer on the Romantic poet Friedrich Hölderlin. The problem Vischer faces is that on the one hand he is committed to a democratic standard of cultural excellence, yet on the other hand he is evaluating a great poet who himself rejected this democratic understanding. Vischer explains the gap by admitting that his philistines are full of 'weakness', and so falls back on an aristocratic understanding of culture after all (18). For Nietzsche, this is an opportunity to reveal to the philistine world that the work of the human spirit is inescapably aristocratic, that it necessarily involves the rank ordering of human excellence.

3 David Strauss as the 'anti-genius'

David Friedrich Strauss (1808–74) was a famous left–Hegelian theologian and philosopher, whose *Life of Jesus* (1835), alongside Ludwig Feuerbach's *The Essence of Christianity* (1841), deeply

---

[6] See, for instance, Nietzsche 2004: 35, 49–50, 67.
[7] This critique of democratic culture continues throughout his career. See especially BGE aphorism 202; Clark 1999.

challenged Christian faith in the nineteenth century. Nietzsche himself read the *Life of Jesus* and was heavily influenced by it (Young 2010: 56–7). In 1872 Strauss published *The Old Faith and the New*, an attempt to found a new faith based on modern science and philosophy. Strauss calls on fellow writers to 'found a non-ecclesiastical, a purely humanitarian or rationalistic' community (1997: 1.6).

The book has four parts. The first two are critical of the 'old faith'. Part one ('Are We Still Christians?') summarises the main critiques of Christianity. Strauss argues that the many internal inconsistencies in the Bible, as well as the contradictions between biblical teachings and modern science, make it impossible for modern people to be Christians any more. In part two ('Have We Still a Religion?'), Strauss extends his critique from Christianity to natural theology in general, offering several arguments against the main philosophical arguments for the existence of God. He also develops a natural history of religion that is indebted to Hume and Feuerbach, which claims that religion as such is an attempt to explain and master an alien nature. Modern natural science can allow us to cast off such myths and gain actual control over nature.

The latter half of the book is Strauss's positive statement of the 'new faith'. Part three ('What is Our Conception of the Universe?') draws on Darwin and other modern science of Strauss's day to develop a naturalistic account of the universe. No supernatural forces exist in this world, and human life and civilisation are the results of billions of years of a blind evolutionary process, a cosmic accident. Part four ('What is Our Rule of Life?') turns from science to ethics, arguing against Schopenhauer's atheistic pessimism and defending a humanistic optimism much indebted to Kant. Strauss holds that our sensuous natural desires incline us towards egoism, while our humanity drives us towards cooperation and mutual respect. For Strauss, then, each ought 'to bring himself, as an individual, into abiding concord with the idea and the destiny of mankind', and ought to 'promote in all other individuals also, this permanently enduring kind' (1997: 2.51). Strauss's new faith, then, is a kind of naturalistic, evolutionary Kantianism.

Nietzsche's overall criticism of Strauss does not concern his Darwinian naturalism. In fact, in unpublished writings written just

before the Strauss essay, Nietzsche announces his own naturalistic
view of the world and the 'truth' of 'Darwinism'.[8] In the second
Observation, Nietzsche will describe the 'deadly truths' that modern
science has revealed that challenge all supernatural claims about
humanity and the universe (153). Nietzsche, like Strauss, sees in
modernity the irreversible trend towards the demythologising of
culture. Instead, Nietzsche's overall criticism centres on the terrible implications for culture of Strauss's ethics. As Nietzsche points
out in an unpublished remark to the essay, although Christianity
might not be true in its metaphysics, it had a salutary influence
on culture. In his blithe critique, Strauss 'ignored the best part
of Christianity, the great recluses and saints – in short, its genius'
(KSA 7.27[1], UW 157). Strauss 'believes in modern culture', but
in fact 'ancient culture was a much greater one' even with all its
myths, and 'yet Christianity still asserted its dominance over it'
(KSA 7.27[2], UW 158). In sum, though Christianity was based
on myth, it nevertheless fostered human excellence. By contrast,
Strauss's culture, though rooted in the truths of modern science,
nevertheless obstructs excellence.

   In section 3 of the 'David Strauss' essay, Nietzsche outlines his
critique. Nietzsche will first discuss the 'word of the confessor' –
the substance or 'content' of Strauss's views – and then turn to the
'act of writing' – the form or style of Strauss's 'literary product'.
Nietzsche's aim in both cases is to reveal the weaknesses of philistinism found in Strauss's 'confessions' [*Bekenntnisse*].

   Much of this introductory section is playful. Nietzsche plays on
Strauss's suggestion that he is offering a new *Glaube* – which can
mean 'faith' or 'belief' in German – by imagining that he is making a public confession and 'composing the catechism "of modern
ideas"'. Strauss is in this way no different than the old faith. As a
philistine, however, he has spent his life gaining knowledge, and so
he is not qualified to even make a confession of faith. The 'poverty
and vulgarity' of what results engenders a 'yawn' in the audience
rather than the passionate drive to create this new faith (20). The
most extended joke that Nietzsche makes is to compare Strauss to

[8] See the first pages of 'Homer's Contest' and 'On Truth and Lies in an Extra-Moral Sense'; see
also his note on 'Darwinism' which he 'considers to be correct' (KSA 7.19[132], UW 44).

the 'poodle' in Goethe's *Faust*. Famously, in part one of the play, a poodle comes to Faust in his study, and transforms one scene later into Mephistopheles. The poodle is the harmless animal, yet one that turns into someone quite dangerous, indeed into the 'spirit that denies forever' [*der Geist, der stets verneint*] (*Faust* line 1338). Strauss embodies this negative philistine culture, and the growth and expansion of it from a 'poodle' into a massive 'hippopotamus'.

Nietzsche concludes the section by revealing why he chose David Strauss and *The Old Faith and the New* as his target. It is because Strauss is a 'founder' of 'religion' (21). He is what I will call the 'anti-genius'. The genius or exemplar for Nietzsche is the human being who can reshape and found a new culture, while exemplifying its excellence. Strauss exemplifies the philistine culture and expounds a doctrine to give it unity. He also is 'the philistine who believes himself to be, or acts like, a genius', as Nietzsche says in a notebook entry to the essay (KSA 7.27[46], UW 169). Yet like philistine anti-culture, which prohibits rather than promotes creativity, the anti-genius exemplifies such lack of creativity. Rather than fostering other geniuses, Strauss sees himself as the final voice at the end of history, a figure who wilfully effaces rather than distinguishes himself. As such, unlike the genius who transforms the world, Strauss has no effect on anyone – 'no religion destroyed, no universal avenue built'. Strauss is a form of medicine that induces a kind of deep forgetfulness and bovine bliss (22)

4–5 The 'heaven' of the new faith

As a 'founder of the religion of the future', Strauss is unique among philistines in attempting to found a new faith. Yet as an anti-genius, Strauss eschews 'fanaticism' and does not 'stimulate, elevate', nor serve as the 'guiding light of our life', but instead puts 'fanaticism under the control of reason' (22). As we will see, Nietzsche argues that this project is impossible, because abstract reason cannot found culture. To make this case, he examines three features of Strauss's argument – his view of art (the conception of 'heaven' in sections 4–5), his view of virtue (the 'courage' engendered by artistic culture in sections 6–7), and his

DAVID STRAUSS THE CONFESSOR AND THE WRITER

view of nature and ethics (the Darwinian naturalism underlying his view in sections 7–8).

Nietzsche begins his assessment of Strauss's new faith by examining his vision of the perfect or end state, what in the old faith was 'heaven'. Strauss's naturalism means that this condition will be a 'heaven on earth', a state not provided by God's grace but through human effort, one that will achieve 'all the higher interests of humanity' (23). These 'higher interests' consist in the improvement of historical and natural science, as well as edification through art. Unfortunately, Nietzsche argues, Strauss and the philistines satisfy these interests in bourgeois and democratic ways, that is, through means that enervate the soul rather than elevating it. The philistines promote historical studies by reading newspapers and discussing them over 'daily visits to the beer hall'; they improve scientific studies with a 'stroll through the zoo', and artistic edification with trips to the 'theater and concerts' (24).

Strauss's heaven consists in the daily activities of the philistine anti-culture, but there is a higher end that this anti-culture serves, namely, a particular way of life, the anti-genius, that 'ideal image of the philistine' (25). Again, in this way, Strauss partially embodies the true genius in that he legislates a purpose for culture. Nietzsche identifies this 'heaven of heavens' in the two appendices to Strauss's book, in which Strauss evaluates the great classical geniuses of poetry and music. Nietzsche discusses Strauss's first appendix on 'our great poets' in the remainder of section 4, and his second appendix on 'our great composers' in section 5.

In the first appendix, Strauss discusses the contributions of the classical German poets – Lessing, Goethe and Schiller. Strauss's portrait of these geniuses arouses Nietzsche's bemusement and ire. He pokes fun at Strauss's treatment and understanding of the poets throughout, stressing the artificial character of his portrait. Strauss's poets are not the youthful leaders inspiring a new generation, but old dotards who stifle creativity. Nietzsche mirthfully sums this criticism up by recounting a friend's 'dream' about Strauss's poets:

> He dreamed of a wax museum: the classical authors were all standing there, elegantly copied in wax and pearls. While they moved their arms and eyes, a screw inside them squeaked.

There he saw something utterly uncanny, an unceremoni-
ous figure from which hung a volume and some yellowed
paper and out of whose mouth a piece of paper protruded
on which the name 'Lessing' was written; as my friend
approaches he becomes aware of something horrible: it is
the Homeric chimera, Strauss from the front, Gervinus from
the rear, and chimera in between – in summa, Lessing. (26)

The wax figures represent the artificiality of Strauss's portrayal.
They bear some resemblance to the great living poets of the past
from a distance, but when you look more closely, you realise how
far they are from the real thing. Moreover, these wax figures are
not vivifying in the way the poets themselves were – when they
move, they do not arouse action, but instead a screw inside them
squeaks. Finally, the chimera was a mythic beast, part lion, goat
and serpent, representing a chaotic assemblage of conflicting
parts. Strauss and fellow literary historian Georg Gottfried Gervinus (1805–71) admired Lessing because, Nietzsche suggests, of
his 'universality', that he was a 'critic and poet, archaeologist and
philosopher, dramatist and theologian' (27). However, they failed
to grasp Lessing correctly, instead inserting into Lessing their
own aspiration to be a cultural jack of all trades. The result is not
Lessing himself, but a hideous figure of Gervinus, Strauss, and a
monster with the name 'Lessing' slapped on top.

In the final long paragraph of section 4, Nietzsche turns from
playfulness to anger as he reflects on the consequences of philistine
anti-culture for these geniuses. He focuses particularly on Gotthold
Ephraim Lessing (1729–81), the important dramatist and critic of
the German Enlightenment. For Nietzsche, Lessing demonstrated
'universality' not willingly, but out of 'compulsion' (27).[9] Lessing
was 'troubled, tortured, and suffocated by the vulgar narrowness
and poverty of his circumstances', particularly by his 'learned contemporaries', who taught him to learn everything about everything
in an enervating, philistine fashion. The emerging philistine anti-
culture hence fought against the promotion of genius, hampered

---

[9] See Kaufmann on Nietzsche's reappropriation of Lessing in these sections (1978: 137f.).

his development and grounded his 'eternal flight which was his purpose in life', and finally made his 'flame' burn 'out too quickly'. Similar fates befell the classicist Johann Joachim Winckelmann (1717–68) and, of course, Friedrich Schiller, that 'glorious, divine plaything' whom the philistines 'broke' (28). Culture is supposed to promote the genius's flourishing. The anti-culture actively resists it.

Nietzsche returns to his playful jokes about Strauss in section 5 on the great German composers. Strauss compares Haydn to 'honest soup' and Beethoven to 'confection', revealing first of all his commitment to the levelling, democratic standard of digestive 'healthiness' in culture (29). He reuses the example of Wilhelm Heinrich von Riehl's *House Music* to further illustrate the philistine democratic taste. Riehl was a critic and historian of folk music, who published in 1860 a two-volume collection of simple music to be played in middle-class homes, in contrast to the salon music of aristocratic taste (Arrowsmith 1990: 25 n.8). Nietzsche's most sustained criticism of Strauss's judgement concerns Beethoven. For Nietzsche, Strauss fails to appreciate the 'Baroque' character of Beethoven's music and the 'formless' nature of the 'sublime' in his work (31). In all his judgements on classical art, Strauss ruins it. Nietzsche thus returns to his recurring joke that Strauss's new faith recycles the practices of the old faith. In this case, Strauss lights a 'small sacrificial fire' and 'tosses the most sublime works of the German nation' so as to 'consecrate his idols in their smoking incense' (31).

Nietzsche offers a deeper analysis of the reappearance of the old faith in the new in the final paragraph of section 5. There, he connects philistinism once again to its slavish devotion to public opinion with its 'insipid, insecure, and easily misled' judgements. For Nietzsche, the public 'takes pleasure' in the philistine's skewering of the classics 'as if they were godless obscenities'. The public 'takes pleasure' in their 'candid confessions and admissions of sins', especially when it is those 'great intellects' who were 'supposed to have committed' them (32). Nietzsche suggests here that what drives the old Christian faith and the new philistine faith is the same thing: namely, a democratic hatred of rule and the desire for freedom we saw at the end of section 2. The public longs for this kind of faith because they can finally exercise control over the cultural tyrants who had controlled them.

In sum, Nietzsche's strategy in these sections is to employ reason to reveal the myth at the heart of the putatively rationalistic culture. The myth is that philistine culture possesses the great exemplars of German history as its founding geniuses. Instead, by examining the portrayal of these geniuses, we find they are either artificial constructs or masks for the philistine anti-genius Strauss himself. By juxtaposing the classical and philistine period, Nietzsche reveals a gulf that cannot be bridged, one that can be drawn on to reassert the aristocratic conception of culture once again.

6–7 The 'courage' of the new faith

In the second part of his assessment, Nietzsche shifts from the goal of the faith to its means, the development of moral character or virtue. Or, as Nietzsche asks, 'how much courage does this new religion inspire in its believers?' (32). The virtue of courage appears throughout the essay, already in section 1. There, Nietzsche spoke of the 'natural courage' demonstrated by the Germans on the battlefield. However, Nietzsche argues, courage must be turned inward, against the 'inner enemy', a spiritualisation of natural courage to found and promote culture (6). Culture requires more than the soldier's courage to risk his life, but rather the cultural leader's courage to risk honour and reputation so as to create something novel. Strauss's faith manifestly fails to cultivate this spiritual virtue.

Nietzsche argues that Strauss's new faith is cowardly in two ways. First, it fails to face up to the truth, and instead cloaks itself in myth (section 6). Second, the new faith fails to take any real action to transform the world (section 7). On the contrary, it accommodates itself to the fears of the middle class. Despite these failures, 'this lack of character and strength masquerad[es] as character and strength' (44). Strauss affects courage, and fools German philistines.

In section 6, Nietzsche argues that the Straussian faith flees the truths discovered by the modern world. Strauss expresses his naturalism in various ways and in different metaphors, including saying that the 'universe ... is a machine ... it consists not merely in the movement of pitiless cogs, but also gushes soothing oil' (33). There is no God to provide redemption or meaning to the sufferings of this world. The universe is 'nothing but a rigid mechanism'. These truths are difficult to handle for human beings who have lost a 'compassionate and merciful god'. The philistines thus 'grow alarmed at the rigid and pitiless mechanism of the worldly machine and, with trepidation, ask their leader for help' (43).

For Nietzsche, Schopenhauer's pessimism represents the philosophy most in line with the truths of modern naturalism, but it does not provide solace for the philistines. According to Schopenhauer, the evils of the world greatly outnumber the good, and so we would be 'better off if the world did not exist' (36). Strauss seems to recognise the power of Schopenhauer's view as well, since he engages in a battle with him throughout his book. Yet instead of cultivating courage in facing up to the evils of the world as Schopenhauer does, Strauss offers 'soothing oils' that distract our attention from them and tranquillise our minds (33). In particular, he adopts the views of 'Hegel and Schleiermacher' and transforms them into a 'shameless philistine optimism' (36). For Strauss, the world may possess evils, but it is 'ordered in an absolutely reasonable and purposive manner, and hence ... it embodies a revelation of eternal goodness itself' (41). Reason emerges and progresses gradually in history, transforming evils into good, thereby consoling our fears about a cruel, indifferent world.

Nietzsche revives in this section his critique of 'optimism' from *The Birth of Tragedy* against Socrates' assumption of the rationality and goodness of the world. For Nietzsche, this optimism fails to respond adequately to Schopenhauer's pessimism, being unable to demonstrate that reason directs the world nor how reason can redeem us from evil. Nietzsche identifies a particular argument that Strauss makes in *The Old Faith and the New* as evidence of this cowardice – because the pessimist thinks the world ought not exist, then he also thinks that 'philosophical thought, which forms a part of this world, would be better off if it did not think'. By declaring the 'world to be bad', the thought also 'declares itself to be bad', to be offering a 'bad thought' (36). As Nietzsche points out, this argument is sophistical, relying on an ambiguity between a bad argument and a bad thing, between truth and goodness. It is perfectly consistent to state the harsh truth that it would be better for us not to know this harsh truth. Strauss presents himself as a

courageous defender of the goodness of the world, which masks
the basic cowardice behind his optimism.

Nietzsche concludes section 6 with a second argument against
Strauss's optimism. Optimism is not just 'absurd' but it is also a 'truly
invidious form of thought, a bitter mockery of the nameless sufferings of humankind'. Optimism arouses Nietzsche's 'indignation'
because it does not adequately redeem the suffering of the world,
and so does not offer a challenge to Schopenhauer's pessimism.
Instead, it is a kind of opiate, a distraction from suffering, a way for
us to look upon life 'cheerfully and take the weaknesses of humankind so lightly'. Nietzsche indicates here that for him suffering is
indeed the basic philosophical problem of the modern age, and that
mere illusion and distraction do not suffice to answer this problem,
contrary to the claim of some scholars (e.g. Hussein 2007). To be
redeemed, suffering must serve a purpose. For instance, Nietzsche
castigates Strauss for misunderstanding Beethoven's brooding melancholy. Strauss simply counsels Beethoven not to take the evils of
the world so seriously. Strauss also misunderstands the 'dreadfully
serious impulse toward self-denial and the pursuit of ascetic sanctification characteristic of the first centuries of Christianity'. For
Strauss, this impulse was the result of a kind of 'hangover' from too
much indulgence in previous centuries. Nietzsche uses these examples to show that Strauss has little understanding of the role that
suffering can play in our inner, spiritual lives, driving us to create
and develop higher states of the soul and thereby to redeem this
suffering. It is more evidence that there is no inner life among the
philistines, that they are shallow beings. Strauss's remarks about Beethoven and Christian asceticism reveal a false courage, in which he
confesses his shallowness without 'being ashamed in the least' (37).

Section 7 turns from truth to action. For Nietzsche, the new
faith vitiates the courage necessary to act and achieve the good in
modern culture. Of course, as with the truth, so too with 'ethics',
Strauss affects courage (38). He 'speaks boldly, even brazenly' about
Christianity, suggesting that 'Jesus can be described as a fanatic who
in our day and age would scarcely escape the madhouse' (37–8).
However, this courage is not 'natural and originary' but rather
'acquired and artificial'. Strauss is all talk and no action – he 'never
manages to carry out an aggressive act, only to utter aggressive

words'. Strikingly, Strauss unleashes 'uncouth and thundering' criticisms of Christianity, but then 'announces with admirable candor that ... he does not want to disturb anyone else's solace' in their Christian faith (38). For Nietzsche, the transformation of culture by geniuses is necessarily active – they transform fundamentally how a people understands itself and what its highest aim is. To aim to transform culture but then to deny that one wants to change anything suggests a lack of courage, the virtue of risking one's honour and reputation to ennoble humanity. Instead, Strauss risks nothing and accomplishes nothing, except for fostering a spiritual cowardice.

Strauss also demonstrates cowardice in his circle of fellow philistines. The philistines universally praise 'Darwin as one of humankind's greatest benefactors'. He transformed our view of nature, but how do his findings transform our ethics? Here, Nietzsche says, 'was a real opportunity to exhibit natural courage', to draw out from the Darwinian struggle for existence the 'privileged right of the strong' and a 'moral code for life'. Strauss would have had to summon up an 'inwardly undaunted sensibility' that is 'born of a love of truth' to distinguish himself from his fellow philistines, whose democratic sensibilities blunt the sharp edges of Darwin's implications for ethics (39). Instead, Strauss shows 'weakness' in his 'cowardly accommodation' to these philistines (44). He suggests that the highest life for human beings is to reject our animal instincts, to devote ourselves to humanity and cooperate with others rather than struggle with them.

Strauss accordingly combines 'impudence' towards the old faith with 'weakness' in the new faith, 'audacious words and cowardly accommodation, this careful weighing of how and with which words one can impress a philistine' (44). For Nietzsche, this cowardice provides 'ghastly', 'dreary' prospects to 'father the next generation' and produce 'a truly German culture'. The new faith – as an anti-culture – cultivates the opposite of spiritual courage, a tendency to conform to the judgements and cater to the needs of the middle class. Accordingly, Nietzsche imagines the result as a barren ground 'strewn with ashes, all stars extinguished', where 'spring will never come again' (44). The cowardice of the anti-culture actively resists the promotion of creative daring and lively new ideas and art. Yet it fools itself into believing that it possesses courage after all, which makes defeating this anti-culture so difficult.

7–8 The 'world' of the new faith

In the second half of section 7, as part of his discussion of courage, Nietzsche digresses to address the question, 'How do we conceive the world?' This digression is crucially important to Nietzsche's argument, because here he challenges the ethical foundation of Strauss's view. It also reveals Nietzsche's deep neo-Kantian commitments. As we will see, for Nietzsche, culture aims at the best life for human beings, and so culture requires a justification of its particular account of the good. Strauss thinks that he offers a rationalistic justification for that view of the good. Nietzsche argues, by contrast, that this justification fails, and the new faith rests just as much on myth as all previous cultures. As he proceeds to argue in section 8, the new faith avoids the most fundamental ethical questions about the 'why, whence, and whither' of existence (47).

For Nietzsche, it is 'just as easy to preach morality as it is difficult to establish it' (40). Strauss, by contrast, thinks it is easy to do both. Nietzsche offers three arguments against Strauss's moral theory. First, he argues that Strauss's ethical views are too formalistic and hence empty. Strauss claims that 'all moral activity . . . is the self-determination of the individual according to the idea of the species'. Nietzsche translates this as 'live like a human being and not like an ape or a seal'. Unfortunately, Nietzsche points out, there are many 'diverse and manifold' ways to be a human being, from the 'Patagonian savage' to 'Master Strauss' himself (39). For Nietzsche, there are no universal natural dispositions of the human being as such – human beings are plastic, infinitely malleable based on the culture in which we are educated. In this way, Nietzsche is no Aristotelian naturalist, but rather, as we will see in the second and third parts of the *Observations*, he adopts a historicist approach to human nature. As such, 'live like a human' offers no determinate ethical guidance.

Second, Nietzsche argues that Strauss's ethical views are incompatible with his naturalistic view of the world. Strauss purports to found his ethics on a Darwinian naturalistic view that humanity is not distinct from, but 'wholly a creature of nature'. At the same time, however, Strauss implores: 'never forget even for a moment . . . that you are a human being and no mere creature of nature'. According to Nietzsche, when Strauss comes to ethics, he gives up his effort of scientific explanation and makes the 'leap into imperative'. This imperative is groundless and, Nietzsche points out, it actually runs contrary to the natural tendencies of organic beings in a Darwinian world. Strauss implores us to set aside differences and work for others. Yet, Nietzsche points out, humanity only 'evolved to the heights' by 'adhering to a completely different set of laws; namely . . . by constantly forgetting that other similar creatures possess the same rights [*berechtigt*], by feeling himself to be the stronger and gradually bringing about the demise of other specimens [*Exemplare*] displaying a weaker constitution' (40). Strauss thus does not explain why human beings ought to turn wholly contrary to their natural dispositions.

Third and most fundamentally, Nietzsche turns to the ground of Strauss's ethical view. Strauss argues that we should live as he suggests because we would thereby live in accordance with our natural destiny, in accordance with a benevolent nature that guides the evolutionary project. For Strauss, we are not a 'wild chaos of atoms governed by coincidence', but rather 'everything springs . . . from one primal source of all life, of all reason, and of all goodness' (40–1). God is not outside the world, but immanent 'within us'. Nietzsche sees in this evolutionary pantheism a 'Hegelian devotion to the real as the reasonable, that is, to the *idolatry* [*Vergötterung*] *of success*' (41, original emphasis). The world possesses an inner rationality progressing inexorably towards the good of humanity. For Strauss, the task of the philosopher is to discern the aim of the world, and this aim should guide the conduct of our lives. On this view, Strauss's ethics is grounded on the will of nature, in much the same way that traditional Christian ethics is grounded on the will of God.

Nietzsche's objection to this argument reveals his Kantian lineage. He states that

an honest natural scientist believes in the absolute adherence of the world to laws, without, however, making any assertions whatsoever about the ethical or intellectual worth [*Werth*] of these laws: in any such assertions he would recognise the supremely anthropomorphic demeanor of a reason unable to adhere to the constraints of what is allowed. (translation altered)

In other words, even if Strauss is right that the world is ordered in such a way, this order does not justify that we ought to act in accordance with the world. There is a gap between the 'is' of scientific explanation and the 'ought' of practical philosophy which Hume had recognised long before. For Strauss's argument to succeed, Nietzsche continues, he owes us a 'complete cosmodicy', that is, a justification of the goodness of the cosmos, akin to traditional 'theodicy' which looked for a justification of the goodness of God (41). Only by establishing that the cosmos is indeed good, rather than, as Schopenhauer thinks, a rather rotten place to live, can we have reason to act in accordance with it. Indeed, Strauss's own half-hearted dabbling in such a cosmodicy – arguing with Lessing that God permitted error in order to maintain human striving – makes the world 'the showplace of error than of reason', vitiating Strauss's view of the rationality of nature (43).

In section 6, we already came across a hint that Nietzsche strongly distinguishes practical from theoretical reason, and adopts a Kantian idealist approach to ethics in contrast to Strauss's materialism, which Nietzsche dubs the 'crudest sort of realism'. Strauss tries to ground his ethics on the structure of the world, but if he knew his *Critique of Pure Reason* better, Nietzsche points out, he would know that this project is impossible. Strauss 'hasn't the foggiest notion of the fundamental antinomies of idealism and of the extreme relativity of knowledge and reason. Or: it is precisely reason that should inform him how little reason can discern about the in-itself of things' (35).[10] Famously, for Kant, the traditional metaphysical arguments about the eternity of the world, freedom of the will and the existence of God are impossible to settle with theoretical reason. The antinomies in the Transcendental Dialectic

[10] Nietzsche reworked these remarks about his Kantian idealism in several unpublished drafts of this section, revealing that Kant's transcendental idealism (as filtered through contemporary neo-Kantians) is driving Nietzsche's thinking. See KSA 7.27[37], 27[77].

show the limits of both metaphysical idealism and materialism – that is, we can have no knowledge at bottom of the basic constituents of the universe, whether those basic constituents are ideas or matter. As such, we cannot work from a theoretical account of the world to a moral account of how we should live. Theoretical reason hence should discipline itself to hold fast to its own limits. Strauss oversteps the legitimate boundaries of reason in the name of reason – Nietzsche, following Kant, reveals the groundlessness of his claims and calls on Strauss to re-establish the limits of our theoretical reason.

To sum up: in the first argument, Nietzsche points out that Strauss has little understanding of the diversity of human aspirations in history; in the second, he shows that Strauss fails to ground these aspirations in a continuity with our natural dispositions. In the third, he holds that ethical justification does not derive from the structure of the world. As we will see, Nietzsche sets out in the second and third essays of the *Observations* to develop an ethical theory that accommodates historical variation, reveals continuity with nature, but most importantly justifies ethical value based on the practical structure of human freedom.

In section 8, Nietzsche investigates the implications of Strauss's ethical view of the world. In particular, he examines the 'scholarly person', one of the bedrocks of the philistine culture. Under the spell of Strauss's hopeless metaphysical optimism, Nietzsche argues, scholars do not think of their 'existence' as 'something hopeless and questionable, but rather a firm possession guaranteed to last forever'. For Nietzsche, by contrast, we do not have decisive answers to these questions, and it is the sign of human excellence that we face the yawning of 'the most terrifying abysses' and ask 'why and to what purpose? Whither am I going? Whence do I come' (46). In asking these questions, Nietzsche thinks, we do not follow some plan or purpose given to us, but freely and radically question our own destiny. Since scholars slavishly follow Strauss, they evade these questions, and 'toil' with a 'frantic pace' in a 'painful frenzy' to get the next book or article published. They can never answer the question as to 'what is the purpose of their labor', nor why they must 'toil like those who are impoverished'. The scholar in this way is like the slave, where tasks are 'foisted upon them by need and the afflictions of life' (47). The slave on this view is unfree because he fails to question his role in the world, accepting unquestioningly the role given to him by some authority.

The scholarly industry offers Nietzsche another example of the anti-culture at work, in which the 'development of a new culture has been made impossible'. Scholars develop an entire system of knowledge, in which they determine the standards of truth and significance, and they educate the next generation to inherit these standards. Nietzsche worries that we now need a bright 'lantern' to find the 'pure devotion to genius', the genuine commitment of culture. Indeed, Nietzsche points out that this anti-culture resembles the 'pomp of culture' superficially. He recalls the military discussion of section 1 in stating that scholars have 'impressive apparatuses [that] resemble arsenals replete with enormous cannons and other weapons of war'. Like the physical military virtues of Prussia, the militarisation of the intellect also proves 'the least useful' in achieving culture (48).

8–12 Strauss as a bad writer

In the last third of his essay, Nietzsche turns from his assessment of the substance of Strauss's book to its style, from Strauss the confessor to Strauss the writer. He discusses the genesis of Strauss's style (section 8), the structure of the book (section 9), its overall style (section 10), its rhetorical strategies (section 11), and he concludes with a lengthy list of examples of Strauss's bad prose (section 12). We can offer a briefer overview of this portion of the essay. However, it is still important, because for Nietzsche style cannot be wholly divorced from philosophical substance. The highest ideal of culture – the genius – must marry artistic or philosophical substance with a fitting form of work and art. As such, we learn a great deal in this part about Nietzsche's developing principles of style.

In the second half of section 8, Nietzsche transitions to Strauss's style of writing by examining the scholarly world whence he came. As Nietzsche observes, there is a 'wheezing and frantic race of contemporary scholarship', and so scholars can spend no time cultivating their style (50). As a result, the scholar is 'tasteless, thoughtless, and aesthetically crude' (49–50). Worse, however, is that scholars come to regard good style as foreign and bad, and laud the ponderous and abstract style that they are used to. Strauss straddles the scholarly world and the emerging world of bourgeois 'public opinion' (50). Strauss mimics the style of the chattering classes, who in turn celebrate him as a true stylist, indeed even as a 'classical writer' – in this way again, the philistine culture projects its own standards back into the classics, deluding itself into thinking that the classics and the philistines share common standards. As such, 'philistine culture celebrates a triumph' in Strauss's reflection of its own mediocre style (51).

In section 9, Nietzsche evaluates the overall structure of Strauss's book. For Nietzsche, the first task the writer faces in 'build[ing] his house' is to sketch the 'architecture' of the book. That is, the writer must 'construct a whole', a 'vision' of 'a totality' which provides a 'general direction' along with the 'proper proportions' of parts in service to the whole (52). Nietzsche gives a good insight here as to what he thinks are the formal virtues of a book, namely, the classical features of beauty, a whole with diverse parts yet 'harmonious proportions' (53). This gives us a clue to Nietzsche's own formal ideal in the construction of the *Observations* as a whole.

Strauss's book fails in two ways to achieve structural excellence. First, the overall logic of the book is, for Nietzsche, incoherent. It is not clear why Strauss begins with Christianity when 'even today the greater part of humanity is Buddhist and not Christian' (53). Nietzsche also argues that the fourth part of Strauss's book does not follow from his third part. As he argued in section 7, there is a logical gap between the findings of natural science (in Strauss's part 3) and Strauss's ethical theory (part 4) – 'the modern natural and historical sciences in their entirety have absolutely nothing to do with Strauss's faith in the cosmos' (56). This gap is obscured by Strauss's failure to distinguish 'between faith and knowledge', the *Glauben* of part 4's new faith and the *Wissen* of part 3's Darwinism. The second structural deficiency is aesthetic rather than logical (56). Strauss structures his book not like a castle, to withstand the 'heavy artillery of scholarly evidence' with which his fellow philistines might object (57). Rather, it is like a 'garden house surrounded by the arts of horticulture' (58) which provides a 'charming and colorful picture' to win over the bourgeois sensibilities of his audience (56). Nietzsche concludes the section with an amusing extended metaphor, imagining Strauss as a party host walking his guests through his utterly conventional garden house (58–9).

In section 10, Nietzsche characterises Strauss's overall stylistic type. He notes that Strauss seeks to imitate Voltaire and Lessing throughout his book. These latter writers share a 'simplicity of style'. For Nietzsche, 'it has always been the mark of a genius, who alone enjoys the privilege of expressing himself simply, naturally, and with naivete'. However, when Lessing or Voltaire adopt this stylistic type, their simplicity hides the fact that they require 'excessive power' to wrestle with the most difficult questions of 'the value of existence and the responsibilities of humanity' while avoiding 'a thousand abysses'. This type thereby 'runs simply and with impetuous or graceful leaps along such a path, scorning those who carefully and fearfully walk with measured gait' (60). This stylistic principle animated Nietzsche's own writing throughout his career, and is memorably embodied in Zarathustra's tightrope walker who knocks a slower rival off his path.

Strauss's style is indeed simple, yet it fails to treat the most comprehensive human questions in anything remotely like a satisfactory manner. As such, Strauss compliments himself for being 'scantily clad' in the simplicity of his writing, but it is a nakedness that is not attractive in the least. In fact, Nietzsche holds that Strauss wears nothing but a 'mask of genius', one that resembles 'Voltaire's and Lessing's features', but has no grace underneath (61).

Section 11 delves into the rhetorical strategies employed in Strauss's work, and Nietzsche focuses on Strauss's tone, use of metaphors and sentence length. Nietzsche adheres to the principle that 'everything that is truly productive is offensive' in tone, because creative, productive spirits upend conventional pieties, and so their tone will reflect their transgressive content. By contrast, Strauss delivers a 'universally appealing' tone, employing the 'incessant, regular drip of the same expressions and the same words' that appear in the newspapers (64). The genius brings a tone and voice that is utterly new, whereas by contrast Strauss and the philistine write in a 'flat, hackneyed, powerless, and common' form, endlessly producing writing like 'the wage laborers of language' who 'take revenge on language itself'. The popularisation of the philistine writing style supports the anti-culture, such that 'what is powerful, uncommon, and beautiful falls into disrepute' (65).

Nietzsche also criticises Strauss for artificial innovation in his use of metaphor. Strauss pervasively uses modern things such as the 'railroad, the telegraph, the steam engine, the stock market' in his metaphors, so as to appear scrupulously up-to-date and so to flatter the self-congratulatory sensibilities of the present (66). Finally, Nietzsche notes Strauss's tendency to use 'long sentences and . . . broad abstractions' when outlining his argument, but then he 'prefers tiny sentences . . . that follow hot on the heels of one another' when persuading the reader to accept the argument (67). This mixture of the deadeningly abstract and the sober, punchy 'dryness' is thoroughly tasteless for the aristocratic ear, according to Nietzsche, but it suits the democratic sensibilities of the audience (68).

Finally, in section 12, Nietzsche supports his claims with more than 70 examples from Strauss's text of 'Solecisms, Mixed Metaphors, Obscure Abbreviations, Tastelessness, and Stilted Language' (68). Nietzsche glosses each example with an amusing observation about Strauss's bad writing. This section reinforces how closely Nietzsche read the texts he studies, how much care he thinks an author should expend on style, and indeed how closely Nietzsche expects his own readers to read his works.

The argument, in sum, of this first essay is that modern politics and modern democratic norms combine to create a formidable obstacle to genuine culture. One of the strongest dangers of this tendency is the self-deception of the intellectual class. They think they have achieved the pinnacle of culture, when in fact they have created an anti-culture. Every culture produces a genius, and the philistines point to David Strauss. Yet Strauss is an anti-genius. Anti-culture and anti-genius systematically obstruct rather than foster true culture and true genius.

'David Strauss' comes first in the *Observations*, then, because it establishes the acute problem that the remainder of the *Observations* must solve. In the course of the essays, Nietzsche will develop a theory of the genesis of culture (second essay), and then replace this anti-culture and anti-genius with true culture and genius (third and fourth essays, respectively). Yet 'David Strauss' also begins Nietzsche's project in the *Observations*, generally overlooked by scholars, not of embracing but of dispelling illusion and self-deception. Nietzsche challenges the philistines' champion in order to undermine their illusory self-glorification. He reveals the groundlessness of this culture and hence urges readers to reconsider the problem of the value of existence that is the task of culture. He also reveals the sloppiness of Strauss's writing to awaken once again humanity's distinctively aristocratic feature, our capacity to rank or evaluate the higher and lower.

3
On the Utility and Liability
of History for Life

'On the Utility and Liability of History for Life' is the most studied of all the *Observations*, and for good reason.[1] It offers profound philosophical reflections on the role of history in a fulfilled human life and flourishing culture, on the historical nature of human thought and character, and a searching critique of a culture oversaturated with knowledge and information. It anticipates Nietzsche's own genealogical method and Heidegger's account of the historicity of human beings.

There is, however, a pervasive misunderstanding about the argument of the essay. According to the most common reading, in 'Utility and Liability' Nietzsche bemoans the advancement of human knowledge and the Enlightenment and instead calls for wilful belief

---

[1] The literature can be roughly divided into several interpretive camps: first, the 'ontological' reading, which holds that Nietzsche is giving an account of the nature of being, particularly of human beings (see Heidegger 2016; Bambach 1990); second, the 'postmodern' reading, which emphasises Nietzsche's critique of modernity and his historicising of all truth claims (see Lacoue-Labarthe 1990; Foucault 1984; Borchmeyer 1996; Habermas 1993); third, the 'ethical' reading, which focuses on Nietzsche's view of the 'value or moral significance' of history for the good or examined life (Berkowitz 1995: ch. 1, 27; Lampert 1993: ch. 11; Zuckert 1976). Jensen (2016) has also offered an epistemic reading, that Nietzsche is centrally concerned with exploring the conditions for historical knowledge. As we will see, I prefer the 'ethical' reading of the text, which can incorporate many of the insights from the other camps. For excellent background on the text's genesis and historical context, see Emden 2008: ch. 3; Jensen 2016; Salaquarda 1984; Brobjer 2004.

in myth and illusion.[2] This reading fits with a broader account of Nietzsche's early period, in which he celebrates ancient mythic culture and denigrates modern science (Franco 2011: 7). It also establishes Nietzsche as part of a broader 'Counter-Enlightenment' that includes Herder, de Maistre and Sorel, among others, and that seeks to curb reason in the name of Volkish tradition or throne and altar (Smith 2016: ch. 12).

Other studies have criticised such claims about the 'Counter-Enlightenment' and Nietzsche's early period (Norton 2007; Church 2015a). In this chapter, I challenge this 'mythic' interpretation of 'Utility and Liability'. Although Nietzsche celebrates 'myth' in *The Birth of Tragedy*, he uses the word only once in this essay in an off-handed way (100). Nor is Nietzsche anti-science. In a note to section 6 of the essay, Nietzsche proclaims himself 'against mythology' and proposes to 'explain the history of nations ... in a wholly material manner, according to an analogy with colliding complexes of atoms' (KSA 7.29[75], UW 228). He recognises the virtues of modern historical and scientific knowledge, while also developing a justification to guide and limit the accumulation of knowledge in culture. This justification is based on our highest human need to confer value on our existence. In sum, Nietzsche values modern culture, but thinks it has taken a wrong turn. He seeks to correct its course by drawing on the insights of the ancient world.

The misunderstanding about 'Utility and Liability' stems in part from how scholars have read the essay. They think that Nietzsche discusses the 'utility' of history in sections 2–3, in his famous discussion of monumental, antiquarian and critical history, and then the 'liability' of modern history in sections 4–9.

---

[2] Habermas 1993; Hübner 1996: 29; Breazeale 2000: 71; Yack 1992: 335; Dannhauser 1990: 81; Ottmann 1999: 36. Exceptions include Berkowitz, who argues that 'the general aim of Nietzsche's histories is to discover and display nonhistorical or enduring knowledge about human nature and the rank order of desires, human types, and forms of life' (1995: 28); Lampert, who claims that Nietzsche 'did not advocate the conscious holding on to illusion' (1993: 281); and Emden, who rightly points out that if Nietzsche 'believed science and scholarship to be life-rejecting, it is rather bizarre for him to continue throughout his life to read a considerable amount of material that ... falls into the categories of science and scholarship' (2008: 140).

After all, Nietzsche provides just such an outline of the essay in his notebook (KSA 7:29[153, 160], UW 259, 261–2). Thus, this reading goes, Nietzsche rejects the modern approaches to history discussed in sections 4–9 and adopts the traditional understandings of history in 2–3 with their attendant illusion and myth.[3] This is a mistaken way to read the essay, however. As we will see, in sections 4–9 Nietzsche does not confine himself to the 'liability' of history alone. In section 6, for instance, he has a remarkable discussion of the exemplar of justice. Instead, Nietzsche thinks that the traditional types of history can be transformed and improved through the encounter with modern history. As Walter Kaufman (1978) has suggested, Nietzsche is a more dialectical thinker than is often appreciated, and here we have a good example. Nietzsche does not reject modern history in favour of ancient so much as dialectically synthesise the two.[4] This account thereby helps overcome the recurring scholarly dispute about whether Nietzsche is for or against modernity (Meyer 1998) – he is for modernity, insofar as it incorporates the insights of the ancients.

In terms of the structure of the *Observations* as a whole, 'Utility and Liability' continues the critical project set out in 'David Strauss' of clearing the obstacles to genuine culture. Whereas 'David Strauss' challenged the superficial public culture of modern 'philistines', 'Utility and Liability' drives to the core of modern culture, its unconditional valuing of truth and knowledge. In addition, this essay begins to lay the foundation for the positive project of the *Observations*, namely, to offer an account of the nature of genuine culture and to give a philosophical justification for it based on the value of human existence. 'Utility and Liability' most importantly glosses the role that individual exemplars play in redeeming humanity – the foundation of Nietzsche's positive project – which will be central to 'Schopenhauer as Educator' and 'Richard Wagner in Bayreuth'.

---

[3] See, for example, Lemm 2010: 174f.; Smith 1996, 85. Berkowitz reads the three types of history as 'pure species' discovering 'enduring truth' (1995: 32).

[4] Nor does Nietzsche reject the ancient types of history as argued by Jensen (2016: 146).

Structural overview

1   Life
2–3   The utility and liability of ancient history for life
4–9   Modern history's utility and liability for life and the
        incorporation of the ancient uses
10   Redemption of modern life

Foreword: the philosopher in the historical age

The 'Utility and Liability' essay is the only *Observation* that begins
with a Foreword, an oddity that calls for an explanation. The Foreword accomplishes what many introductory sections do – namely,
it states the main theses of the essay. Nietzsche offers two arguments. In the first paragraph, he states the basic normative claim
that governs the whole of the essay – the 'value' [*Wert*] of history is derived from the 'needs' [*Bedürfnisse*] of 'life' [*Leben*] and
'action' [*Tat*]. History can serve life's aims, but too much instruction
in history can 'inhibit activity', and so should 'arouse our intense
hatred'. Too much history is an 'intellectual superfluity and luxury'
that comes at the expense of our 'most basic necessities'. As human
beings accumulate ever more historical knowledge – which we
do, Nietzsche observes, in the modern age – 'life atrophies and
degenerates'. This degeneration manifests itself in two forms – the
withdrawal 'from life and from action' into oneself, and the increase
of egoism, which uses history to 'whitewash a selfish life and cowardly, base actions'. In this paragraph, Nietzsche also points to the
basis of his main normative claim in his account of our distinctively
historical nature. For Nietzsche, we are not ahistorical animals for
whom history is irrelevant, but nor are we superhistorical gods –
the 'pampered idler in the garden of knowledge' – without needs
(85). Rather, human beings have needs, which can be promoted or
undermined by history.

Nietzsche presents the second overall argument in the third paragraph, in which he discusses the effect of history not on individuals,
but on the community, on the 'age' or the 'people'. Here he argues
that the 'historical cultivation' [*historische Bildung*] of our modern age
is indeed a 'virtue' in which we 'justifiably [*mit Recht*] take pride'.

Nietzsche's admiration of the modern age is often overlooked in accounts of this essay. However, he argues, we have cultivated our historical skills too much. They have become a 'hypertrophied virtue', which turns into an 'infirmity' and threatens to 'cause the demise of a people' (86). This critique of modern culture, as we will see, builds on his cultural criticism of the first *Observation*.

However, the Foreword does not simply present Nietzsche's theses. It also reflects on himself as an author in this historical age. It comments on his 'unfashionableness' and how his thesis will be (negatively) received. Nietzsche predicts that some will greet his views with sympathy, but yet diagnose him as an immature thinker. These reviewers will judge that Nietzsche has 'not experienced' historical knowledge 'in all its purity and originarity', and has not defended it with 'confidence and maturity'. Others will condemn his views as 'unnatural' and wrong, claiming that thereby Nietzsche proves himself 'unworthy of that powerful historical orientation of our age' (86).

After reading the 'David Strauss' essay, we might expect Nietzsche to comment on his unfashionableness stridently and with pride. His tone is quite different here, however. He does not present himself in combat, but on the contrary, he admits that his unfashionableness will 'tend to promote rather than injure' the convention of the age, since it will occasion many authors to 'say flattering things' in their self-defence. Moreover, he admits – no doubt in jest – that 'I stand to gain something for myself that is worth even more than propriety – to be publicly instructed and set right about our age' (86). As such, in this essay he announces that he will adopt a more sober and less polemical style, reminiscent of Socrates, suggesting that he remains open to public correction and even asking permission 'to speak up'. He appeals to the common authority of Goethe throughout the foreword to motivate inquiry into the question at hand. He concludes with a self-effacing 'exculpation', tracing his own views back to his personal 'experiences' and his training as a scholar of Greek antiquity (86).

This change of rhetorical strategy is appropriate given the shift in his target. 'David Strauss' took aim at German culture and its public intellectuals. A polemical tone can be effective in challenging a superficial culture from the perspective of a profound one. However, 'Utility and Liability' deepens *Unfashionable Observations'* cultural criticism, striking at the very basis of modern culture. Nietzsche needs to be more apologetic in his approach in order to begin 'to work against the time and thereby have an effect upon it' (87). As such, he includes a Foreword to convey this shift. In this sense, the Foreword marks another beginning for the *Observations* – if the aim of 'David Strauss' was to destroy the superficial 'anti-culture' of modern Germany, Nietzsche must now set about confronting the deeper obstacle to culture that the modern age presents us, namely, its pursuit of truth.

There is a final reason for a Foreword, which speaks to its philosophical rather than rhetorical purpose. One of the main challenges that Nietzsche faces in writing such unfashionable reflections is the way in which the historical age he is challenging will respond by historicising his own putative untimeliness. Nietzsche himself describes this very process, playfully imagining the historical age's own response to his essay, which would be to claim that his historical 'feeling' [*Empfindung*] has not yet come to 'maturity' and 'purity' or that it is an 'unnatural' development, and that the airing of these disputes will ultimately culminate in his being 'set right about our age'. In other words, Nietzsche purports to leap outside of his age, but the historical critics, shaped by Hegel, deny that such a Herculean leap is possible, insisting that we are always a 'child of our time' and that history will eventually correct Nietzsche as well. Nietzsche must offer such self-reflective comments in order to defend his 'unfashionableness' against the historical charge (86). As he suggests in 'Schopenhauer as Educator', Nietzsche considers himself a 'stepchild' of his age, shaped by it but also able to surmount it with the help of deeper cultural influences (194). In this Foreword, he suggests that as a 'student' of Goethe and 'of ancient Greece', he is able to transcend his time by imagining alternatives posed by the great German or Greek thinkers (86). In sum, then, a Foreword is necessary in order to justify the standpoint assumed by the essay as a whole – illustrated by its famous opening reflections on human nature – that the philosopher is not imprisoned by the age, but can transcend it.

1 Life

This first section discusses the distinctive nature of humanity, a recurring theme in Nietzsche's corpus. For Nietzsche, our relationship to history makes us unique, and he expounds on our historical nature by distinguishing us from ahistorical animals (see A, below). Our humanity consists in our capacity to create value and organise our historical experiences into a meaningful whole, what Nietzsche calls our 'shaping power' [*plastische Kraft*] (B). As human beings, we long for wholeness, to organise our lives and our culture in a systematic, meaningful way, a longing that Nietzsche describes as 'love'. Yet at the same time, we have the capacity to critically evaluate our values – since we are evaluating beings – and so we also long for perfection, to hold the best or truest values, a longing that Nietzsche describes as 'justice'. These two deep desires come into conflict (C).

Many readings implicitly interpret Nietzsche as an Aristotelian – that is, human beings are driven by the needs of 'life' towards some natural end, and so we can draw normative conclusions about how we should live and relate to history based on this telos.[5] This Aristotelianism is mistaken, and it partially accounts for the popularity of the 'mythic' interpretation – if nature guides us towards illusion, then we ought to embrace it. By contrast, I read Nietzsche as a Kantian in the following sense. Our nature does not guide us towards one single end, but rather our fundamental needs conflict with one another. Kant identified the tension between the ends of reason (freedom) and of nature (happiness), and Nietzsche recognises a similar tension. Since our fundamental needs conflict, our nature gives rise to the question of the value of our existence as such, a question driving Kant and Schopenhauer's practical philosophy (D). In a later note, Nietzsche states that identifying this 'fundamental problem [*Grundproblem*]' is the contribution of

---

[5] See, for instance, Solomon: 'Nietzsche was indeed, like Aristotle, a self-proclaimed functionalist, naturalist, teleologist ... standing very much opposed to the utilitarian and Kantian temperaments ... Nietzsche's functionalism is most evident in his constant insistence that we evaluate values, see what they are for, what role they play in the survival and life of a people' (1998: 332). See Gerhardt (1988) for an excellent account of 'life' in this essay.

'Utility and Liability' (KSA 12.2[124]). This problem Nietzsche had already discussed in *The Birth of Tragedy*. In the *Observations*, Nietzsche develops a new type of 'aesthetic justification of existence', namely, the beautiful exemplars or geniuses of humanity rather than particular tragic works of art.[6]

1A *Humanity versus animality (pp. 87–9)*

The section opens with a reference to the title of the book as a whole. Nietzsche asks his sceptical reading public to 'consider [*betrachte*]' the 'herd as it grazes past you' (87). His rhetorical approach is ingenious. Continuing the self-effacing strategy of the Foreword, Nietzsche begins the text by invoking the scientific method of his readers – knowledge is gained primarily through empirical observation, and so Nietzsche asks the reader to test his observations against her own experience. Additionally, by beginning with a reference to his own work – *betrachte* – Nietzsche enlists his readers in his own unfashionable project. By observing the world in this way, he implicitly promises, the reader assists him in justifying his conclusions, and will be led to Nietzsche's unfashionable conclusions as well.[7] As we will see, part of the drama of the *Observations* is the enlistment and education of Nietzsche's readers – by 'Wagner in Bayreuth', Nietzsche is speaking to a fully mature audience, ready for action.

What distinguishes humanity from animality? Animals 'cannot distinguish yesterday from today'. They live in the 'moment', driven by instinct to 'leap about, eat, sleep, digest, leap some more' (87). The 'animal lives ahistorically, for it disappears entirely into the present' (87–8). Human beings, by contrast, have the 'burden of the past' and of memory, so that all our actions are mediated by thoughts about other times and places. We live historically. That we are not simple brutes prompts each of us to 'boast about the superiority of his humanity [*Menschentums*] over animals', but at the same time we 'look enviously upon their happiness [*Glücke*]' (87). The animal and the 'child' live in 'blissful blindness' (88),

---

[6] See Church (2015b) for further elaboration of this point.
[7] See Jensen (2016: 44–5) for more on the opening use of *betrachte*.

neither 'melancholy nor bored', but rather complete with 'happiness' (87). By contrast, as we grow into adulthood, we look at childhood as a 'vision of lost paradise' and suffer from the 'great and ever-greater burden of the past; it weighs him down or bends him over, hampers his gait as an invisible and obscure load' (88). We chase after the happiness of the simple life, but the 'ghost' of the past 'once more' returns and 'disturbs the peace'. This 'chain' of the past is a 'cause for wonder', because these memories are nothing substantial, but rather 'gone in a flash' only to return later to destroy our happiness (87).

Despite the fame of these opening observations, few scholars have critically examined Nietzsche's argument.[8] It seems wrong, first of all, to claim that animals or children live ahistorically – they can learn and possess many memories that prompt them to act. But more importantly, it seems implausible to portray them as happy – some fortunate animals and children may be, but many live in unimaginably harsh circumstances. On the other side, why does the past necessarily make us unhappy? After all, the past can be a source of great joy for many of us.

These objections, however, misconstrue Nietzsche's argument. Nietzsche recognises that animals can learn and that they can suffer. 'Schopenhauer as Educator' portrays a 'beast of prey' as 'seldom satisfied' and with 'gnawing torment' (209). Instead, Nietzsche's view is better understood if we trace it back to an account of human nature held by Jean-Jacques Rousseau and expressed in the classical German thought of Kant, Hegel, Schiller and Goethe. On this view, animals and children live pre-reflectively, driven by natural instinct to completion or wholeness. The development of human self-consciousness, by contrast, introduces critical reflection on our experiences and our instincts, interrupting nature's guidance towards wholeness and leaving us incomplete and full of longing. Schiller's distinction between 'naïve' and 'sentimental' poetry applies this view to pre-reflective and reflective art, a distinction that Nietzsche was wrestling with in the 1870s (KSA 7.7[126], 7.29[126]).

---

[8] Jensen claims that 'there is no real argument that Nietzsche presents for our evaluation' (2016: 46).

As such, when Nietzsche describes the happiness of animals, he focuses not on pleasure, but rather animals' wholeness – the animal, driven by instinct, is 'like a number that leaves no remainder', and so it cannot 'dissemble, conceals nothing, and appears in each and every moment as exactly what it is'. Animals can experience pain, but they cannot experience regret or boredom, feelings that involve a division in the self, between what we could or might become or do and what we are. Human beings, by contrast, do experience these feelings, and Nietzsche understands them as rooted in our historical memory, rendering us perpetually incomplete. Our existence is a 'never to be perfected imperfect' (88).

Why does our historical memory render us incomplete? Nietzsche offers two answers based on the normative and the explanatory nature of history. First, the normative nature of history: we human beings are unique in that we evolved the capacity for memory. By memory, Nietzsche does not primarily mean a cognitive capacity, which, as he well knows, animals share in as well. Rather, he thinks of memory in normative terms. When human beings develop the capacity to remember a condition different from the present, we can compare the present and the past. The past can appear to us as superior to the present, or indeed the past can hold out the counterfactual possibility of some superior present that we did not pursue. In an important draft of this section, Nietzsche emphasises this normative consequence of our historical natures. Unlike those living the simple life – the 'farmer', Nietzsche says – we 'compare and measure' ourselves 'in such a painstaking way', such that we cannot 'remain unconscious in matters of self-judgment'. We gaze on the 'previous picture galleries of all ages', and thus each of us is 'constantly reflected back upon himself, forcing him to make comparisons and ask himself what business he has being in these rooms at all?' (KSA 7.29[172], UW 265).

The normative nature of memory gives rise to all sorts of emotions in human beings, including melancholia and boredom (87). The feeling of regret, for instance, is one in which alternate possibilities from our past confront us – why didn't I choose that university or career or spouse? In the very moment in which we think we have achieved wholeness in our choices of life, our reflection critically evaluates the alternatives we could have pursued, suggesting that our life could always be better – 'over and over a leaf is loosened from the scroll of time, falls out, flutters away – and suddenly flutters back into the human being's lap' (87). This memory drives us on an endless, fruitless quest towards perfection. As such, we develop a distinctively human need for perfection – for our life to be of the incomparably highest value – even though it is our lot 'never to be perfected' (88). That is, we seek not just life merely, but a good, valuable life, in 'search of the unattainable goal' (KSA 7.29[172], UW 265).

Nietzsche thus identifies the two fundamental or what he will call 'genuine needs' [ächten Bedürfnisse] of humanity, for wholeness and for perfection or value (167). However, the problem of the human being is that these fundamental needs conflict. Nature does not give us guidance for what a good life is, but rather we human beings introduce such standards, which vary from historical culture to culture. Thus, any claim to the good life can be contested by a past or present standard, and there is no impartial judge, no super-culture outside all cultures, to adjudicate such conflicts. Our criti-cal reflection, in other words, reveals the foundationless character of all our claims to the good, driving apart our two basic needs. Accordingly, Nietzsche describes human existence as 'something that lives by negating, consuming, and contradicting itself'. By pursuing perfection, we can never achieve wholeness, because we cannot hold on to a standard of the good life that can organise our past, present and future into a unified, achievable purpose or aim. Instead, only death eliminates the conflict between our needs, though it does so by 'suppress[ing] the present' (88).

The second reason why historical memory renders us incom-plete is because it explains away and thereby destroys our free agency. Nietzsche asks us to 'imagine the most extreme example' of historical memory, someone who can never 'forget' anything. 'Such a human being' would 'see becoming [Werden] everywhere' and 'would no longer believe in his own being, would no longer believe in himself . . . and would lose himself in this stream of becoming'. History provides explanations for all things. It might seem as if par-ticular individuals such as Napoleon drove history forward, but the closer we look at history, the more we see that a multitude of causes outside of any individual's control determined events – large-scale political, economic and social forces or biological forces, or some interaction of both. The more we learn about history, the less we see any permanence or agency within it. Like Heraclitus, we eventually see only flux (89), and if we discover the 'laws' regulating history, the 'only result would be determinism, and the acting human being would be violently reduced once more to a sufferer' (KSA 7.29[40], UW 207).[9]

The first, normative feature of historical memory, Nietzsche states, prevents us from 'know[ing] what happiness is'. This second, explanatory feature is 'worse' in that it prevents us from 'do[ing] anything that makes others happy'. It prevents action because 'action requires forgetting', it requires that we think that human agency is possible in the world. If we see only flux as the 'true student of Heraclitus', then 'in the end [we] would hardly even dare to lift a finger' (89). Why act if all our efforts will have a transient effect, undone by history? For Nietzsche, to act and promote wholeness we must assume we can introduce permanence in the world, or else the flux of history will constantly transform us as well. We must therefore 'believe [*glaubt*] in [our] own being' and each must 'believe in himself' as an agent who possesses an identity that endures over time and that can introduce enduring effects into the world (89). As we will see, Nietzsche develops a justification for belief or faith [*Glaube*] in free agency in the form of an exemplar – he does not ask for a groundless leap of faith.

1B *Life and the shaping power (pp. 89–91)*

To overcome these problems and satisfy both needs for wholeness and perfection, Nietzsche argues we must cultivate the 'ability to forget' (88–9). For Nietzsche, 'there is a degree of sleeplessness, of rumination, of historical sensibility, that injures and ultimately destroys all living things, whether a human being, a people, or a culture' (89). He here notably extends his analysis from individuals to communities, arguing that the same account holds for both – a people is an organic, living thing in much the same way as an individual. Both, Nietzsche states in a series of metaphors in this

---

[9] See Meyer (1998: 15f.) on Nietzsche's view of becoming in the early period writings.

section, require a 'closed and complete ... horizon' for their historical memory (90), or an 'enveloping cloud of mist' that prevents too much history (91).

What do these metaphors mean? In a way, 'forgetting' is a misleading description of what Nietzsche discusses in this section, and should itself be taken as a metaphor. It is not that individuals or cultures passively forget experiences or events, but rather that they actively interpret historical events as part of their particular identities. Nietzsche names this capacity the 'shaping power [*plastische Kraft*]' of an individual or community, and describes it as 'that power to develop its own singular character out of itself, to shape and assimilate what is past and alien, to heal wounds, to replace what has been lost, to recreate broken forms out of itself alone' (89). Here, Nietzsche recalls his discussion of culture from section 1 of 'David Strauss', in which he lauded the self-determination of French culture in contrast to German. In this account of the shaping power, Nietzsche is describing the fundamental nature of individual and collective agency that makes possible such self-determination.

The shaping power is not a capacity distinctive to human beings, but rather is an important capacity shared by animals and humans. Indeed, it is a 'universal law' that 'every living thing can become healthy, strong, and fruitful only' by 'drawing a horizon around itself' (90).[10] In the case of animals, the shaping power is biological. The animal is an organic system of interdependent parts which has certain instinctual aims. The 'shaping power' is a metaphor to refer to the organism's ability to control its environment, pre-eminently by ingesting parts of the world and converting the food into resources for its own functioning. The organism's shaping power transforms the external world, hostile and alien to itself, incorporating it into parts of itself, into its inner world. Of course, sometimes the organism may be overwhelmed by the environment, when, for instance, it is assailed by a stronger organism that ingests it. At that point the organism's shaping power fails,

---

[10] Meyer insightfully connects the plastic power back to the tension between the Apollinian and Dionysian from *The Birth of Tragedy* – the Apollinian establishes historical horizons, and the Dionysian destroys these horizons (1998: 99–110).

its interdependent parts and structure destroyed and reconverted into functional parts of the stronger organism that shapes it.

In human beings and communities, the shaping power has the same formal character, which explains why Nietzsche describes our activity with biological metaphors and terms such as incorporation. However, our shaping power works on a different substance – rather than biological, it is normative in character, or what he will call a '*moral* nature' [*sittlichen Natur*] later in the text (167, original emphasis). In addition to having an underlying organic or biological structure, the individual or community possesses a normative structure. That is, each individual and community cultivates a 'singular character' (89), organised by a particular set of 'valuations' (92), that is, norms about what is worth pursuing and achieving in life. These valuations are structured into a rough unity so as to confer a coherent character on each, such that there is a clear normative aim distinguishing one individual or culture from others, and a set of subsidiary norms guiding the other aspects of life for each. These norms also guide 'judgement' in responding to new events and experiences (90).

We employ our shaping power, then, just as in the case of the organism, to control the normative world. The organism struggles for existence, fighting against a hostile world by transforming its alien character into itself. The human individual or community also fights a spiritual battle within the normative conflicts in the human world. History presents us with many competing visions about what is good and worthy in a human life, and nature provides us with no objective criteria by which to judge the best.

As such, the first task of the human shaping power is to 'develop its own singular character out of itself', to give itself its own distinctive set of values for it to pursue, abandoning the natural state of normative anarchy (89). This first task, then, involves conferring normative meaning on ourselves, especially our biological desires and lives, transforming their meaning from natural urges to those shaped and willed by us as something valuable or worthless. For instance, some cultures use their shaping power to brand some desires as sinful or cowardly, and they introduce duties that individuals ought to fulfil in order to live a good or worthwhile life, not just the life of an animal.

This autonomy or self-determination connects Nietzsche with the Kantian tradition.

The second task of the human shaping power involves its relationship to its competitors: 'to shape and assimilate what is past and alien, to heal wounds, to replace what has been lost, to recreate broken forms out of itself alone' (89). Nietzsche envisions a struggle with 'alien' competitors over our normative structure. In such challenges to the authority of our normative order, the shaping power 'incorporates into itself all that is past ... transforming it, as it were, into its own blood' (90).[11] For instance, a culture employs its shaping power to reinterpret the meaning of its own conflicted history into a unified story, or to classify alternative ways of life as aberrant or unnatural, or to regard other cultures as barbaric or evil. In all these cases, an individual or culture negates the external or alien character of some experience or action, and instead confers meaning on it, such that it becomes part of the normative structure of its character, in service to its overall aim. Later in the text, Nietzsche uses ancient Greece as the pre-eminent example of a culture able to incorporate 'a chaos of foreign – Semitic, Babylonian, Lydian, and Egyptian – forms and concepts' into a harmonious, self-determined moral order (166).

As in the case of organisms, so too can human individuals and communities be weaker or stronger, measured by the efficacy of their shaping power. The weakest shaping power could 'bleed to death from a single experience, a single pain', unable to confer meaning on it within its system, but rather overwhelmed by its alien, meaningless character (89). By contrast, the strongest shaping powers are 'little affected by life's most savage and devastating disasters' because the strong 'roots' of their 'innermost nature' are able to 'incorporate into [themselves] all that is past' without 'limit' (90). The stronger the shaping power, Nietzsche asserts, the 'healthier' the individual or culture. One is 'vigorously healthy and robust, a joy to look at', when one becomes able to forge a unity or values for oneself, as in the case of the Greeks (91).

---

[11] See Lemm (2013) on the notion of 'incorporation' [*Einverleibung*].

How then, does a strong shaping power satisfy our basic needs? It satisfies our need for wholeness, because stronger individuals or cultures achieve a 'tolerable level of well-being and a kind of clear conscience' from their 'closed and complete . . . horizon' (90). The self-determined individual or culture is not divided against itself, but becomes a dynamic unity. It also satisfies our need for perfection by giving us our own standard of value. Its closed normative structure allows the individual or community to 'forget' their normative competitors. Our closed horizon means that we assume ourselves to be the objective judge of all normative claims, the standard according to nature, as it were, and according to which all other normative systems are deviations. We are the normative centre of the universe, and so have discovered the key to leading a valuable life. An individual and culture synthesises these needs by making its normative end or aim the basis for its unity of character – every culture has a distinctive aim, and all its parts are unified in a functional way to serve that aim, or, in terms that we have seen already, 'culture is a unity of artistic style that manifests itself throughout all the vital self-expressions of a people' (9).

Nietzsche summarises his argument beginning at the bottom of p. 90. For him, we pay too much attention in contemporary culture to historical knowledge and not enough to our genuine needs. Our most basic need, the need for wholeness, requires that we 'live to a certain degree ahistorically', and so this need must be regarded as 'more significant and more originary', since it is the 'foundation upon which something just, healthy, and great [*Rechtes, Gesundes und Grosses*], something that is truly human [*wahrhaft Menschliches*], is able to grow at all' (91). However, our ahistorical nature must be balanced against our distinctively human, historical nature, our need for wholeness against our need for perfection. Our historical nature is like the 'bright, flashing, iridescent light . . . generated within that enveloping cloud of mist', and when we do 'utilize the past for life', only then do we 'become a human being' (91). Indeed, our historical nature has value of its own, because it is the very condition for the possibility of exemplarity. As he puts the point in a notebook entry, the burden of history has this positive effect, that it 'drives us with the disquiet of a ghost to ascend tirelessly the entire stepladder of all that human beings call great, amazing, immortal, divine' (KSA 7.29[98], UW 242). For Nietzsche, then, human beings can get the balance wrong in either direction, either by forgetting too much and becoming an animal without the possibility of doing 'something, just, healthy, and great', or by remembering too much and becoming paralysed by history.

1C *Justice and love (pp. 91–2)*

Nietzsche illustrates his argument with a vivid example of a 'man seized and carried away by a vehement passion for a woman or for a great idea'. This example reveals that, though the shaping power can balance our two fundamental needs, there nevertheless remains an enduring tension between the two. He describes this tension now as one between love and justice.

The man 'seized' by love has his 'world change', in the sense that 'all his valuations [*Wertschätzungen*] are changed and devalued' (91–2). The love he feels becomes his overriding aim, which then transforms the norms he follows and the judgements he makes about the world around him. Yet this single-minded longing makes him 'blind' to competing alternatives, and his 'memory turns inexhaustibly round and round in a circle'. Love promises wholeness because the man in love does not compare his beloved to anything else, in which case he would become divided against himself. Rather, his *eros* propels him to unify with his beloved. Accordingly, love makes his agency possible, giving him the belief or faith that his activity can have an enduring effect in the world: acquiring a lasting love. Love is the 'womb' of all 'deeds', and the 'best deeds occur in such an exuberance of love' (92).[12]

At the same time, however, this condition, representative for Nietzsche of all limited horizons, 'is the most unjust [*ungerechteste*] condition in the world', as it is 'narrow, ungrateful to the past'; the man struck by love is 'blind to dangers, deaf to warnings'.

---

[12] I use the term *eros* here interchangeably with 'love' to underline the connection between Nietzsche's and Plato's view of love, a point drawn by Nietzsche himself in several notebook entries (KSA 7.19[10], 7.21[14], 8.5[22]). In addition, as Kaufmann noted, the *Symposium* was the young Nietzsche's '*Lieblingsdichtung*' (1978: 160).

Love requires that we act 'without knowledge [*wissenlos*]', so that the man 'is unjust to whatever lies behind him'. Thus, Nietzsche strikingly concludes, 'everyone who acts loves his action infinitely more than it deserved to be loved, and the best deeds occur in such an exuberance of love that, no matter what, they must be unworthy [*unwert*] of this love, even if their worth were otherwise incalculably great' (92). In sum, then, acting in service to life – following our *eros* towards wholeness in our overriding aim – is unjust.

Why is life unjust? Nietzsche points out that the condition for the possibility of 'every just deed [*rechten Tat*]' is an 'ahistorical' horizon (92). The man in love acts without right or justification [*Recht*] for two reasons. First, he does not justify the choice of his overall aim, his particular beloved. Why choose this beloved rather than another? The man remains 'blind' to alternatives, fails to critically evaluate his choice, and ultimately accepts his beloved without reflection. The man does not justify that his beloved deserves his love. The second reason is that he then makes partial or biased judgements about the world based on his unjustified final end. His beloved colours his world, clouds his vision and obscures his beloved's faults. His partiality thus distorts the world as it is. For instance, consider Nietzsche's example of an 'isolated alpine valley' culture (90). This culture is driven by love for its particular ideal, and its members shape the world and act based on this ideal. The culture is healthy according to the basic need of life, but it is unjust because 1) it uncritically accepts its ideal as authoritative (according to nature, the gods, ancestors, or any other authority external to it), and 2) it makes partial judgements about the world that distort it. In these senses, the man in love or the alpine culture embrace the 'ahistorical' and hence their animal natures – they relinquish their distinctively human critical capacity that freely transcends every authority given to us from the outside. They fail to be free in the sense of becoming their own self-determining normative authority.

Accordingly, Nietzsche's example provides us with some guidance about his fundamental views of justification. Like Kant, Nietzsche examines not only the 'quid facti' about the values pursued by individuals and cultures, but also the 'quid iuris', the question of what justifies the pursuit of such values. Also like Kant, he denies that we can justify these values with reference to some external authority, even a deity, or some pressing desire, such as love; rather, we must justify them according to our free-dom. We can see in this first section that *Recht* requires 1) a self-determined justification of the end or ideal of one's action, and 2) a justification of the judgements that one makes about the world. In this way, Nietzsche does not simply enjoin cultures to embrace illusion. On the contrary, he argues that from the perspective of *Recht*, all such illusions are unjust, and that we must provide a new justification for modern culture. 'Utility and Liability' outlines the conditions for such a justification; the theory of exemplarity in 'Schopenhauer as Educator' supplies this justification.

1D *The suprahistorical and the value of existence (pp. 92–6)*

Thus far, Nietzsche has been discussing animals' ahistorical nature and humans' historical character. We have seen that the plas-tic power draws on both the ahistorical and historical to forge a unique character that temporarily satisfies our fundamental needs for wholeness and perfection. However, Nietzsche recognises that putting history in service to life is at the same time deeply unjust. In the final pages of this introduction, Nietzsche introduces a third approach to the past, the suprahistorical, one that offers a just approach to history, though one that prevents us from 'continuing to liv[e] on and tak[e] part in history' (93). Nevertheless, in a few draft outlines to this essay, Nietzsche regards the 'ahistorical' and the 'suprahistorical' as 'remedies for life harmed by history' (KSA 7.29[157, 160], UW 260, 262).[13]

Nietzsche describes the 'suprahistorical' standpoint as an 'elevat[ion]' [*erheben*], a term connected to the 'sublime' [*erhaben*]. We achieve this standpoint by recognising the limits and injustice of each 'ahistorical atmosphere' surrounding historical individuals and cultures. By critically examining the horizon of the individual, then

---

[13] See Jensen (2016: 14f., 57–9) on the genesis of Nietzsche's notion of the suprahistorical. Jensen is rather critical of Nietzsche's notion; I try to justify its importance here.

the community, we finally ascend to the perspective of humanity as a whole. This ascent to the universal is similar to that of modern scientific history which Nietzsche will go on to discuss, in the sense that modern historians seek an 'objective' account not just of any one particular history, but of humanity's history as a whole. However, the 'suprahistorical' standpoint differs essentially in its aim and its method. Modern scientific history pursues knowledge for its own sake. The 'suprahistorical' person elevates himself beyond each culture in pursuit of the good life, or, as Nietzsche puts it, of an answer to the question posed by our distinctively human need: 'why and to what purpose do people live?' (93). In its method, modern historical science shares with natural science the search for knowledge, defined as the understanding of the facts and lawful regularities that govern the causal order of the world. However, the 'suprahistorical' standpoint seeks 'wisdom', Nietzsche's term for the understanding of the categories or 'types' that underlie the many varied manifestations of these types (94).

In other words, the 'suprahistorical' perspective regards the 'past and present' as one and the same, that despite the great 'diversity' of cultures, 'they are identical in type, and as the omnipresence of imperishable types they make up a stationary formation of unalterable worth and eternally identical meaning'. Whereas the modern scientific historian seeks endless knowledge about the 'hundreds of different languages' that divide cultures, the 'suprahistorical' person recognises that these languages are means to achieve 'the same constant types of human needs, so that anyone who understood these needs would be able to learn nothing new from these languages'. The scientific historian gathers knowledge of the surface of things, while the 'suprahistorical thinker illuminates the entire history of peoples and individuals from the inside', regarding the expressions of a culture as 'different hieroglyphs' that indicate a fundamental inner meaning shared by humanity (94).

As such, the 'suprahistorical' individual answers the question of the purpose and value of existence differently than the 'historical' person. The 'historical' individual – the individual or culture enclosed within a horizon – locates the value of existence in his successful efforts in time. The man in love, for instance, takes as the 'meaning of existence' the achievement of his beloved, the

unfolding 'of a *process* [*Prozesses*]' (93). By contrast, the 'suprahistorical' thinker is the one who 'does not seek salvation [*Heil*] in a
process, but for whom instead the world is complete [*fertig*] and
has arrived at its culmination [*Ende*] in every individual moment'.
The passage of time is irrelevant, because the fundamental types
of human beings are enduring. The suprahistorical individual
achieves wholeness and perfection through the contemplation of
the completeness and culmination of the enduring types (94). By
contrast, the historical person achieves wholeness and perfection
through the 'active and progressive [*Tätigen und Fortschreitenden*]'
pursuit of his distinctive aim (95).

Who are these 'suprahistorical' persons? The suprahistorical
standpoint is that of art (e.g. the poet Giacomo Leopardi, 94), religion (e.g. the Hindu religion (KSA 7.30[2]) and philosophy (KSA
7.29[197]), each of which takes as its object humanity as a whole
rather than particular individuals. Nietzsche's debt to Hegel's analysis of art, religion and philosophy as constitutive of absolute spirit
is recognisable here, despite his critique of Hegel later in the essay.
Indeed, Nietzsche regards the achievement of this standpoint as
a 'sublime [*erhabene*] breach with nature, a striking lack of utility'
(KSA 7.29[197], UW 272), as it freely transcends the needs of life
entirely and seeks the truth behind all things. Indeed, Nietzsche
identifies the freedom achieved through the 'suprahistorical' perspective to be one of its main benefits – he cites Barthold Niebuhr
in support of the view that without assuming this perspective, we
'will be enslaved by the presence of any powerful intellect that
places the loftiest passion into a given form' (93). This elevation
liberates us from the wilful ignorance of every historical perspective. At the same time, by transcending life in this way, one ceases
to take 'history overly seriously' and no longer acts within it, recognising the impossibility of changing the essential order of things
(93). Accordingly, the impotence of the 'suprahistorical' reasserts
the 'antithesis between life and wisdom', between our needs for
wholeness and for perfection.

Nietzsche implores his readers to 'leave the suprahistorical
human beings to their nausea and wisdom', since we are focusing
on the historical point of view 'today' (94). However, we are left
with the question of which perspective is better, the historical or

suprahistorical? Which, for instance, does Nietzsche adopt? Many scholars, especially in the post-modernist tradition, have assumed that he adopts an essentially historicist perspective.[14] However, consider the fact that this entire section itself has been a suprahistorical analysis: Nietzsche has unearthed the basic 'types' of beings – humanity and animality – the fundamental 'types' of needs – wholeness and perfection – and the three main 'types' of perspective on the whole – ahistorical, historical and suprahistorical. Nietzsche will proceed in the next eight sections to describe four sub-types of the historical perspective – monumental, antiquarian, critical and modern scientific. Finally, he will base his entire positive ethical project on the enduring exemplars of humanity, in contrast to the Hegelian view of humanity's progress.

In all these ways, Nietzsche adopts a suprahistorical perspective. However, he does not simply embrace this perspective, because it rejects any role for human agency in the world, and thus must endure 'nausea'. Nietzsche recognises that humanity can transform itself, and introduce new types – the most important example of our self-transformation for him is the transition from pre-modern closed communities to modern culture's destruction of all horizons. As such, in my view, Nietzsche aims to synthesise the suprahistorical and historical perspectives. The suprahistorical can provide a universal perspective on the enduring human types. The historical can examine how humanity changes over time, particularly through the activity of individual exemplars. This history of exemplars can thereby provide a justification for faith in human freedom. If past exemplars were capable of transforming the nature of things, so can future exemplars. In this way, Nietzsche sets out not only to contemplate humanity, but actively to transform culture to generate continued human freedom.

2 Monumental history

Sections 2–9, then, expand on the 'historical' approach to satisfying life's need for wholeness and our distinctively human need to

---

[14] See, for example, Foucault 1984. Jensen (2016: 68) claims that the suprahistorical is a late development and is quickly rejected by Nietzsche. I follow Berkowitz (1995: 31) and Ansell-Pearson (2013: 245), who note Nietzsche's admiration for the suprahistorical.

lead a valuable existence. Nietzsche argues that there are different types of history, and that these types can be combined in different ways. Sections 2–3 discuss the ancient or pre-modern types of history – monumental, antiquarian and critical – while sections 4–9 examine the modern scientific approach to history. For each type, there are benefits (or utility – *Nutzen*) and dangers or disadvantages (or liability – *Nachteil*). Most scholars focus on the benefits of pre-modern history and the disadvantages of modern scientific history.[15] Although Nietzsche himself emphasises the utility of ancient history and the liability of the modern scientific, he nevertheless recognises utility and liability in every type. In my view, Nietzsche suggests that through balancing these different types in culture, we can enjoy the benefits and minimise the deficiencies of each.

Sections 2–3 are some of the most commented-on portions of Nietzsche's entire corpus.[16] My main contribution will be to argue that these initial types of history are ancient or pre-modern types.[17] Nietzsche identifies three types of ancient or pre-modern history based on three 'needs [*Nöten*]' (108). The need to 'act and strive' is satisfied through monumental history; the need to 'preserve and venerate' is fulfilled through antiquarian history; those who 'suffer' and are 'in need of liberation' require critical history (96). Nietzsche orders these types in this way because they form a cycle, which in its totality realises the active life of the historical perspective.

2A *Utility of monumental history*

Nietzsche begins his analysis of monumental history by stressing its great importance, that 'above all, history pertains to the active and powerful human being'. As we saw in section 1, the

---

[15] See, for example, Dannhauser 1990: 78.

[16] Niemeyer's entry on 'Utility and Liability' in the *Nietzsche-Lexikon* provides a good overview of the genesis of each type of history (2009: 155–7). See also Lemm (2010: 174f.), Jensen (2013: ch. 4), Emden (2008: 150–73) and Meyer (1998: 159–90) for helpful readings.

[17] That these forms of history are ancient in nature helps explain why, as several commentators have pointed out, Nietzsche does not maintain these categories in his later work (Jensen 2016: 69; Brobjer 2004).

'historical' perspective finds the value of existence in the realisation of a historical process. This perspective calls, then, for the active life precisely to realise this process. The active life, however, requires 'exemplars [*Vorbilder*], teachers, and comforters' to 'emulate and improve' on in its own 'great struggle [*grossen Kampf*]' (96). Thus, history that recounts past monumental deeds has utility in inspiring active individuals, and so is the primary type of history, as it drives individuals towards fulfilling the active life.

Since monumental history functions to serve the active life, much of Nietzsche's discussion concerns the nature of the active life. The 'person who takes action' has as 'his goal ... some kind of happiness [*Glück*] – not necessarily his own, but often that of a people [*Volkes*] or of all of humanity [*Menschheit*]'. What does Nietzsche mean by this aim of the active life? As we saw in the first section, human beings vainly seek happiness, burdened as we are by history. Cultural horizons provide happiness for us by limiting our exposure to history. However, these horizons are not natural, but rather artificial. They must be created by someone, and for Nietzsche, the founder of a new cultural order is the active person. By founding artificial orders in which human beings can find happiness, the active life serves a people and even all of humanity.

To achieve this goal, the founder's 'path leads through human minds [*Gehirne*]' (97). Nietzsche speaks of minds rather than bodies because the active person uses his shaping power on the spiritual or normative thoughts of a people, rather than forcing their bodies into submission. The active person transforms the valuations of an aggregate of human beings, making them into a cultural unity. As such, the monumental action is not in service to selfish aims or self-aggrandisement, nor is it undertaken through physical violence, as is so often suggested by readers of Nietzsche and the *Übermensch*. Rather, the active life aims to eliminate the wretched natural condition of human beings by forging a shared spirit. In this way, Nietzsche's account belongs to the tradition of modern political thought about founders that includes above all Machiavelli's *The Prince*, chapter 6, and Rousseau's *Social Contract*, book 2, chapter 7.

But why, we might ask, is the happiness of a people or of humanity the aim of the active life? It is important to recognise that though the active person seeks the happiness of others, he does not do so selflessly. The founder performs 'great' deeds ultimately because he will win 'fame' – his deeds will be recorded by monumental historians and he will 'serve later generations as a teacher, comforter, and admonisher'. In this way, he does not live the mere life of an animal, but the free, self-determined life of a human being. His life has value because he extends 'the concept of "the human being" [*Mensch*]' and he gives 'it a more beautiful substance [*schöner zu erfüllen*]' (97).

Let us expand here on Nietzsche's reasoning, because it offers insight into his positive ethical view. Nietzsche could have said that monumental deeds are those that 'extend the concept' of a particular culture, which we might expect given that the aim of the historical perspective is to complete a historical process. We might think here of the deeds of statesmen and citizens of the ancient world who sought to expand the greatness of an Athens or a Rome. Nietzsche does not, because such individuals and their deeds are not active in the deepest or most far-reaching sense. To be active, an individual has to create something new in the world, and so has to shape and remake the world around him. As such, an individual who unreflectively internalises his culture's aim as his own aim is shaped decisively by that culture. He is not then fully active, but rather passive at the deepest level. This does not mean that the active individual needs to create himself *ex nihilo* – this is impossible – but rather that he transcend existing cultural limits and generate a new aim for a new culture in dialogue with other great individuals who also transcend their limits. In this way, the great deeds of individuals 'form links in one single chain' (97). Accordingly, for Nietzsche, the standard of 'greatness' is not internal to any one culture, but is constructed out of the many foundings by active human beings across time. These are the 'few individuals in whom humanity will culminate' (KSA 7.29[73], UW 226). In this way, Nietzsche is not a 'relativist' about value, as he is so often understood to be.[18]

---

[18] Jensen is right that Nietzsche does not 'draw up an explicit set of criteria by which to judge whether someone is "great"' (2016: 114), but he does develop a theory of exemplarity, and we can ground our judgements of greatness based on instances of exemplarity. See Ansell-Pearson (2013: 246–7) on this passage about our faith in humanity and its ethical significance.

The active life strives for greatness so that the individual can create something new in the world and hence express his freedom in the sense of self-determination. By doing something unique and new, moreover, the active person can favourably compare his greatness to all other great deeds in history – historical memory does not thereby lead us into self-doubt as we discussed above. Instead, monumental historical memory actually augments the value of the individual's life as it forges a new link in the chain, a new contribution to humanity's freedom.

However, as Nietzsche recognises, the fame from such deeds can be fleeting, and even the greatest deeds can fade into the oblivion of history's flux or becoming. The active individual suffers from 'resignation' at this thought, which threatens to undermine the value of his existence. If his efforts do not change the fundamental nature of things, then he is not a self-determining agent after all, but passively suffers under the destructive power of history's flux. As such, the active individual 'must be eternally [*ewig*] present in order for' his agency 'perpetually [*ewig*] to have this effect' (97). For Nietzsche, then, monumental history is so important, because it promises immortality for the monumental deed, by retelling it generation after generation. If monumental history is regarded highly, the active individual need not 'hold existence in high regard' as the 'common human being does'. Those 'on the way to immortality and to monumental history' can treat mere existence with 'sublime derision', because when they go to 'their graves' they leave behind only 'waste, refuse, vanity, and animality', which 'had always oppressed them' and 'now would fall into oblivion after long being the object of their contempt'. Death is in fact a positive good, because it rids us of our animality and liberates our humanity. This thought – reminiscent of Plato's *Phaedo* – does not entail that human beings have an immortal soul freed from the cage of the body. Rather, it is that 'one thing will live on: the signature of their most authentic being, a work, a deed, a rare inspiration, a creation' (98). The active individual will not live on in a disembodied form, but his deed will as the founder of a particular cultural order. Indeed, this immortal act gives him more 'worth' than 'an empire because he has a more salutary effect for all of posterity' (KSA 7.29[1], UW 188).

This desire for immortality, Nietzsche argues, is not the 'tastiest morsel of our self-love, as Schopenhauer called it'. Indeed, we will not be around to experience our own immortal fame, so it cannot be a matter of self-love. Rather, Nietzsche argues that fame, the aim of the active life, amounts to the 'belief [*Glaube*] in the coherence and continuity of what is great in all ages'. Fame is a 'protest against the change of generations and against transitoriness', humanity's rejection of becoming and its creation of artificial, enduring being (98). Monumental history, then, collects all these great actions and puts them into a story that 'forms a mountain range of humankind through the millennia', and that keeps all such great moments 'alive, bright, and great', which expresses the 'belief in humanity [*Glauben an die Humanität*]' (97). Nietzsche uses in these important passages the German term *Glaube*, which can also be translated as 'faith', because he is making an argument for practical faith akin to Kant's in the *Critique of Practical Reason*. For Kant, the possibility of moral action justifies a rational faith in his postulates of practical reason and in the hope for the moral perfection of humanity. For Nietzsche, here, the greatness of an action – the fact that human beings are capable of setting aside personal advantage to live for humanity's expansion – justifies a faith that humanity will keep such actions alive eternally in memory and will inspire new ones. Monumental history, then, inspires the active individual by 'banish[ing]' the 'doubt', and instead conferring on him the faith that a valuable human life is possible despite the natural contradictoriness of his existence (98).

2B *Liability of monumental history*

Nietzsche insists that monumental history is always possible for human beings, because the active life is always available to us. He states that one might think that 'no more than one hundred productive human beings, educated and working in the same spirit [*Geist*]' could revive monumental history (98). However, he casts grave doubt on this project, suggesting that there are tremendous obstacles to it in the modern age. Monumental history belongs to Polybius and other ancient historians (96; Jenkins 2014). Schiller and Goethe, by contrast, found their 'age ... so wretched' that there were 'no useful qualities in the lives of the human beings' around them. In part, monumental history faces the overwhelming force of modern scientific history which encourages 'curious tourists or meticulous micrologists climbing about on the pyramids of past great ages'. The modern historical approach does not regard history as edifying, but as the source of scientific knowledge and 'diversion or excitement, saunter[ing] about as though among the painted treasures in a gallery' (96). History does not inspire, but rather becomes an ever greater weight fettering the ambitious. Monumental history is thus pre-modern in nature.

There are two more problems internal to monumental history itself that render its retrieval in modernity exceedingly difficult. First, monumental history inspires human agency by 'disregard[ing] all causes' and focusing only on 'effects in themselves' as 'exemplary [*vorbildlich*] and worthy of emulation'. As Nietzsche puts it, 'what is celebrated at popular festivals and at religious or military commemorations is really just such an "effect in itself": this is what disturbs the sleep of the ambitious' (99). Monumental history is what we might call the 'great man view of history', that individuals are the self-making propulsion of history, and so any individual at any time can become such a great man if he works hard enough – or gathers together 'one hundred' of his fellows to do the same. The problem with this understanding, Nietzsche argues, is that there are myriad causes behind all monumental deeds. On p. 99, Nietzsche points out the multitude of differences among different cultures, and he concludes that no moment is 'wholly identical' with the past (100). As such, this salutary faith in self-moving individuals is a myth – some cultures and conditions are more conducive to producing great deeds than others. Nietzsche makes this point here to suggest that monumental history's disregard of causes is particularly vulnerable to modern scientific history. The latter uncovers the causes of all things, including the many causes of great deeds. Monumental history requires the myth of the 'great man', and modern scientific history thoroughly destroys this myth, endangering monumental history in modernity.

The second problem of monumental history follows from the first. Since monumental history effaces the causes behind actions, this tendency can be abused by 'talented egoists and wicked fanatics'. These individuals can employ monumental history to serve their particular ends by transforming history into a 'pure fiction' that deifies them. Under such fictitious history, 'entire large parts of' history 'are forgotten, scorned, and washed away as if by a gray, unremitting tide, and only a few individual, embellished facts rise as islands above it' (100). Thus, monumental history can function usefully to inspire individuals to live a valuable life, but it also has the danger of allowing individuals to abuse it so as to lead an egoistic life. Nietzsche points out here that the 'antiquarian and the critical views' of history serve as salutary checks on monumental history's tendency to be abused.

Nietzsche suggests that this problem of egoists and fanatics is ancient in nature by offering the example of the 'disciples of Pythagoras' (100). Yet he proceeds to argue that there is a modern version of this problem that is much more dangerous, and he draws on his critique of contemporary 'cultural philistines' from the 'David Strauss' essay to do so. For Nietzsche, the problem of the modern age is not that nefarious individuals will appropriate monumental history, but that the democratic mob will do so. Already in his analysis of the active life, we can see the tension that exists between the founder and the people, those who must be shaped but who are 'frightened and short-lived animals who ... want only one thing: to live at all costs' (97). The 'dancing mob' gains its freedom from the rule of the few (101) by appropriating the cultural 'weapons' of its master (100). It 'deploys the authority of the monumental derived from the past' to condemn and prevent all new founders from emerging. As such, the demos pretends to embody 'good taste' despite the fact that it is a 'jury of aesthetic do-nothings' (101). These cultural philistines abuse monumental history as the 'costume under which their hatred of all the great and the powerful people of their age' is expressed (102).

3 Antiquarian and critical history

3A *Utility of antiquarian history*

Antiquarian history 'pertains to the person who preserves and venerates, to him who looks back with loyalty and love on the origins through which he became what he is'. In several ways, the preserving person – he who needs antiquarian history – is the polar opposite of the active individual. The active individual radically reshapes the world around him in his own image; the preserving person 'preserve[s] for those who will emerge after him the conditions under which he himself has come into being' (102). Rather than shaping the things of the world in his image, he 'is possessed by them'. The active individual makes his distinctive individuality central to the value of life – his *eros* is for the beautiful or noble deed; the preserving person 'looks beyond his own transient, curious, individual existence and senses himself to be the spirit [*Geist*] of his house, his lineage, and his city' – his *eros* is for his community. Finally, the active individual longs for greatness; the preserving individual confers 'dignity and sanctity' on 'small, limited, decaying, antiquated things', the non-human things such as the 'wall' and 'towered gate' of the city and the common experiences and 'festivals' that constitute the everyday identity of a people (103). As such, as opposed to the record of great deeds of individuals, antiquarian history is the record of the common experiences, 'land and native customs' of a people (104).

Despite these differences, both forms of history serve life by securing happiness and conferring value on existence. Antiquarian history provides happiness by making the community into a whole, a 'we', rather than an agglomeration of individuals. It knits together the past, present and future generations, such that the preserving person can 'greet across the distance of darkening and confusing centuries the soul of his people as his own soul'. It connects the people to the things around them, the parts of the city that the people built, the 'barren mountain ridges' from which the people arose, and the 'tiresome habits' that constitute the character of the people (104). Through this history, the preserving person 'rediscovers himself in all of this', in the 'spirit [*Geist*] of his house' (103). The recognition that we are parts of a whole satisfies our desire for wholeness.

Antiquarian history also confers 'worth [*Wert*]' on the existence of a people despite its otherwise 'modest, rough, even wretched conditions' (103). For Nietzsche, this history shows 'that one's existence is not formed arbitrarily and by chance, but that instead it grows as the blossom and the fruit of a past that is its inheritance', which in turn 'thereby excuses, indeed, justifies [*gerechtfertigt*] its existence' (104). As we have seen, the 'historical' life justifies existence through realising a cultural process or aim. A culture is like an organism – here, Nietzsche envisions, a tree. Every part of the organism is essential for its growth and expansion, which is why reverence for even the most common item in one's history is essential. Indeed, each member of the culture should feel reverence for the whole community because it is only through this precise arrangement and interaction of all its parts that the member of the community was possible at all. Furthermore, the growth and development of the organism to this point was not accidental, but necessary. All past events have led up to and converge on each individual member, which thereby invests each member with a weighty responsibility to do his part for the growth of the organism into the future. The existence of each individual member is thereby justified because he is necessary to the continued process and its ultimate conclusion – he is irreplaceable, set 'apart from all other human beings', not fungible in his unique contribution to the whole (KSA 7.29[178], UW 268).

Indeed, Nietzsche argues that once a people begins to lose antiquarian history, attenuating its connection and loyalty to its own tradition – as, for instance, by embracing the 'adventurous joy of migration' – there are 'dreadful consequences' to happiness and the value of life. Instead of feeling a sense of wholeness in the community, the people 'succumb to restless, cosmopolitan craving for new and ever newer things' (104). They become divided within themselves, the unity characterising their culture broken between the past and an imagined future. If they also lose a sense of providential destiny and sever the link with the past, each new person becomes a contingent rather than a necessary link in the chain of history, thereby losing the justification for his existence.

Although monumental and antiquarian history differ sharply from one another, Nietzsche suggests that they can coexist in the same culture and even in the same historian. In his discussion of antiquarian history, for instance, he strikingly revisits three examples from the previous section – Goethe, the Italian Renaissance and Barthold Niebuhr. Each of these examples either performed great deeds (Goethe, Renaissance) or lauded them (Niebuhr), and here we see that they also embrace antiquarian history. As such,

Nietzsche argues, these forms of history can balance and complement one another. They need not exist in permanent tension. For example, antiquarian history benefits the active life because it provides it with some context and limits to its striving. As we saw, monumental history has the tendency to efface the historical genesis or conditions for great deeds, which allows egoists to destroy history and replace it with their own ego. Nietzsche here imagines that as the active 'Goethe stood before Erwin von Steinach's monumental work ... he recognized this German work for the first time, "exerting its effect out of a strong and rugged German soul"' (103). A due reverence for the past – which illuminates the conditions for the genesis of one's deeds – is necessary to elevate the ego out of itself, such that the active person seeks happiness for others, not just for himself.

3B *Liability of antiquarian history*

On the other hand, antiquarian history needs monumental history to redress its main problem. Namely, since antiquarian history regards everything in a culture's history as necessary to its growth and development, it 'regards everything to be equally important'. Thus, it can generate 'no criterion for value and no sense of proportion for the things of the past that would truly do them justice [*gerecht*] when viewed in relation to each other'. However, the problem is that 'whatever is new and in the process of becoming' needs to be shaped or transformed to maintain the overall unity of culture. The shaping power works by distinguishing between what is of value and what is not, what will be incorporated and what will be forgotten. Yet since there are no unimportant things for antiquarian history, it meets everything new 'with hostility'. Eventually, a 'people's sensibility hardens' as antiquarian history 'no longer conserves but rather mummifies' life (105). For Nietzsche, to stay alive, a people requires new deeds and experiences in order to grow and progress towards the aim internal to culture.

Otherwise put: for Nietzsche, the active life is primary for the historical perspective, whereas the preserving life is secondary, since it maintains and transmits what the active life brought into existence. If the preserving life makes itself primary, it destroys

the conditions for the possibility of the active life, and then eventually destroys anything it could preserve. Nietzsche expresses
this thought in his image of a culture's death through too much
antiquarian history – 'the tree gradually dies an unnatural death'
because its corruption begins 'at its crown' – those great deeds
squelched by antiquarianism – then 'moving down to its roots',
which contain the many objects of antiquarian reverence (105).

Monumental history thus benefits antiquarian history by
injecting the latter with new life, that is, with great deeds that
help foster growth and development. Monumental history also
provides a culture with the standard of excellence missing from
antiquarian history. This standard of excellence allows a people
to judge what is significant and insignificant in its own history,
and thereby to provide space for the active individual to shape
its history so that it moves onward towards the valuable end that
distinguishes it as a unified culture.

Like monumental history, however, antiquarian history is pre-
modern in nature. Nietzsche discusses the spirit of the 'house' and
the 'city' [Stadt], not the modern state [Staat] (103). His own description of the functional unity of the city reflects the famous accounts
of the Greek polis offered by Friedrich Schiller in the *Letters on the
Aesthetic Education of Man* and G. W. F. Hegel in the *Phenomenology of
Spirit*. Antiquarian history can persist in some forms into modernity
– as with Goethe – but it is endangered by the rise of modern scientific history. Antiquarian history differs essentially from the latter
because it focuses all its attention on its national history, ignoring
every other community with its 'extremely limited field of vision'
(104). Modern scientific history explodes all national boundaries
in its cosmopolitan pursuit of the truth, thus casting suspicion on
antiquarian history. Like Schiller and Hegel, Nietzsche too suggests
that ancient communities dissolve in modernity.

Nietzsche's account adds to Schiller's and Hegel's, however, in
that he thinks antiquarian history can lend support to modern
scientific history while also ushering in its own undoing. As we
saw, 'antiquarian history degenerates from the moment when the
fresh life of the present no longer animates and inspires it'. 'At
this point', Nietzsche says, the preserving person's ethical disposition, his 'piety', 'withers', and thereby he loses his connection to

the community and withdraws into himself. However, the 'habit' of antiquarianism that he has developed 'persists without it and revolves with self-satisfied egotism around its own axis'. Thus we 'view the repugnant spectacle of a blind mania to collect, of a restless gathering together of everything that once existed'. In his habitual search for 'bibliographical minutiae', the preserving person fuels the pursuit of modern scientific history, though now without any happiness or sense of value in life (105).

3C *Utility of critical history*

Though critical history was a late addition to Nietzsche's composition of this essay, scholars have rightly recognised that it plays an important role in his argument, and in the eventual development of his genealogical method (Nehamas 2006; Breazeale 2000; Emden 2008). The precise role that it plays has not, however, been identified. In my view, critical history is the tertiary type of history in what turns out to be an ancient, cyclical 'historical' existence. Monumental history is primary as its great deeds found a culture; antiquarian history is secondary in preserving that cultural order; critical history is tertiary in demolishing an ossified cultural order in order to liberate the active individual to perform new great deeds. The cycle then continues. Nietzsche's own order of presentation tracks the overall logic of the 'historical' existence – the active life propels a people into the future, the preserving life maintains the past, and the liberating life casts off 'the affliction of the present' (102).

Let us expand on critical history's benefits. Nietzsche recognises that the problem of antiquarian history is too severe for monumental history to check alone. As a culture grows older, the reverence for the past increases, and the number of conditions responsible for creating the present expands. Eventually, there arises a 'demand' that features of culture 'be immortal' (106). This deepening reverence for the past is combined with two further obstacles to new deeds: 1) the entrenched egoistic interest of 'a privilege, a caste, or a dynasty', who would be the beneficiaries of the past's apotheosis (107), and 2) the common people's aversion to the shaping power of the few active individuals. The ambitious few and their monumental history, in other words, are no match for the numbers of the many, their need for the status quo, and powerful oligarchic class interest.

Critical history thus pertains to the person 'who suffers and is in need of liberation' from the ossified status quo (96). The liberator must 'shatter and dissolve a past' or 'take a knife to' the cultural tree's 'roots' and 'cruelly trample on all forms of piety' (106–7). The liberator is unlike the active and preserving persons, who are motivated by love. Instead, the liberating person seeks justice – he brings the 'past before a tribunal, painstakingly interrogating it, and finally condemning it'. Nevertheless, in levying his judgement, this person is driven by the needs of 'life and life alone' (106).

In his discussion of this section, Breazeale argues that life is a 'notoriously vague and controversial standard' upon which to base judgement, and that Nietzsche offers 'no such clarification or argument' to support it (2000: 63). Yet this criticism is unfair to Nietzsche, since he himself recognises that life provides no clear standards for judgement. Indeed, Nietzsche even describes life here as that 'dark, driving, insatiable power that lusts after itself' (106). Life achieves its end by giving rise to human cultures that are self-reflecting, in the sense that they legislate values as ends that they consciously seek. Furthermore, life produces a multitude of different cultures, which themselves have quite different normative standards in service to their many ends. As such, Nietzsche does not owe us a justification of the liberator's judgement – rather, the liberator owes his culture a justification for his judgement, and this justification will be internal to the standards of the community. This justification will appeal back to the founder, who created a cultural order that aims at an overriding value. The liberator will criticise the antiquarian for arresting the community's progress towards that aim, and so his judgement will be justified according to the end of the community itself. This is the sense in which the liberator serves the life of the community, since 'human violence and weakness' always interrupts a culture's course towards its end (106). Of course, Nietzsche recognises too that there may be would-be or overzealous liberators who judge too harshly or destroy too much, but again, the standard for assessing their judgement is not given from the outside, by Nietzsche, but rather from the inside, from the overriding aim of the culture.

One of the ways to see this point is that Nietzsche specifically distinguishes between the judgement of the liberator – whose standard emerges from 'life and life alone' – and the 'tribunal' of 'justice itself' (106–7). Nietzsche admits that 'in most instances the verdict would be the same', but he here importantly recognises two distinct normative authorities. We were already introduced to this second normative authority – that of 'justice itself' – in the first section. This is the 'suprahistorical' perspective, in which the human being ascends from the partial 'historical' perspectives of each culture to the 'pure fountain of knowledge'. Nietzsche repeats the judgement of justice here as well, that 'living and being unjust are one and the same thing'. However, he draws a more radical conclusion here than he does in the first section: 'For everything that comes into being is *worthy* [*wert*] of perishing. Thus it would be better if nothing came into being' (107, original emphasis). Here Breazeale's question about Nietzsche's standard becomes appropriate – how does Nietzsche justify this judgement? Nietzsche appeals to 'human violence and weakness', 'heavy artillery', and castes and dynasties, though these examples hardly help in justifying a general standard (106–7). In my view, the best way to interpret the judgement of justice is to return to the contradictory nature of humanity at the beginning of section 1. Human beings lead a contradictory and hence miserable natural existence. The fact that we create illusions for ourselves to manage our fundamental contradiction does not eliminate it – rather, our contradiction re-emerges clearly in the violence and oppression that we cause to one another, which then raises the question of the value of our short existence when we seem hell-bent on snuffing it out. Nietzsche, then, does not justify these judgements based on a vague standard of life as Breazeale assumes, but rather on the contradiction of human nature, that we are living, embodied beings, but also free beings capable of transcending the needs of life.

3D *Liability of critical history*

This contradiction can be seen again clearly in the main problem with critical history, which concerns human freedom. The liberation implicit in the history is supposed to serve life, but human freedom can transcend the aims of life itself. As Nietzsche points out, 'we are, after all, the products of earlier generations', and so 'we are also the products of their aberrations, passions, and errors – indeed of their crimes' (107). Human beings have no natural character – as we have seen, culture is our artificial creation. Everything that we call 'nature was once a second nature', an artificial set of habits, dispositions and values that become thoroughly internalised (108). However, 'if we condemn these aberrations' of our nature and 'regard ourselves as free of them', then we have no internalised, given character to fall back on. Instead, we have to 'cultivate a new habit, a new instinct, a second nature, so that the first nature withers away'. But 'second natures are usually feebler than first natures', so it is difficult to lay the conditions for great deeds. Moreover, 'it is so difficult to set limits on this negating of the past' (107). Human freedom has no limits – once it has been uncaged to negate the past, every new culture receives critical judgement and condemnation as soon as it is introduced.

Nevertheless, Nietzsche states that occasionally critical history stays within the bounds of life, and the knowledge of the historical nature of human character – that it is 'second nature' all the way down – is a 'consolation' (108). It consoles because it reminds the active person that there is no limit to human creativity, to the shaping power of humanity. If there were a first or given nature of human beings, some deep immutable structure manifest in our culture, then the active individual would not be able to act in a fully self-determining way. Nietzsche's discussion here is short and elliptical, but he suggests that monumental history is crucial to keep human freedom within its boundaries. The promise of the great deed of the active person provides the path for human freedom to find satisfactory expression, in contrast to constant, radical and unsatisfying negation. As we saw above, critical history is unique among the types in not providing guidance to happiness or the value of existence. Monumental history's promise for both may thereby keep freedom within its bounds.

Like the others, Nietzsche sees critical history, with its criticism of privilege, caste and dynasty, as pre-modern. Modern scientific history, as we will soon see, adopts a value-neutral perspective towards history. It does not stand in judgement; it only seeks to know, to learn about the past. Accordingly, critical history is not scientific in this sense; its judgements, based on life and hence the standards internal to culture, have no objective justification. Like the other forms of history, critical history requires incorporation through modern scientific history.

4 The transition from ancient to modern history

Nietzsche begins this section by clarifying the audience for his three forms of ancient history. We might expect the audience for monumental history to be only the ambitious few, for antiquarian history only the many. On the contrary, Nietzsche argues that 'every human being and every people needs ... a certain knowledge of the past, sometimes as monumental, sometimes as antiquarian, and sometimes as critical history'. Everyone requires all three forms of history so that each can check and balance the others in the ways described above. At the same time, Nietzsche observes that sometimes an individual or culture will have greater 'capacities or needs' for one type or another (108), in which case a different balance ought to be struck so that no one form of history predominates. In such a case, what is otherwise useful history becomes a 'most devastating weed' (102).

In the rest of this section, Nietzsche shifts from the ancients to 'our own time' (108), by which he means all of 'modern' culture, of which 'present day ... Germans' are only one example (111–12). This transition section compares the peak of ancient cultures – the 'ancient Greek[s]' (111) – with modernity, or 'we moderns [*wir Modernen*]' (110). 'Modern' culture's pre-eminent distinguishing feature, for Nietzsche, is its embrace of the aim of modern 'science' (109). In his unpublished essay 'On Truth and Lies in an Extra-Moral Sense', composed at the same time and in the same notebook as 'Utility and Liability', Nietzsche describes this ideal as the 'drive for truth' (TL 254; cf. 'Utility and Liability', 124). This drive is the 'powerfully hostile star' that has reconfigured the 'constellation of life' of ancient cultures (108). Modern culture's shaping power has thereby fundamentally transformed the valuations and character of the ancient way of life.

Modern culture is qualitatively different from ancient cultures – 'no past generation' has 'ever witnessed' this 'spectacle' – because in it 'life no longer rules alone and constrains our knowledge of the past'.

In place of life, our distinctive freedom allows us to transcend its needs and place truth as the rule and ideal of our culture. In pursuit of truth in all domains, we 'demand that history be a science'. Scientific history demands that we tear down 'all the boundary markers' established by ancient culture, since these distort our judgement. It demands that we reach 'as far back into the past as the process of becoming extends, as far back as infinity' (109). Every moment in human history is to be impartially analysed and catalogued in the comprehensive pursuit of universal truth. History does not serve any of life's needs, but this type of history should pursue only truth. If the ancient types of history found their exemplars in Polybius, Herodotus or Livy, this modern scientific history is best expressed in the scholarly approach of Niebuhr and Ranke.

Most readers of this essay focus on the bad consequences of this cultural revolution. Yet Nietzsche declares that the 'star' of modern science is 'brilliant and magnificent' (109). Its immense discoveries contribute to deepening the 'inner being' of the Germans, which proves itself 'to be finely receptive, serious, powerful, sincere, good, and perhaps even richer than the inner being of other peoples' (113). Modern science, after all, allows humanity to emerge from a condition of myth-making and partiality and address the concerns of universal humanity. It is animated by our distinctively human concern for perfection, which demands that we free ourselves from all constraints. I begin with these benefits not only because they have been overlooked, but also because Nietzsche's argument that follows can only be understood against the backdrop of the utility of modern culture.[19] As we will see, Nietzsche does not think it possible or desirable to return to the ancients, but rather wishes to check modernity's excesses with the ancient types, thereby exploiting the utility of both.

However, it would be wrong to minimise the bad consequences of modern culture, because Nietzsche discusses them at such great length. The problems of modernity begin with the way modern science undermines the basic need of life, our need for wholeness.

---

[19] For an exception in the scholarship, see Zuckert on the 'virtue' of modernity in representing the 'first step to complete historical self-consciousness' (1976: 57).

Recall that life drives individuals and cultures to employ their shaping power to form a unity out of diverse experiences, interests and dispositions. Modern scientific culture, however, accumulates immeasurably vast amounts of knowledge from 'inexhaustible sources', such that 'alien and disconnected facts crowd in upon' individuals and culture. In response, 'nature struggles as best it can to receive, order, and honor these alien guests, but they themselves are involved in a struggle with one another'. No individual's or culture's plastic power is expansive enough to encompass the 'indigestible stones of knowledge' streaming in from modern science, and so they are overwhelmed by it. With their plastic power overwhelmed, individuals and cultures embrace the 'habituation to such a disorderly, stormy, and struggling household', which 'gradually becomes second nature' (109).

We moderns thereby fail to form a unified character, and instead constantly display a 'remarkable antithesis between an interior ... and an exterior' (109). The 'chaotic inner world' created by this immense body of knowledge within us prevents us from performing 'visible' actions (110). We become, in Nietzsche's famous image, 'walking encyclopedias' (110–11). In his discussion of contemporary Germany – which for Nietzsche represents the best specimen of this division between the content and form in our character – he claims that the infinite, inner depth of the Germans has led them to regard all 'convention as a disguise and deception', a limit on what is limitless. However, individuals still must emerge from an inner life to exterior action, and must act based on some judgement and principle. Yet as we have seen, there is no 'natural' basis for normative judgement, even though the Germans think they rely on this basis (112). Unable to generate a 'self-revelation of this inner being' (113), Germans simply adopt judgement and principle unreflectively from 'French convention' (112). Our modern exterior lives are determined by 'indifferent convention, a pitiful imitation, or even a crude caricature' (110). Accordingly, our division prevents any 'measure of self-overcoming [*Selbstüberwindung*]', and instead makes us into abstract beings (112). Our story, Nietzsche says, might be entitled 'Handbook of Inward Cultivation for Outward Barbarians' (111).

In this section, Nietzsche deepens his critique of contemporary culture from 'David Strauss'. He connects this discussion back to the previous essay by approving of his own definition of culture – oddly, as if it were 'termed' by someone else – as the 'unity of artistic style that manifests itself throughout all the vital self-expressions of a people' (111). Section 1 of 'Utility and Liability' helps us understand why culture must be a unity – namely, to achieve wholeness. It also explains why culture unifies 'vital self-expressions [*Lebensäusserungen*]', since culture is the expression of life's needs. Here in section 4, Nietzsche recalls his claim from 'David Strauss' that genuine culture involves the 'cultivation' [*Bildung*] of the human spirit (110), and his denial that what we currently call 'cultivation' is in fact *Bildung* – it is instead 'modern cultivatedness [*modernen Gebildetheit*]' (111). He deepens his discussion from that essay by locating the source of 'cultivatedness' not only in the local political and cultural concerns of the Germans, but also in the effects of modern science itself.

What is to be done? Nietzsche's final paragraph of the section begins his transformation and incorporation of the ancient approaches of history. In this paragraph, he suggests that these reflections on modern culture will be 'terrible' to an 'observer' who needs 'faith [*Glauben*] in the authenticity and immediacy of German feeling'. Nietzsche judges this observer a 'great, productive spirit [*grosse productive Geist*]', that is, the aspiring active individual from section 2 who seeks to perform great deeds. This active individual, however, despairs at the loss of wholeness in modern culture, the destruction of the 'unity of national feeling', such that 'he is no longer needed by his people as a whole' (114). The active individual's 'heart is full of compassion for all', but the 'instinct of his people no longer embraces him; it is useless for him to stretch out his longing arms' (114). In his despair, he must turn to critical history's task of liberation, so that 'as judge he can at least condemn what he, a vital and life-giving being, regards as destruction and degradation'. However, Nietzsche asks, 'what means should he employ?' Nietzsche suggests that he cannot simply return to the old type of history, but that 'all that remains for him is his profound knowledge [*tiefe Erkenntniss*]' (115). That is, only by employing – not rejecting – the infinite knowledge of

modern science can he effect the liberation from modern culture
necessary to 'sow the seeds of a need' for a distinctively modern
form of monumental history, one that will forge a new wholeness
or 'unity' for the 'German spirit [*Geistes*]' (115). In other words,
Nietzsche points to a form of critical history that incorporates
rather than denies modern science, one that works from the perspective of modern science rather than retreating from it. In section 6, Nietzsche will expand on this transformed type of history.

5 The decline of the active life in modernity

The first paragraph of section 5 provides a topical overview of sections 4–9. As we will see, each topic is a distinct liability caused by
the 'excess' of historical knowledge (115). In addition, the structure of Nietzsche's presentation is causal and cumulative: each
liability results from the previous one, culminating in a 'cunning,
egoistical praxis through which ... vital forces [*Lebenskräfte*] are
paralyzed and ultimately destroyed' (116). In sum, the liabilities are:

1 *Section 4*: the loss of wholeness ('such an excess produces the
   previously discussed contrast between the internal and the
   external').
2 *Section 5*: the loss of value in life ('and thereby weakens the
   personality').
3 *Section 6*: the inability to achieve its own ideal ('this excess leads
   an age to imagine that it possesses the rarest virtue, justice, to a
   higher degree than any other age').
4 *Section 7*: the inhibiting of cultural growth ('this excess undermines the instincts of a people and hinders the maturation of
   the individual no less than that of the totality').
5 *Section 8*: the false belief in the culmination of world history
   ('this excess plants the seeds of the ever dangerous belief in the
   venerable agedness of the human race, the belief that one is a
   latecomer and epigone').
6 *Section 9*: the destructive belief in universal egoism ('this excess
   throws an age into the dangerous attitude of self-irony, and
   from this into the even more dangerous attitude of cynicism')
   (115).

Section 5's liability flows from section 4's. Section 4 claimed that the 'influx of foreign influences' has 'degenerated' into a 'cosmopolitan carnival of gods, customs, and arts' in the soul of the 'modern human being'. As our inner life exponentially expands, it becomes increasingly difficult to shape a wholeness of individual and cultural character. In section 5, Nietzsche argues that this decline in character leads to the loss of the capacity for action. Modern individuals have become 'spectator[s]' to history, such that their character cannot be shaped by monumental action. Indeed, Nietzsche remarks that 'even great wars and great revolutions can scarcely change anything even for a moment', because 'before the war is even over . . . it has already been served up as the latest delicacy to the exhausted palates of the history-hungry'. Modern scientific culture has a bottomless stomach for knowledge. Or, to employ a different metaphor, its horizon is limitless. Thus, no individual can shape a coherent character for himself, and for the same reason the active individual cannot shape a coherent character for culture as a whole. Scientific culture resists all efforts at closing horizons by turning around and reflectively analysing any action that attempts to close the horizon, thereby anticipating and transcending its limit. As such, all 'deeds' become 'sudden claps, not rolling thunder. Even if you accomplish the greatest and most wonderful things, they will still descend silent and unsung into Orcus' (116). Nietzsche describes this inability to act as 'weak personality', though it is important to remember that this inability is not due to a weakness of will. Rather, it is because our inner life is far too capacious to shape into a unity.[20]

Nietzsche discusses a second way in which excess knowledge stultifies action. The endless drive for knowledge prevents modern culture from standing 'in prolonged awe at the sublime [action] as the incomprehensible' expression of a single active person; in contrast, the scientific culture seeks immediately to 'understand, calculate, or comprehend in a moment' that seemingly miraculous deed (116). 'Even if something that is most astonishing should

---

[20] See Heidegger, who discusses the notion of 'personality' at length, tracing it back to Kant (2016: 101–5).

occur', Nietzsche bemoans, 'the mob of the historically neutral is always on the spot, ready to survey and supervise the author from afar.' What results is a torrent of 'critique [*Kritik*]', which leads to an analysis of the 'history of [the deed's] author', until eventually the mundane causes of the deed are revealed, the miraculous dispelled (120–1). Under the atmosphere of relentless historical critique, however, 'art takes flight' (116). It does so because even would-be active individuals internalise the relentlessly reflective self-consciousness of modern culture. In doing so, each individual 'has destroyed and lost his instinct; he can now no longer trust in the "divine animal" and give it free rein when his rationality wavers . . . The individual thus becomes hesitant and uncertain and can no longer believe in himself' (117). As we saw in sections 1 and 2, the active individual must think of himself as a self-moved mover. Modern historical science reveals to all of us that we are neither self-moved nor can we move anything.

This unending self-critique leads to nothing being stable in the individual's inner life, and so in his outer life he clings to 'mere abstractions and shadows: no one runs the risk of baring his own person' to critique. Instead he 'disguises himself behind the mask of the cultivated man, the scholar, the poet, the politician' (117). He becomes an actor playing these roles. He is not 'honest' to himself (117), and thus is not '"free" [*frei*] – that is to say, truthful to themselves and truthful to others in both word and deed' (118).[21] To be truly free, Nietzsche here argues, involves the self-determination of one's character, that one's actions express one's inner life; one is unfree when one is forced to play a role in one's culture. Nietzsche singles out philosophy as a prime example in modern culture. The ancients considered philosophy as a way of life, so that the philosopher would 'fulfill the law of philosophy in himself'. In the modern age, we are bombarded by knowledge about the history of philosophy, and philosophy becomes a public role, a mask that is 'political and policed, limited by governments, churches,

---

[21] In a *Nachlass* entry, Nietzsche expands on what it would mean to be 'honest' to oneself: 'to take possession of oneself, to organize the chaos . . . toss aside everything foreign and grow from within your own self, do not make yourself fit the mold of something outside yourself' (KSA 7.29[192]).

academies, customs, and human cowardice to scholarly pretense'. Philosophy 'has no rights' to call itself philosophy 'if it seeks to be more than just an inwardly restrained knowledge without effect' – it is untrue to itself and hence not free (118).

Adopting a public mask for one's identity makes one unfree, but it also, Nietzsche points out, is arbitrary. When one chooses the mask of a scholar of 'Democritus', on what basis does the scholar make this decision? 'Why not Heraclitus? Or Philo? Or Bacon? Or Descartes?' Furthermore, why choose to become 'a philosopher?' 'Why not a poet, an orator?' In other words, the inner chaos of modern culture undermines any principle of judgement for choosing one life as better than another. This makes even the choice of what role to play an unsettled matter, a constant object of self-scrutiny. With no principled basis of choice, the possibility of action in history becomes even more remote, and so individuals in modern scientific culture eventually become 'eunuchs', for whom 'one woman is just like any other'. Nietzsche means by this metaphor that for this culture there is no *eros* to 'draw you upward' towards some ideal, since there is no basis on which to choose an ideal, nor the opportunity or ability to act in service of it. Personality becomes ever weaker until it is 'snuffed out . . . reduced to eternal subjectlessness – or, as they say, to "objectivity"' (120).

If section 4 dealt with the effect of modern scientific history on our need for wholeness, this section concerns its effect on our need for value in life. As we have seen, the 'historical' existence confers value on its life through a process towards an end. Yet modern scientific history undermines any principled basis for a single end, and undermines the cultural mechanism for achieving this end through action. Despite its bleak assessment, this section nevertheless offers a glimmer of hope. Namely, Nietzsche identifies a contradiction at the heart of the scientific culture – for a culture that prizes truth at all costs, individuals become remarkably untrue to themselves. Furthermore, scientific culture prides itself on its freedom from partial, shaped horizons, but individuals reveal themselves to be deeply unfree, unable to determine their own personalities. Nietzsche employs this and other self-contradictions to guide modern culture towards genuine freedom.

6 Justice and the new history

In section 5, we saw that modern scientific culture fosters souls who celebrate themselves as 'objective'. In this section, Nietzsche proceeds to distinguish two different senses of 'objectivity' – first, one can do 'justice' to the things in the world, judging what is valuable in itself and what not (A); second, one can adopt a thoroughly disinterested perspective on the world, discovering what is true and what is false (B). Nietzsche argues that modern scientific culture achieves only the 'semblance of justice [*Schein der Gerechtigkeit*]' and the 'semblance of that [disinterested] artistic power' (129). However, despite scientific culture's failure, Nietzsche thinks that modern culture nevertheless succeeds in creating the possibility of something greater, what he calls 'great justice'. Great justice does not reach back to pre-modern types of history for its realisation, but is the 'most noble kernel of the so-called urge to truth' (124). It synthesises and incorporates pre-modern critical and monumental history through the modern pursuit of knowledge (C).

6A *Great justice and the semblance of justice (pp. 121–5)*

Pre-modern cultures are bounded by horizons, which makes their judgements unjust to everything outside their horizons – they do not accurately portray what is truly good and bad, but rather confer value judgements from their own limited perspective. They refer to other cultures, for instance, as barbaric or evil. In contrast, modern scientific culture claims to display the virtue of justice 'to a higher degree than the human beings of other ages' (121). To assess this claim, Nietzsche distinguishes two features of virtue – '[a] the urge and [b] the strength for justice'. First, Nietzsche holds that to properly display a virtue one must first act out of the right 'origin', 'cause' or motivation. To be virtuous means to do the right thing for the right reasons. If I display 'generosity' to someone only because I calculate that doing so will better satisfy my egoistic aims, then I do not truly possess the virtue of generosity (122). I only display the 'semblance' of it (129).

Why does Nietzsche hold this Kantian view, that virtue requires the right motivation? He does not justify his claim here, but it follows from his argument about being true to oneself in the previous section. As we saw, human freedom as self-determination requires the 'self-revelation of [our] inner being' (113), that we adhere in our external actions to a principle determined by our inner character. Having the right motivation is integral to virtue because it is essential to self-determination. In the case of justice, Nietzsche argues that most modern individuals seek justice from 'the most different impulses ... such as curiosity, fear of boredom, disfavor, vanity, desire for amusement, which have nothing whatsoever to do with truth' (123). Their pursuit of justice, then, is just a 'semblance', since it is motivated by natural needs – such as the desire for amusement – that drive our will only contingently towards the truth (129). By contrast, Nietzsche argues, 'only insofar as the truthful person has the unconditional will [*unbedingten Willen*] to be just is there anything great in that striving for truth'; that is, only by adhering unconditionally to the principled commitment to truth can we display justice (123). In this case, our action is determined by an inner principle that we have given to ourselves, and thus we are self-determining and true to ourselves. Nietzsche's use of the term 'unconditional will' points explicitly back to Kant's categorical imperative, with its unconditional demand for autonomous moral action, and its related claim that heteronomous determinations of the will by natural incentives have no moral worth. Nietzsche's argument about virtue here adopts the same form as Kant's – that virtue requires autonomy, and that virtue becomes only the 'semblance' of itself through heteronomy.

The second feature of virtue is the 'strength' to undertake it. One may have the right motivation to be virtuous, but if one does not have sufficient shaping power, one cannot become virtuous after all. In the case of justice, the scholarly historian had the wrong motivation; here, Nietzsche identifies the 'fanatics' as those with the right 'urge to justice' yet who 'lack the power to judge', and so lead to the 'most horrible afflictions' that 'have befallen humanity'. As such, Nietzsche recognises that the modern age has produced not only weak, 'eunuch' scientists, but also revolutionaries. The modern age's great virtue – escaping the partiality of each and every culture – can sadly lead to a great danger, those fanatics who from this perspective condemn and destroy all limits. Nietzsche in fact 'excuse[s]' his contemporaries for respecting the scholar more than the fanatic, because in his judgement the fanatic is more dangerous than the scholar to social and political order, which is the precondition for any higher life at all (123).

Nietzsche describes the truly just individual in one of the most remarkable passages of this essay.[22] He declares that 'no one deserves our veneration more than those who possess the urge and the strength for justice'. The just individual is the '*most venerable* exemplar [*ehrwürdigste Exemplar*, original emphasis] of the human species'. Justice is the 'rarest of all virtues' as it 'unite[s]' all other virtues into itself, 'just as an unfathomable sea receives and absorbs all the rivers that flow into it from all directions'. Nietzsche here identifies justice as the highest or most supreme virtue, as well as the complete virtue – the one that synthesises all other human excellences into a systematic whole – for human beings. As such, this is an absolutely critical passage for Nietzsche's positive ethics, and for his argument in this essay. Indeed, the just individual promises the ultimate satisfaction of both of our fundamental desires: our desire for value in life through the achievement of the highest human excellence and our desire for wholeness through the completeness of all human excellences.

What is justice? For Nietzsche, justice is the pursuit of the 'truth', the transcendence of what is good and bad according to all cultural horizons, and the longing for knowledge of what is good and bad simply. The purpose of justice is not for 'cold, inconsequential knowledge' itself (122), nor is it for any 'egoistic' aim such as 'the captured prey and the pleasure of the individual hunter' (123). On the contrary, Nietzsche describes three ultimate aims for the pursuit of truth: truth as 1) the 'ordering, punishing judge' [*ordnende und strafende Richterin*], 2) 'the sacred legitimation [*heilige Berechtigung*] to shift all the boundaries [*Grenzsteine*] of egoistic possession', and (3) 'Last Judgment' [*Weltgericht*].

---

[22] Surprisingly, this passage has received little attention – Heidegger (2016: 131–63) offers the most extensive treatment.

First, Nietzsche contrasts the just individual with the 'cold demon of knowledge', by which he means an imagined godlike creature who is wholly detached from the needs of life and so can pursue knowledge for its own sake. The just individual is a human being and hence finite, embodied, with the contradictory need for value in life alongside the need for wholeness. The just person, then, does not concern himself with what is 'inconsequential', but rather with what is significant or valuable in life. The just individual must first and foremost be a 'judge' of what is most valuable in human life, and thereby 'order' human things in accordance with an index of value, and 'punish' human beings who fail to live up to this index (122–3). Yet second, the just individual's judgements cannot be arbitrary in the way all pre-modern individuals and cultures at bottom are – he must offer a 'sacred legitimation' [*heilige Berechtigung*] of his judgements to demonstrate that they are not his particular, partial perspective, but that they explode all horizons 'of egoistic possessions'. Finally, third, the just individual's legitimation must at the same time be a 'Last Judgment', a translation of *Weltgericht* that rightly captures the theological resonance of this concept. However, this translation overlooks Nietzsche's reference to Schiller's 1786 poem 'Resignation', which contains the line 'World history is the supreme court' [*die Weltgeschichte ist das Weltgericht*], as well as Hegel's appropriation of it in the *Philosophy of Right* (1991a: 371).[23] With the notion of *Weltgericht*, both Schiller and Hegel envision a this-worldly form of judgement and redemption for the sufferings of humanity. Nietzsche follows them by seeing the just individual as engaged in a redemptive act – even though natural human existence is not worthwhile, the life of the just individual confers value on it, redeeming the senseless suffering it has endured. Nietzsche's comments are all quite abstract and elliptical given the importance of the subject, and will have to wait until 'Schopenhauer as Educator' to give the exemplary individual more flesh.

Justice, then, is the highest virtue for human beings because it involves the transcendence of all local or particular cultures, as well as action in accordance with our highest capacity, our

---

[23] See Emden (2008: 165–7) for further discussion on this connection.

freedom. It is the complete virtue because it synthesises the three exemplars of ancient history – the active individual, the preserving person and the liberator – as indicated by the three aims of justice. First, the just individual orders and punishes, as a monumental individual does. Yet he avoids the problem of the unjust active individual precisely by incorporating justice – he is an erotic 'judge', thereby combining love and justice. Second, the just individual legitimates the order he creates, elevating individuals out of their natural egoism. Nietzsche's use of the term 'sacred' [*heilige*] points back to the 'dignity and sanctity' [*Würde und Unantastbarkeit*] that the preserving individual confers on an order (97), and he speaks of the just man as deserving our 'veneration' [*Verehrung*] (122), reflecting the preserving individual who is also the 'one who ... venerates' [*Verehrenden*] (96). Finally, the just individual serves as the world's court or *Weltgericht* of humanity, and thus embodies critical history's liberator. The liberator confers justice on a people, freeing it from the obstacles to its aim. The just individual also redeems humanity by leading it to a valuable and happy existence.

Finally, justice is a distinctively modern virtue. 'Great justice' is the 'most noble kernel of the so-called urge to truth' (124). Modernity's universality makes possible the highest and most complete virtue, and so Nietzsche could not possibly advocate a return to the pre-modern types of history. Instead, he sees in the urge to truth the possibility of a new virtue that can transform and synthesise the ancient approaches to history. He thereby 'sublates' these approaches, employing all three meanings of this Hegelian term: he *negates* the ancient approaches, while still *preserving* and *elevating* them (see Hegel 1991b: 154). From the perspective of this ideal, modern scientific culture falls woefully short in not summoning the will nor strength of the virtue of justice. Nevertheless, Nietzsche points out, modern culture shares some features with the just individual, and so all is not lost. Our culture 'has cultivated ... a sensibility so tender and sensitive that absolutely nothing human is alien' to us, and our 'lyre can echo in kindred tones the sounds of the most diverse ages and persons' (124). Modern culture, then, should not be destroyed, but rather reformed to build a better modern culture.

6B *Objectivity and the return of the suprahistorical (pp. 125–30)*

There is another, epistemological sense in which modern scientific culture considers itself objective. That is, the 'historian observes all the motives and consequences of an event with such purity that it has absolutely no effect on his subjectivity'. In other words, the historian tries in his judgements to jettison his shaping power, the power in all living things that actively transforms the object in accordance with the needs of the subject. Instead, this scientific observer aims passively to mirror the object, describing it as it is in itself, not its nature as shaped by him. Nietzsche uses the analogy of the disinterested perspective on art, 'that detachment from personal interest with which the painter, in a stormy setting among lightning and thunder . . . contemplates his inner picture'. The historian aims not to actively shape, but to submit himself to a 'total immersion in things' (125).

For Nietzsche, this subjectless approach to history is impossible, a 'mythology' (126). His claim rests on his underlying neo-Kantian epistemology. That epistemology, outlined in 'On Truth and Lies in an Extra-Moral Sense', holds that the natural world itself is an anarchic chaos of sensation, a 'mysterious X of the thing-in-itself' (TL 256). The only way that we can make sense of the world is by first transforming our 'nerve stimulus' into an 'image [*Bild*]' (TL 256), an activity of 'artistic transference' in the sense that each individual shapes the chaos of sensation into something coherent. Second, then, to communicate with one another, we must 'dissipate intuitive metaphors into an abstract pattern, that is, to dissolve an image into a concept' that can be intelligible to more than one person (TL 258). As such, knowledge of concepts does not tell us anything about the world in itself, but rather about the world we have constructed. Indeed, this construction of concepts 'made of spiders' webs' raises us much higher than all the animals, because animals build things out of material that they 'collect from nature, while man builds out of the far more delicate material of concepts which he has first to manufacture out of himself' (TL 259).

These thoughts find their way here as Nietzsche argues that history, like nature, is an anarchic chaos of events. Historians then try to make sense of history by discovering causes that drive it and laws that govern it. Yet the flux of nature means that there are no underlying general laws driving history. Instead, the historian 'weave[s] isolated events into a totality', and must 'spin his web over the past and subdue it'. Rather than being the passive recipient of history, the historian exerts 'the most powerful and most spontaneous creative moment in the inner being of the artist' in conferring order on the chaos of history (126). Objectivity as a goal of history is, in this sense, impossible.[24]

But if objectivity is impossible, then is all history a subjective matter? Do we always read the past through the lens of the present? No – Nietzsche here retrieves the ideal of the suprahistorical perspective from section 1 to describe the proper approach to history. Recall that the suprahistorical is distinctive in identifying enduring types across history. Here, Nietzsche argues that history's 'value lies precisely in its ability to intelligently circumscribe, to elevate a well-known, perhaps even commonplace theme, an everyday melody, heightening it into a comprehensive symbol, and thereby intimating in the original theme a whole world of profundity, power, and beauty'. To discern in a theme a 'comprehensive symbol' requires not the purging of the subjective shaping power, but on the contrary a 'great artistic power'. But nor does it necessarily require that we must read the past in a parochial fashion. Such an artistic power requires 'a creative floating above things, a loving immersion in the empirical data, a poetic elaboration of given types' (128). For Nietzsche, 'ages and generations never have the right to be the judges of all prior ages and generations'. On the contrary, 'this unpleasant mission always falls only to individuals, even to the rarest individuals, at that' (129). Only individuals have the capacity to transcend horizons and to identify patterns and commonalities among them.

The crucial point Nietzsche makes here is that the suprahistorical perspective is in a deep sense more 'objective' than the scientific approach to history. The purpose of examining history

---

[24] See Jensen for a helpful elaboration of Nietzsche on art and historiography, and his relation to other nineteenth-century figures (2016: 88–104).

is not just for knowledge's own sake, but rather to discern what is truly, 'objectively' great, noble or worthwhile in human life. Scientific history, unfortunately, provides no guidance, as it is unable to distinguish between the significant and insignificant. 'Only from the highest power of the present', by contrast, 'can you interpret the past.' By adopting the suprahistorical perspective, one can 'divine what in the past is great and worth knowing and preserving'. Accordingly, the suprahistorical historian gains genuine wisdom about how best to live, and then can 'recast what is age-old into something never heard of before, to proclaim a general truth with such simplicity and profundity' (129). For the suprahistorical person, the past is the 'voice of an oracle' in the sense that its meaning must be interpreted by a wise person looking for general patterns (130).

Nevertheless, Nietzsche insists, we should not jettison scientific historians. Indeed, 'we should not look down on those laborers who cart, heap, and winnow', but rather 'should recognise them as necessary apprentices and journeymen in the service of their master'. That is, contrary to some scholars' claims, Nietzsche is not critical of science, but on the contrary sees it as crucial work. The scientific historians should serve to carry out the research agenda set by the suprahistorical historian – the latter identifies certain broad types and the labourers set out to locate these types in the varied cultures across history. Nietzsche's claim, though, is that culture should not 'mistake' these scientific historians 'for great historians' (130). The error, then, of modern scientific culture is not to unleash the drive for truth, but rather to herald the scientific historian as the peak of that culture – Nietzsche's task in 'David Strauss' and 'Utility and Liability' is in part to lower the cultural status of scholars, scientists and public intellectuals, and to elevate great artists, saints and philosophers.

6C *A New monumental-critical history (pp. 130–1)*

The last paragraph is unusual in that it is a rousing exhortation to the reader to 'look ahead', 'set yourself a great goal', 'draw around yourselves the fence of a great, all-embracing hope, of a hopeful striving', and 'create within yourselves an image [*Bild*] to which the future should conform' (130). However, this section has been an assessment of the primary virtue of the modern age, and Nietzsche has concluded that modernity has failed to live up to its own high ideals. Accordingly, an exhortation to his contemporary readers is most needful.

Particularly surprising, however, is that Nietzsche revives the language of monumental history here, calling for the 'architects of the future' to set themselves a 'great goal', and bolster their ambition with a 'great-all-embracing hope' for success (130). Indeed, Nietzsche counsels reading histories of 'great men' and revisits his once doubtful hope that 'with a hundred such unmodernly educated human beings … the entire noisy sham cultivation of this age could now be silenced once and for all' (130–1). Notice, however, that this monumental history differs from the ancient version, as it is based on modern scientific history. This architect of the future will employ scientific historians in the service of his task. Moreover, this architect can 'sit in judgment of the past', unlike the pre-modern monumental individual, incorporating an element of critical history (130). This modern architect benefits from the suprahistorical perspective afforded him by the universal scope of modern scientific history.

How does this pinnacle, the new monumental history, fit with the higher peak of justice discussed at the beginning of the section? In my view, Nietzsche presents the architect of the future as preparatory for the just individual. The architect's aim after all is merely to 'silence' the 'noisy sham cultivation of this age', to adopt a 'great, all-embracing hope' without necessarily carrying it out (130–1). By lowering the status of modern scientific historians, this architect can begin to elevate the cultural status of the just individual. In doing so, this new monumental individual prepares the way for the emergence of the just individual. Several scholars have argued that Nietzsche himself takes up the mantle of critical historian (Zuckert 1976: 62). It seems more appropriate to see him as adopting this new modern monumental-critical history, since his task is to deflate the pretensions of the present and to prepare the way for a better future. In addition, he fits this new type of history by adopting a suprahistorical perspective, one not driven by religion but by the universal scope of modern science.

7 Arrested growth and development in modernity

In his account of modernity thus far, Nietzsche has discussed its failure to achieve its ends – both the fundamental needs of humanity, the need for wholeness (section 4) and for value in life (section 5), and the ideal that modernity sets for itself, objectivity (section 6). In section 7, he shifts from ends to means, to modern scientific culture's liability for its growth and development. He specifically highlights modern scientific culture's ideal, 'historical justice', as stunting the growth of culture (131).

Nietzsche's argument reaches back again to his discussion of horizons and limits in section 1, and particularly to his account of the tension between justice and love. For Nietzsche, 'only in love, only in the shadow of the illusion of love, does the human being create – that is, only in the unconditional belief [*unbedingten Glauben*] in perfection and justness' (131). *Eros* drives individuals and cultures to inner development, inner self-overcoming, on the path towards their ideal. They employ their 'creative instinct' to shape the world around them in service to their end. However, the condition for the possibility of this *eros* is that we have unconditional faith in the value – or 'perfection and justness' – of the ideal. To use Nietzsche's earlier example, we must have unconditional faith in the worthiness of our beloved to produce deeply heartfelt and creative poetry for him or her. If we begin to have doubts about the worthiness of our beloved, this deflates our love and hence our creative instinct, and our poetry suffers.

More broadly, 'historical justice' dampens our love for our ideals by bringing 'to light so much falsehood, coarseness, inhumanity, absurdity, and violence that the pious atmosphere of illusion, in which alone everything that wants to live is actually capable of life, vanishes' (131). Nietzsche uses the example of Protestant Christianity to illustrate his point. In the nineteenth century, a theological movement led by Friedrich Schleiermacher agreed with modern historical challenges to Christian dogma and institutional order – even the notions of God and the immortality of the soul were unnecessary, they claimed – and insisted that Christianity in its truest form involves an inexpressible feeling of the divine.

As a result, Christianity 'permits us "to empathize with all actual and even with some merely possible religions"', and the '"true church" is supposed to be one that "becomes a fluid mass where there are no defined outlines, where each part is sometimes here, sometimes there, and in which all things peacefully mingle"' (133, citing Schleiermacher). Yet for Nietzsche, this form of religion is based on modernity's relentless criticism, such that there is very little love or unconditional faith left. Any determinate claim made on behalf of the religion is subject to the same corrosive critique, and so members of this religion cease to be inspired by anything that they share in common, as each must retreat to the private inner life of faith. Religions can never 'become mature' without 'a protecting and enveloping cloud' of 'illusion [*Wahn*]' (134).

A further consequence that Nietzsche discusses is that modernity's arrested development leaves individuals in the natural state of egoism. Cultures shape individuals to 'serve the purposes of the age', and pre-modern cultures employ history to educate individuals to maturity. Pre-eminently, this involves elevating individuals out of their natural love of themselves, particularly through antiquarian history which demonstrates the rootedness of the individual within the community, engendering loyalty and veneration. However, modern historical culture puts individuals 'to work at the earliest possible moment; they are supposed to go to work in the factory of general utility before they are mature – indeed, so that they do not become mature' (134). Because of the culture's immaturity, it can only conceive of the satisfaction of egoistic interest as the end of human life, hence the aggregation of all egoistic ends – 'utility' – as the end of the community. As such, modern culture structures ever more features of life in utilitarian and economic terms, seeking to maximise utility as far as possible. The pre-eminent model for such utility-maximisation is the 'factory' with its 'division of labor' and authoritarian 'rank and file' rule (136).

Nietzsche uses contemporary scholarship as his example of an arena of life colonised by this utilitarian logic. He argues that modern culture does not allow scholars to become mature because this 'would be a luxury that would divert a great deal of energy away from "the labor market"'. Instead, 'young people' are 'whipped onward through the millennia' in their training, gaining a tremendous breadth of knowledge but no depth of wisdom (134). Then, the new scholars are thrust into the 'factory of scholarship' where they engage in endless scholarly drudgery – long hours of work at low pay with no clear satisfactory goal in mind. In this sense they are like 'slaves', with no leisure time and performing their duties not for the sake of themselves but for the sake of the scholarly machine as a whole (136). They are like parts of the machine rather than human in themselves. Accordingly, they internalise the egoism pervasive in culture as a whole, not working for the common good but demanding 'honors and advantages for themselves' (136). Finally, none of the products of this factory improves life, but rather damages it, as witnessed in scholars' attempt to 'popularise' their work (137).

Does this section suggest that modern culture ought to embrace 'illusion' and throw away truth? I think not. Nietzsche's point in this section is rather narrow, concerning only the preconditions for creativity and cultural growth. Moreover, he is not advocating that we invent ideals and not investigate their basis. Instead, he argues that creativity requires 'unconditional belief in perfection and justness' (131). For pre-modern cultures, this unconditional faith had no justification, which is why it suffers under the modern scientific gaze. However, Nietzsche here leaves open the possibility of a justified unconditional faith in perfection, one that need not be deflated by the discoveries of modern historical culture. Indeed, as we will see, the life of exemplary individuals provides just such a justification for this unconditional faith, rendering the pre-modern baseless faith unnecessary.

8 Modernity's philosophy of history

Section 7 discussed the growth and development of culture, but growth points towards an end point, as well as an account of how to make the developmental process as a whole intelligible. Section 8 examines the nature of this developmental process. As Nietzsche claimed in section 1, history confers value on existence through the process of development towards an end. Modern culture is distinctive in its drive towards truth, and this drive eventually critically reflects on modern culture itself. As a result, modernity comes to think that it represents the old age of humanity. However, this self-understanding does not hold up to modernity's own critical scrutiny turned against itself (A). In response, modern culture concocts a Hegelian account of historical progress that sees the present as the culmination of history, a secular-providential account that Nietzsche critiques with his own version of the problem of evil (B).

8A *Ironic self-consciousness and the old age of humanity (pp. 137–42)*

Modern culture casts its critical gaze on all past ideals. However, modernity's impartiality and universality means that it eventually points its cannon against itself, and thereby it develops a 'superior, critical consciousness that attains a certain ironic perspective on [its] own necessary inner nature'. Modern culture in its origin proclaims itself superior to all ancient cultures by transcending them, but it finds itself unable to defend this judgement when it is subjected to its own criticism. As such, it continually harbours doubts about all of its claims. For instance, Nietzsche suggests that his contemporaries, though supporting a historical-scientific education for the youth, nonetheless display a lingering scepticism about it. This 'ironic self-consciousness' forces modern individuals always to adopt a stance of detachment from the very claims and policies that they propose (138).

This ironic self-consciousness reinforces all the problems we discussed above; most importantly it impedes action and growth, making us the 'anemic offspring of powerful and cheerful generations'. But our detachment from the present also leads us to 'retrospection', living in the past by 'seeking comfort in the past by means of memories'. In these ways, our culture is not full of youthful vigour and hope, but exists in perpetual old age, appearing 'to confirm Hesiod's prophecy that one day humans would have gray hair already at birth'. Our 'historical cultivation' thus gives us the 'belief' [*Glauben*] that we represent the 'old age of humanity', that humanity was once youthful, energetic, but unenlightened, and now we have become old, knowledgeable, but without a future. This belief is, of course, a faith [*Glauben*], that is, not something demonstrated by historical knowledge. Nietzsche traces this faith back to the 'Christian theological conception' of the Middle Ages and its belief in the inevitable 'imminent end of the world' and its reminder of the 'memento mori' (139).

What results from such a philosophy of history, Nietzsche claims, is a 'profound sense of hopelessness'. There is no future for modern culture, a view 'inimical to all attempts to sow the seeds of the new, to engage in daring experiments, to desire freely'. This hopeless view of history 'opposes every flight into the unknown, because it finds nothing to love or hope for there' (139). Throughout this section, Nietzsche seeks to destroy all philosophies of history that cling to an 'end of history' thesis, precisely because such an end vitiates originality and onward movement in a historical process that gives life meaning. He claims here that the 'human race is a tough and tenacious thing' and cannot live only one life, from youth to old age (138). 'Lateborn offspring', Nietzsche says at the end of the section, can always create something new and thereby rejuvenate humanity, such that 'coming generations will know them only as the firstborn' (146).

Nietzsche's deeper criticism, however, is immanent to modern culture itself. He argues that modernity's philosophy of history does not stand up to its own criticism. Its view of the process of history must 'be understood historically, history itself *must* solve the problem of history, knowledge *must* turn the goad upon itself'. The problem with modernity's philosophy of history is that it cannot be demonstrated scientifically, and so its very 'faith' can be traced back to its human, all too human origins. Such a history will undermine the unconditional faith in the 'justness' of the claim, as we saw in section 7 (131). Moreover, the fundamental problem with this philosophy of history is that it does not provide a completion of a process at the end of history, only a perpetual decline. From the 'historical' perspective, our efforts are only valuable insofar as they contribute to the realisation of the ideal central to our culture. As such, 'without heirs' who will complete the moderns' task, 'their memory is meaningless'. Modern individuals thus become 'overcome by the gloomy inkling that, since no future life can justify it [*Recht geben*], their life is an injustice' (142). Nietzsche here offers a glimpse of the task of a genuine history, as he points back to section 6 with its idea of the exemplary just individual, who must justify life to redeem existence.

Nietzsche then offers an alternative philosophy of history for modern culture. Our historical cultivation is universal in nature, and so we moderns can appreciate the ways in which the German people are 'descendants' not only of the 'ancient world' but also of the 'spirit of Christianity' (141). We can incorporate within ourselves such divergent and capacious cultures as these. Indeed, we can 'find no greater or prouder destiny than that of being descendants' of these people (142). At the same time, we need not be 'doomed to being the disciples of fading antiquity'. We can 'recreate in ourselves the spirit of Hellenistic and Roman culture' but 'by means of our universal history'. That is, we do not turn away from modernity back to the ancients, but precisely use its tools to reshape pre-modern cultures, allowing us 'gradually to set our goal higher and farther' than the ancients (141), to 'go behind and beyond' them (142). In this way, we moderns need not lose hope in the future with an 'end of history' philosophy. Nietzsche's philosophy of history is one of endless incorporation and self-overcoming, that the modern age can synthesise the achievements of the past while going beyond them, thereby always grounding the hope for future originality.

8B *Hegelian idolatry (pp. 143–6)*

This alternative, however, has to contend with Hegel. The 'old age of humanity' view was vulnerable to the claim that our activity is meaningless because it has no ultimate purpose. Yet in the second half of the section, Nietzsche argues that modern culture responds by developing its own highest purpose, one supplied by G. W. F. Hegel. According to 'Hegelian philosophy', the 'world process' culminates in modernity as its 'necessary result'. History is the process of spirit becoming 'transparent and comprehensible to himself', and this self-consciousness is nowhere more evident than in the critical self-reflection of modern scientific culture. This view 'deifies this lateborn offspring as the true meaning and purpose of all previous historical events'. History 'justifies' existence through an intelligible process that culminates in the 'Last Judgment' [*Weltgericht*]. From the perspective of the end of history, we can justify and render intelligible the suffering of the past, showing how what seemed unjust was in fact necessary for the development and realisation of spirit. Hegel's philosophy of history, Nietzsche points out, thereby supplants the suprahistorical views of 'art and religion', offering a competing account of the value of human existence in the teleological process of world history (143).

Hegel thus 'instilled in those generations nurtured by his philosophy' a 'naked admiration of success' and the 'idolatry of the factual'. Since every event – regardless of our feelings about it – is necessary for the realisation of history, Hegel's followers reasoned, then we must 'kneel down and bow [our] heads before the "power of history"' (143). We conceive of ourselves as a passive instrument, as a vehicle for history's progress, a 'Chinese puppet to every power – regardless of whether it is a government, a public opinion, or a numerical majority' (143). Hegel's view engenders, according to Nietzsche, a supreme quiescence and celebration of the status quo. However, instead of despairing at their meaningless existence, modern individuals benefit from the faith in their own valuable role in the completion of history. Despite this consolation, Nietzsche argues that the Hegelian philosophy of history destroys our freedom even more profoundly than the 'old age of humanity' view. At least the latter made possible freedom in virtue of the fact that humanity would live on even if in old age – there would be in principle some room for continued human agency. The Hegelian view, by contrast, enslaves each individual to be an instrument of the 'sojourn of God on earth' (143).

However, Nietzsche's challenge to Hegel strikes deeper than the bad effects he sees in the Hegelian philosophy of history. He also argues that it suffers from the same traditional critique of Christianity, namely, the problem of evil. The problem of evil challenges God's providential design by identifying moments of suffering, catastrophes and deaths on a grand scale that could not possibly have been permitted by such a loving and all-powerful God. Nietzsche applies the same critique to Hegelian providential design, identifying certain evils that could not be justified as part of a rational process, thereby casting doubt on the idea that there is necessary progress at all in history.

Nietzsche does not, however, employ the traditional evidence of suffering and death as his predecessor Schopenhauer did. Rather, he draws on the lives of exemplary individuals, again indicating that he holds exemplars to be the basis of his account of normative value. Nietzsche argues that it is 'an insult to morality that someone like Raphael had to die when he was only thirty-six years old: such a person should never die at all'. It is a moral outrage that Raphael 'once lived and will never live again'. Even Goethe, who lived until the age of 82, still died too young: 'I would gladly trade entire wagonloads of fresh, ultramodern lives for but a couple years of the "exhausted" Goethe.' In destroying these exemplary individuals, in other words, history displays its irrationality. It destroys those who bring value into existence, and keeps alive those who lead meaningless lives: 'By comparison with such great people who are dead, how few living people have a right to live at all!' (145). Note here that Nietzsche is not levelling a groundless, elitist judgement about life. As we have seen, Nietzsche holds that human existence as such is without worth, and only those who lead exemplary human lives can redeem it.

In attacking the Hegelian philosophy of history in this way, Nietzsche begins to develop his own distinctive philosophy of history that he would pursue throughout his career. Namely, he holds that history does not have a necessary path, but is contingent. There are many possibilities immanent to any one culture. This philosophy of history, however, should be understood as being in service to Nietzsche's broader ethical theory of exemplary individual self-determination. Nietzsche limits the scope of history so as to allow for individuals to transcend historical determination and shape the course of history according to their free self-determination. He states that 'everywhere the human being is virtuous precisely because he rebels against that blind power of facts, against the tyranny of the real' (145). Individuals are the 'great fighters against history' who transcend 'that's how it is' with a claim about 'this is how it should be' (146).

9 The redemption of humanity

Sections 7–9 concern the development of history – section 7 on the growth of culture, section 8 on the nature of historical development, and now section 9 on the end point or aim of historical development. Pre-modern cultures possessed disparate aims, but each of these aims is based on myth and hence groundless. Modern culture in its universal scope seeks to know the aim of humanity as a whole, encompassing these pre-modern cultures as part of the overall world-historical process. This end of humanity would serve as the 'Last Judgment' or *Weltgericht*, the final court for justifying humanity's existence as a whole. As we saw in the previous section, Hegel's philosophy of history offers the most influential account of this *Weltgericht* for modern culture. However, Nietzsche suggests in this section, Hegel's account was missing a crucial ingredient – namely, the concept of the redemption of humanity. Redemption becomes necessary when beginning from Schopenhauer's and Nietzsche's starting point – namely, that human existence is not worth living, and so requires the contradiction at its heart to be redeemed. To be rational, world history must culminate in human effort that redeems past evil, by showing that evil was necessary for the final realisation of humanity's end. Nietzsche sees Eduard von Hartmann as completing the Hegelian and hence modern project of rendering its historical process rational to itself. Unfortunately, Nietzsche argues, Hartmann's culmination is itself a reductio ad absurdum of any such teleological account (A). Nietzsche finds Hartmann's view comically bad, but the motivation for it – the discoveries of Darwinian natural science – represents a much more powerful support for universal egoism (B). Accordingly, Nietzsche recognises the crucial need for redemption, a redemption not at the end of history, but in the peaks across human history that together represent the 'republic of geniuses' (C).

9A *Hartmann's cynical redemption (pp. 146–53)*

When it was published in 1869, Eduard von Hartmann's *Philosophy of the Unconscious* 'created a sensation and became a philosophical bestseller. The first edition rapidly sold out, and in the next decade the book went through no less than eight editions' (Beiser 2016: 122). In this section, Nietzsche critiques this popular contemporary book in much the same way that he castigated

Strauss's in the previous essay; that is, with a mixture of philosophical argument and playfulness.[25] Like Strauss, Hartmann was a student of Hegel, arguing that nature and history possess an intelligible, rational structure and aim. Both argue that religious faith is an illusion overcome by the modern age. They differ, however, in their assessment of the culmination of human history – Strauss celebrates the end of history as the liberation of humanity, while Hartmann bemoans it as humankind's worst era of suffering.

Hartmann follows Schelling and Hegel in postulating the existence of a universal will – Hartmann calls it the 'unconscious' – that underlies nature and human history, and that develops through history into ever higher stages of complexity and self-reflection. In the first two sections of his book, he sets out to demonstrate the unconscious in nature and in human beings by appealing to the most advanced modern science, especially the work of Charles Darwin. In section 3, Hartmann then traces the development of the unconscious from its origins in plants, animals, and then in human beings. Hartmann departs from Schelling, Hegel and Strauss, and follows Schopenhauer, in arguing that the unconscious will develops in human history through the growing awareness of the 'misery of existence' (1931: vii). At each stage in human history, humanity produces for itself an 'illusion [*Illusion*]' of 'happiness [*Glück*]' that it sets out to achieve – in the 'childhood' of humanity, among the ancients, this illusion consists in the happiness of friendship (1931: vii); in the 'youth' of humanity, among the medieval, this illusion consists in the happiness of the afterlife; finally, in the adulthood of humanity, in 'modern times', the illusion consists in the happiness achieved through human scientific, technological and political progress (viii). Unfortunately, the achievement of the illusion reveals it to be an illusion, thus thrusting us face to face with the 'misery of existence' (vii).[26]

For instance, in the case of the modern age, we harbour the illusion that the advancement of modern scientific knowledge

---

[25] See Salaquarda for more on Nietzsche and Hartmann (1984: 30–45).
[26] Nietzsche does not engage with Hartmann's argument that all illusions are destroyed in the course of human history, casting doubt on the reading that Nietzsche himself embraced illusion.

will culminate in universal happiness. However, Hartmann argues, all such advancements in civilisation bring with them a growth of 'wealth and wants' and hence an increase in worry and dissatisfaction. In addition to increasing 'misery', the 'consciousness of misery' also grows. Scientific knowledge makes us ever more aware of the 'paltriness of life, of the vanity of most enjoyments and endeavors and the feeling of misery'. As such, the 'often-asserted enhancement of the happiness of the world by the progress of the world rests on an altogether superficial appearance' (1931: 2.115). The destruction of this third and final illusion leaves humanity with no illusions left to rest on.

However, Hartmann regards this development ultimately in a positive way, since our inability to achieve happiness through illusion teaches us a valuable lesson. Namely, we finally see the 'folly' of our 'endeavor' for happiness and so forego 'all positive happiness' (1931: 2.117). Hartmann argues that humanity culminates in the longing 'for absolute painlessness, for nothingness, Nirvana' (2.118). Humanity awakens to the irrationality of the will for happiness, and so redeems existence by negating this irrational will at its heart. As Hartmann puts it, the more humanity is 'emancipated from the blind vassalage with which it at first followed the irrational will', the more we 'assume a hostile position in opposition to the will struggling for positive happiness', ultimately leading to the 'destruction of every illusion' and embracing 'the knowledge' that 'every volition leads to unblessedness, and only renunciation to the best attainable state, painlessness' (2.124). Humanity must arduously pursue happiness to discover ultimately Schopenhauer's truth, the vanity of all such pursuits.[27]

For Nietzsche, Hartmann nicely represents the ironic self-consciousness of modern culture. While Hartmann supports the advancements of modern scientific culture, at the same time he evinces a 'self-irony' about it, worrying that these advancements will not achieve what we intend, but will in fact backfire (146). Moreover, Nietzsche interprets Hartmann as taking the next step in the development of modern culture, 'cynicism'. Cynicism for

---

[27] See Jensen for more on the Hartmann–Nietzsche relationship (2016: 135f.).

Nietzsche is an explanatory and normative thesis of universal egoism – that is, every human being, and indeed all creatures in nature, do pursue and ought to pursue only their own interest. Hartmann's philosophy of history sets out to 'justify the course of history', that human history moves in a rational direction such that the 'entire development of the world' is ultimately for the 'everyday utility of the modern human being' (146). Nietzsche is stupefied by the 'self-aggrandizement' in Hartmann's claim, that the 'meaning and solution of each and every riddle of becoming' is the 'modern human being', that the purpose of all things, all plants, animals, all of history, is the egoistic 'modern human being himself, who is capable of surveying this immense distance' (147).

Of course, this philosophy of history is widely shared among the 'overproud European[s] of the nineteenth century', who, Nietzsche declares, are 'stark raving mad' for many reasons he has already detailed (147). Fortunately, Nietzsche can rely on Hartmann himself to demonstrate the self-destructive character of this view of the purpose of history. Indeed, Hartmann is the perfect embodiment of the tendency of the age because he at once attests seriously to a philosophy of history that justifies the cynicism of the present, but also defends an ironic stance towards it out of his belief in the ultimate self-undoing of this cynicism. For Nietzsche, this view is a comic absurdity, but it is one that emerges out of the inner tendency of modern culture. Demonstrating this connection between modernity and this 'parody' of itself is a most 'effective' strategy 'against the excess of historical cultivation' (148). If modern culture produces out of itself this absurdly self-refuting statement, then this is good evidence of its wrong turn.

Nietzsche lampoons Hartmann's theory in several ways. His parody on p. 149 is a good example, as he sarcastically claims that the 'Last Judgment' [*Weltgericht*] justifies the pathetic modern bourgeois. 'Our age is very good', Nietzsche's Hartmann claims, but good 'for those who wish to suffer as severely as possible from the indigestibility of life and for whom the Last Judgment cannot arrive too soon'. The modern age is the 'joyous state in which there is nothing but "solid mediocrity"', in which the 'more significant stage' is the one where the 'worker "leads a comfortable existence"'. Ultimately, the culmination of this historical process towards mediocrity will be 'nausea'. However, Hartmann insists, 'it must be this way', and thus '"as laborers in the vineyards of the Lord, let us strive vigorously onward, for it is the process along that can lead to redemption"' (149).

The point of all this playfulness, Nietzsche tells us, is that Hartmann's text is the 'first to succeed in clearly recognising the ridiculousness of the notion of the world process, and, thanks to the uncommon seriousness of his portrayal, in helping us recognise this ridiculousness with even greater clarity'. Hartmann effects a reductio ad absurdum in the very act of bringing the Hegelian notion of a 'world process' to its completion. The end of history teaches us that we should all commit suicide – and soon. The lesson Nietzsche draws from this reductio is that the very idea of humanity's progressive development is mistaken, and so 'we need not be bothered with why the "world" exists, why "humanity" exists' as if these general concepts have agency of their own (153). To confer agency on the world or on humanity is to anthropomorphise it, and indeed to enchain our own will to another illusory concept akin to a religious divinity. Accordingly, Nietzsche concludes at the end of his survey of the historical point of view that we should reject a basic tenet of the historical perspective, namely, that history culminates in a 'process' that confers value on life (151).

9B *Darwin's deadly truths (pp. 153–8)*

In the second half of the section, however, Nietzsche shifts from his playful, 'cheerful' critique to a decidedly more serious tone (147). He does so because he catalogues a set of 'doctrines [he] hold[s] to be true, but also deadly'. These are doctrines supported by the discoveries of modern natural science – especially the work of Charles Darwin – doctrines that provide a much more powerful justification of cynicism than Hartmann's philosophy. The authority of modern natural science lodges these doctrines deep in modern culture, making them difficult to dislodge. It is here that Nietzsche introduces the most formidable challenge of the modern age, which he proceeds to answer not only in sections 9–10 of this essay, but in the rest of the *Observations*.

The three deadly doctrines are:

1 'Sovereign becoming', that there is no permanence in nature, but only flux.
2 'The fluidity of all concepts, types, and species', that because of the flux of nature, no general concepts can explain particulars; general terms change because particulars change.
3 'The lack of any cardinal difference between human and animal', that because of the fluidity of general terms, there is no permanent difference between human beings and animals (153).

These three doctrines challenge all pre-modern cultural beliefs. Pre-modern cultures demand belief in unchanging truths and free human agency, in enduring concepts and categories, and especially in categorical differences between man and beast. These pre-modern views serve in part to elevate human beings out of their natural egoism. Cultures ground the education of a virtuous character on the cardinal difference between human beings and animals, so that, for instance, the community tells its youth that human beings are by nature rational beings while animals are not, and that the youth are taught to conform to these general norms.

These doctrines are deadly because of their challenge to such beliefs. Nietzsche predicts that if they 'are flung at the people for one more generation in the craze for education, then no one should be surprised if that people perishes of petty egoism and wretchedness, of ossification and selfishness, after first falling apart and ceasing to be a people at all'. These doctrines corrode community – the unity of a culture or a people – by undermining all the dogmatic belief that once raised us out of our egoism. Pre-modern communities supplied humanity with moral capital, but these deadly doctrines steadily deplete this capital. In a short time we will lose moral virtue, lose community, and be thrust back in upon our natural egoism. In that case, what will emerge will be 'systems of individual egoisms, brotherhoods whose purpose will be the rapacious exploitation of the nonbrothers, and similar products of utilitarian vulgarity' (153).

This new order can be 'expressed in Christian terms: the devil is the ruler of the world'. By this metaphor, Nietzsche means that self-interest and 'success' are what drive everything. The 'egoism of individuals, or groups, or of the masses was in all ages the lever behind historical movements'. This new order embraces the devil, rather than seeking ultimately to purge our egoism, as Hartmann suggests. This modern outlook decrees that "'egoism shall be our God'". It argues that living in accordance with self-interest is living in accordance with nature – in all previous eras, we were living under oppressive illusions that robbed us of our sublunary happiness. As such, modern culture sets out to erect 'future history upon egoism', and in particular upon 'prudent egoism'. That is, it will have learned its lesson from Hobbes and history about the self-destructive tendency of 'imprudent egoism' (155). Instead, we recognise that we must suppress 'coarse and dull instincts or desires, or at least' channel 'them in the direction of refined egoism'. We should create 'military and police forces' to protect all of us 'from the horrible eruptions of imprudent egoism' (156). Self-interest can be made to combat self-interest, to paraphrase James Madison. Ultimately, by limiting the excesses of our egoism, we can each maximise our self-interest.

Prudent egoism is a fundamental threat to humanity, Nietzsche suggests in his summary of his major criticisms of the essay on p. 157, now subsumed within its cultural aims. For instance, Nietzsche fears for the education of the 'youth', that they will be made to 'fit the mold of that mature manhood of egoism to which the whole world aspires'. Modern culture makes the youth egoistic precisely through their education in historical knowledge. This 'excess of history' leads to the 'uprooting' of 'fire, defiance, self-oblivion, and love'; 'smothering the ardor of its passion for justice', 'suppressing its desire to mature slowly by supplanting it with the opposite desire to be quickly finished'. The excess of history does this by destroying the youth's 'horizons and perspectives' so that he 'retreats from an infinite horizon into himself, into the tiniest egoistical realm, and is doomed to wither there and dry up'. In a remarkable anticipation of his portrait of the 'last men' in *Thus Spoke Zarathustra*, Nietzsche states that the individual under this education 'compromises, calculates and accommodates himself to the facts; he does not seethe, but merely blinks and knows how to seek his own or his party's advantage in the advantage or disadvantage of others' (157).

It is within this evaluation of prudent egoism that Nietzsche's contempt for the 'masses' discussed in this section should be understood. Nietzsche fumes that

> Only in three respects does it seem to me that the masses are deserving of notice: first, as faded copies of great men printed on poor paper with wornout plates; second as resistance to the great; and finally as tools of the great. With regard to everything else, they can go to the devil and to statistics! (154)

This passage is often cited as evidence of Nietzsche's 'aristocratic radicalism', his view that only the great few matter, and that the many have no worth.[28] This argument misunderstands his point. Nietzsche is not condemning the many per se, but only the 'masses' [*Massen*]. Recall that he thinks that culture is extremely important and valuable, and that a culture is a unified 'people' [*Volk*]. For Nietzsche, then, the problem is not the many, but how the many have been transformed by a culture of egoism. Indeed, in a draft of this section, Nietzsche discusses the great gulf separating the modern masses from the ancient people: 'you should have kept statistics in Athens! Then you would have sensed the difference … If the multitude has a more refined and nobler composition, then the law immediately goes to the devil' (KSA 7.29[41], UW 208). Nietzsche uses 'masses' to refer to the modern many because our egoism has gradually transformed us into a homogeneous, mediocre mass. By contrast, the Athenian people had a dynamic, complex culture. Statistics capture the nature of the modern masses, but not the Athenian people. In sum, then, Nietzsche does not have contempt for the people; on the contrary, he seeks to transform the many such that they form a unified culture as in ancient Athens.

9C *The new monumental history in the republic of genius (pp. 151, 153)*

In a few paragraphs in this section, Nietzsche offers a glimpse into his alternative, positive view. He eschews the approach of Hegel

---

[28] See, for example, Detwiler 1990. Jensen (2016: 135) argues that, for Nietzsche, 'common actors – Das Volk – play a merely oppositional or instrumental role'.

and Hartmann of trying to find an aim for humanity as a whole. Instead, he urges his reader to ask 'yourself why you, as an individual, exist'. Modern natural and historical science offers an account of the efficient causes that brought us about, but it provides no answer as to why we exist – that is, to what end do we exist and what is the value of our existence? As such, each of us must 'try to justify the meaning of your existence a posteriori, as it were, by setting yourself a purpose, a goal, a "reason why", a lofty and noble "reason why"' (153). For Nietzsche, we do not discover why we exist – the world provides no such answers, but rather only drives us to ask the question. Instead, we must invent and produce for ourselves a meaning and purpose for our lives, one that is 'lofty and noble', that lives up to our highest capacities.

Accordingly, Nietzsche does not reject the project of redemption and the *Weltgericht*.[29] On the contrary, he embraces it as necessary to justifying the value of existence. Yet for him, 'only cheerfulness can lead to redemption'. Cheerfulness involves 'avoiding all constructions of the world process or even of the history of humanity'. Instead, we must attend 'only to individuals, who form a kind of bridge over the turbulent stream of becoming'. Only the life of exemplary individuals can redeem existence for human beings, and this is because they 'do not further a process', but 'rather they live timelessly and simultaneously, thanks to history'. As we saw in section 2, for Nietzsche, exemplary individuals are immortal in that their deeds are internalised in culture and transmitted through history forever. They also live 'simultaneously' through history in the sense that each can speak to the others – Shakespeare can write in dialogue with the ancient poets, and Goethe can comment on Shakespeare, and so forth, such that 'one giant calls to another across the desolate expanses of time, and this lofty dialogue between spirits continues, undisturbed by the wanton, noisy chattering of the dwarfs that crawl about beneath them'. Nietzsche describes this as the 'republic of geniuses of which Schopenhauer once spoke'. Accordingly, humanity demonstrates

---

[29] The theme of redemption is under-studied in the Nietzsche literature – for example, there is no entry for *Erlösung* in either the *Nietzsche-Lexikon* (Niemeyer 2009) or the *Nietzsche-Handbuch* (Ottmann 2000).

its victory against becoming, against the purposeless flux of nature and history, by producing exemplary individuals who invent and produce a 'bridge' of being above 'becoming'. Thus, Nietzsche concludes, the 'goal of humankind cannot possibly be found in its end stage, but only in its highest specimens [*Exemplaren*]' (151). These exemplars bind humanity together, dragging us out of our natural egoism in communion with our highest deeds. Nietzsche thus sides ultimately with the suprahistorical justification of existence – finding value in each highest moment in history – rather than the historical processual justification.

In this way, Nietzsche does not seek a standard to redeem humanity within nature, nor in the progress of history, both of which are deeply challenged by the deadly doctrines of modern science. Nor does he return to ancient bounded communities and will illusion, as these communities do not redeem humanity but only provide happiness for their members. In addition, such communities have been steadily undermined by the march of modern culture. Rather, Nietzsche looks to the embodied lives of exemplary individuals for redemption, and in this way synthesises the ancient 'monumental' ethical ideal with the Christian and eventually modern longing for humanity's redemption. If one sets them side by side, one can see the paragraph on p. 151 resonating clearly with pp. 97–8, where Nietzsche discusses ancient 'monumental' history. What is new here, however, is the explicit recognition of the 'turbulent stream of becoming' underneath the great deeds of individuals – the deadly doctrines of modern science have been incorporated into history, yet we can nevertheless erect a republic of genius on top of these doctrines, producing a cardinal difference between humanity and animality where there is not one by nature. These exemplary individuals, 'dispersed throughout millennia, conjointly represent all the supreme powers that are buried in humanity' (KSA 7.29[52], UW 214); in them 'humanity will culminate' (KSA 7.29[73], UW 226).

Nietzsche's account of the redemption of humanity provides guidance for a new monumental history as well. We can reject the tendency of modern scientific history to discern statistical 'laws', which only tell us about the 'movement of society's lower strata, its loam and clay' (154). Instead, history can focus on exemplary individuals, though not as effects in themselves, as in the ancient monumental history. Historians can examine every facet of the origin and life of these individuals. No amount of analysis can ever destroy the self-determining wholeness of exemplary individuals. They can withstand the otherwise corrosive analysis of our historical culture. In this way, once again, Nietzsche does not seek to eliminate scientific knowledge.

10 Fixing modern culture

In sections 4–9, Nietzsche detailed the daunting dangers of modern culture's pursuit of historical knowledge. In the final section, Nietzsche asks, effectively, what is to be done about it? He imagines the progress of modern culture thus far as a 'dangerous and exciting . . . voyage' on the open sea, again underscoring that modernity is not in itself an error, but only that it is without guidance. The ship must find 'shore', must 'land' to overcome 'this infinite hopelessness and skepticism'. Nietzsche thinks that the improvement in modern culture will come gradually, so that at first we need only 'make land; later on we will find the good harbors and make landing easier for those who follow us' (158).

What is Nietzsche's strategy? First, he identifies the audience for his plan for cultural improvement: the youth. Like Socrates, Nietzsche turns to the youth because they have 'not yet been fully shaped' by contemporary culture. The 'instincts of nature' still have not been 'artificially and violently broken' by historical 'education'. As such, they can recognise that the historical scholar and the 'cultivated philistine' are not necessary results of modern culture, that there are other possibilities open to modern peoples (160). Nietzsche does not look to the youth so that he himself can indoctrinate them in 'cultural "propaganda"', as one critic puts it, but rather so that he can liberate them to begin to develop their own genuine culture (Lacoue-Labarthe 1990: 210).

The second part of Nietzsche's strategy is to identify the best means of liberation from the drive for excessive knowledge. Namely, we should turn the very ideal of modern culture against itself: the drive for truth. Nietzsche compares the 'modern German' support for its scientific form of education to Plato's 'necessary lie'. The moderns' noble lie is the 'aeterna veritas' of our 'education' and of our 'type of culture'. The lie consists in the claim that the limitless pursuit of knowledge will result in a better life for humanity. Summarising the main claims of this essay, Nietzsche argues that on the contrary, this pursuit of knowledge undermines our wholeness, our sense of value in life, and destroys our capacity to act. Just as Plato's 'state would have collapsed' (161), so too will our belief in our education collapse, if this lie is revealed as such by a 'necessary truth' (162). Thus, Nietzsche turns the scientific culture's commitment to truth against its own ideal, arguing that it cannot ground the truth of its own aspirations. In revealing this lie, Nietzsche suggests, we will 'unshackle this youth and . . . liberated life' (163).

The third part of Nietzsche's strategy is to point towards a new form of historical education. He states that the 'antidotes' to modern historical education are 'the ahistorical and the suprahistorical'. As he himself recognises, these concepts return us to section 1. The ahistorical 'encloses' one in a 'limited horizon', while the suprahistorical 'diverts one's gaze from what is in the process of becoming to what lends existence the character of something eternal and stable in meaning, art and religion' (163). Science stands at odds with these two perspectives, since science ultimately reveals sovereign becoming, while the ahistorical and suprahistorical discern permanent being. This tension between these different perspectives, Nietzsche argues, will manifest itself in some 'suffering', but it is necessary suffering to place knowledge once again in service to life (164). Nietzsche offers very little by way of specifics about what this new education will look like. I have pointed out passages throughout sections 4–9 that provide some guidance. What it will not involve is a simple return to the pre-modern types of history, but rather a synthesis and transformation of the 'three historical modes described above' in sections 2–3 through modern culture and the notion of the exemplar (165–6). The task of discussing the nature and aim of the exemplary individual remains for the next two *Observations*.

Nietzsche concludes the essay with a 'parable' that could support the 'hopeful individuals' in their pursuit of a new, healthy culture. This parable is that of the Greeks who 'found themselves threatened by a danger similar to the one we face today, the danger, namely, of perishing in a flood of things alien and past'. Yet they did not 'become an aggregate', but 'gradually learned how to organize this chaos by concentrating . . . on their genuine needs, and by letting those pseudoneeds out' (166). Since Nietzsche describes this as a parable, he does not intend for us moderns to return to the ancient model. Rather, it justifies our hope, and it gives a formal characterisation of how to improve.

The final paragraph offers one of the clearest statement of the formal nature of culture in the *Observations*.[30] In it, Nietzsche argues that culture involves the organisation of 'the chaos within' an individual or person into a unity, structured around 'his genuine needs'. Culture is opposed not only to chaos or barbarism, but, as we saw in 'David Strauss', to the outward appearance, the 'dissimulation and disguise' of culture, grounded not in genuine needs but in the 'decoration of life'. The overall problem with the anti-culture of contemporary Germany or the chaos of the modern soul is that it fails to synthesise its 'interior' character with its 'exterior' actions. The 'concept of culture' consists in the 'harmony of life, thought, appearance, and will', a unity that is not given by nature but is produced by human action, a 'new and improved physis' or nature. Nietzsche describes this self-determined unity of culture as an expression of 'moral' strength, since culture does not involve superior strength or intelligence, but a superior commitment to a common set of values. Finally, he concludes by defending the value central to modern culture, 'truthfulness', that can further 'true cultivation' as opposed to mere 'cultivatedness'. Nietzsche hence does not invoke myth or rhetoric to defend his views, but rather follows the value central to modern culture, harnessing that commitment against his contemporaries (167).

Indeed, Nietzsche admits at the beginning of this final section that 'this very treatise exhibits' all the signs of the 'modern character, the character of the weak personality' (158). He himself is a product of the modern age, an expression of its ironic or critical

---

[30] As Jensen (2016: 24–9) has shown, this paragraph was not intended to be the final one of the essay. However, Nietzsche did not object to the publisher's excluding the paragraph, suggesting that he 'authorized its omission, at least passively' (Jensen 2016: 29).

self-consciousness. Yet Nietzsche takes this self-consciousness in a productive direction – instead of leading to perpetual self-doubt and eventually cynicism, he proposes a way forward for modern culture, one that does not reject but builds on and channels modern scientific culture, especially its comprehensive human scope. As several scholars have noted, 'David Strauss' and 'Utility and Liability' serve primarily to critique modern culture. However, these scholars then leap from these 'pre-Nietzschean books' to his later period to grasp his real solution (Lampert 1993: ch. 11, 295; Smith 1996: ch. 7). In so doing, they overlook the second half of *Unfashionable Observations*, treating 'Utility and Liability' as a whole unto itself rather than the second part in an ongoing argument. In my view, Nietzsche begins in the first half of the book to critique modern culture, and in the second half – in 'Schopenhauer as Educator' and 'Richard Wagner in Bayreuth' – to develop a positive vision for a renewed modern culture.

4

Schopenhauer as Educator

The third part of the *Observations* has received far less attention than the second, even though it rivals 'Utility and Liability' as a remarkable work of philosophy. For Walter Kaufmann, this essay 'represents nothing less than the consummation of Nietzsche's early philosophy' (1978: 157). Richard Schacht judges it to be 'one of the most sustained, vigorous, delightful, and radically discomforting works Nietzsche ever wrote' (1995: 153). In my view, 'Schopenhauer as Educator' stands out among his works both early and late for developing the most sustained and lucid argument for culture and its aim, the exemplary individual. Insofar as these ideas remain central to his thought throughout his career, Nietzsche's first foray into them deserves close attention.

The main task of this chapter, then, will be to reconstruct Nietzsche's argument for culture and the exemplar. This case for culture represents the core of his positive view, as well as the response to the problems of modernity that he identified in the first, critical half of the *Observations*. I will argue that Nietzsche's positive ethical view is best understood in Kantian, idealist terms rather than in Aristotelian, naturalist terms. Central to Nietzsche's account is a Kantian notion of humanity – already introduced in 'Utility and Liability' – according to which we must ascend out of our animality by living in accordance with the 'fundamental law' [*Grundgesetz*] given by our 'authentic self' (174).[1]

---

[1] Cf. Schacht: 'Nietzsche is often thought to have advanced a conception of humanity that reduces it to its natural rudiments. But this essay shows that such a view is mistaken, since great significance is attached to the difference between humanity and mere animality, and to culture as its source ... Nature and merely natural existence are viewed as devoid of meaning and standing in need of "justification" and "redemption"' (1995: 159).

In reconstructing Nietzsche's argument, I contribute to an ongoing scholarly debate about 'Schopenhauer as Educator'. On the one hand, I agree with James Conant (2001), who has offered an insightful Kantian reading of 'Schopenhauer as Educator', against Thomas Hurka (2007) and Keith Ansell-Pearson (2013), who have developed naturalist readings of the text. On the other hand, I think Conant goes too far in his egalitarian reading of Nietzsche, and Hurka and Ansell-Pearson are convincing in identifying the elitism in Nietzsche's views. The main focus of this debate has been a crucial passage in section 6 of this essay – which we will return to below – in which Nietzsche asks 'How can your life ... obtain the highest value?' and answers, 'only by living for the benefit of the rarest and most valuable specimens [*Exemplare*]' (216). I will argue below that by attending to the context of this passage in light of the book as a whole, as well as its rhetorical aim, we can settle this debate.

My main contribution in what follows is to show that in this text Nietzsche is neither a democrat nor an aristocrat, but rather defends a meritocracy.[2] The aristocratic reading is wrong in assuming that natural inequalities ought to structure culture, for Nietzsche. The democratic reading is right on this count to claim that any individual is capable of participating in culture and achieving excellence. However, the aristocratic reading is correct to see cultural genius as exceedingly rare. Becoming an exemplar, though in principle open to everyone, is extremely difficult and demanding, because of the many physical, social, economic and political obstacles to our perfection. Yet the aristocratic reading is wrong to think that exemplarity comes from a natural endowment. Instead, human excellence is something achieved and thus merited by human beings, not given by nature. In this way, Nietzsche's theory of exemplarity follows Kant in conceiving of human excellence as the perfection of our distinctively human freedom. Nature is in fact contradictory, and human beings must exert our freedom in order to redeem our irrational existence. The achievement of freedom means that humanity claims responsibility for our fate on

---

[2] For a much more extensive elaboration of this point, see Church 2015a.

earth, and hence merits the honour of being regarded as a self-determining species.

In addition to developing this meritocratic alternative in what follows, I will also correct the scholarly habit of running together Nietzsche's politics with his view of culture. Consider Hurka's gloss on Nietzsche's 'perfectionism':

> Since [Nietzsche's] view is the opposite of John Rawls's famous maximin principle, it can be called a 'maximax' view. Whereas Rawls wants society to maximize the well-being of its worst-off individuals, Nietzsche wants it to concentrate on the best, since only their perfection has value ... [H]e seems to find no value whatever in the achievements of lesser humans, so once the best have developed as far as they can it is a matter of indifference what other individuals do. (2007: 18)

First, Nietzsche is far from indifferent about the many. As we will see, on the contrary, he encourages all individuals to consecrate themselves to culture. Second, Nietzsche does not look to politics to reform culture, as Hurka suggests. On the contrary, politics ought to become entirely independent of culture, in part because the modern state is one of the great enemies of culture. In his later work, Nietzsche may or may not embrace a more comprehensive role for the state to play in culture.[3] Here in his early work, however, he envisions a much more limited role for the state, similar to the liberal views of Schopenhauer and Burckhardt.

Structural overview

1   Freedom as the fundamental value
2–6   The education towards culture
    2   Education of affect
    3   Education of character

---

[3] See Ottmann (1999) for an excellent account of Nietzsche's political thought, early, middle and late.

1 Freedom

At the end of 'Utility and Liability', Nietzsche looked to the youth for the reform and rejuvenation of modern culture. He did so because the older generation was thoroughly corrupted by the scientific and scholarly form of education in modern culture. The youth hunger for something higher, to experience wholeness and to confer meaning and value on their lives. However, there exists no alternative form of education that could guide the youth to genuine culture. 'Schopenhauer as Educator' develops a positive vision of this alternative education. The first section grounds this new modern education on the value of human freedom. Sections 2–6 provide an account of the education and educators towards culture by focusing on Arthur Schopenhauer. Sections 7–8 conclude by examining the practicable conditions for reform.

The first section of 'Schopenhauer as Educator' strikingly parallels the first section of 'Utility and Liability'. In both cases, Nietzsche begins with foundational principles that he builds on in the course of the essays. In 'Utility and Liability', he examines the fundamental distinction between humanity and animality, humanity's basic contradiction, and then the pre-modern way in which human beings healed this contradiction: the use of the shaping power to forge closed communities. What becomes clear in the course of 'Utility and Liability' is that this pre-modern approach to the contradiction of humanity is no longer possible in the modern age. Modernity has destroyed traditional communities and horizons, casting human beings into an atomistic, egoistic cynicism. Humanity needs a new, distinctively modern form of community to replace the religion, tribe and patriarchy of the past, one that can satisfy both our need for wholeness and for value in existence.

The first section of 'Schopenhauer as Educator' thus defends the fundamental modern value – freedom – which will form the basis of a genuinely modern community, namely, culture.

This first section is also remarkable in its clear anti-elitism, as Conant (2001: 230f.) has developed at length. Nietzsche is often understood along the lines of the Hurka quote from above – there are a few, great, godlike individuals, the only ones who possess value, and the vast majority of humanity is bereft of value, akin to cattle. Nietzsche's statement that 'every human being is a one-of-a-kind miracle' should prompt us to re-evaluate his supposed elitism (171).

1A *The fundamental value of existence (pp. 171–3)*

Nietzsche opens 'Schopenhauer as Educator', as he did 'Utility and Liability', with a discussion of the universal, contradictory nature of human beings. On the one hand, each human being is unique. At our birth, we are the result of a distinctive array of causes, which propels us on a life course unique in history: 'no coincidence, regardless how strange, will ever for a second time concoct out of this amazingly variegated diversity the unity that he is' (171). Our conscience 'cries out' to each of us, urging us to 'Be yourself!', to live in 'strict consistency' with this 'uniqueness' (172).

On the other hand, however, we have a tendency to 'conceal' our uniqueness 'like a bad conscience', living instead in accordance with the general 'customs and opinions' of our time. We do so, Nietzsche argues, because being unique is very difficult – it requires 'unconditional [*unbedingte*] honesty and nakedness' that causes 'hardships' in society, exposing us to ridicule or poverty or persecution (171). As such, when a 'great thinker disdains human beings', he does not do so out of an aristocratic contempt for their natures or low birth, but rather because of their 'laziness [*Faulheit*]' (172). In sharp contrast to such an aristocratic outlook, this great thinker has tremendously high expectations for all human beings – that all of us can live up to our uniqueness – and it is only because we wilfully turn against our true selves that we fail to live up to our potential. That is, this great thinker assesses us meritocratically, not aristocratically, holding the many responsible for their poor efforts rather than judging them as lowly, base irruptions of nature.

To clarify the meritocratic character of Nietzsche's claim, let us consider both a parallel and a contrasting argument from his influences, Kant and Schopenhauer. First, the famous opening of Kant's 'What is Enlightenment?' offers a striking parallel with Nietzsche's first section.[4] There Kant claims that 'Enlightenment is the human being's emergence from his self-incurred minority'. Minority or immaturity [*Unmündigkeit*], Kant says, is the 'inability to make use of one's own understanding without direction from another'. It does not result from a natural or inborn deficiency of the 'understanding', as an aristocratic judgement would have it. Rather, it is 'self-incurred', since its 'cause lies ... in lack of resolution and courage', and even 'laziness [*Faulheit*] and cowardice' (WIE 8:35). Kant's and Nietzsche's judgement about our *Faulheit* might strike us as unduly harsh, but, importantly, this judgement is not about individuals in particular, but groups of human beings. Indeed, both philosophers recognise and are sympathetic to the major obstacles that individuals face in trying to escape their slavish state. Kant states that 'it is difficult for any single individual to extricate himself', since slavishness 'has become almost nature to him. He has even grown fond of it and is really unable for the time being to make use of his own understanding, because he was never allowed to make the attempt.' Individuals are trained from a young age not to think for themselves, so they become 'accustomed' to not having 'free movement' of any kind (WIE 8:36). As we will see, much of Nietzsche's essay also details the daunting obstacles to freedom that individuals face. In this way, the target of Kant's and Nietzsche's judgement is rather the community, since we have created a culture and institutions that incline us to laziness and are not willing collectively to change our fate. We, all of us, are to blame. For this reason, Kant and Nietzsche do not rely solely on personal virtues and responsibility to address the problem of laziness, but rather look to systematic institutional and cultural solutions to systemic problems – in 'What is Enlightenment?' Kant, for instance, calls for the creation of a public sphere to foster critical public debate and discussion.

---

[4] See Lemm's (2007: 16–17) helpful analysis of this connection.

Second, consider a contrasting argument from Schopenhauer. Interestingly, like Nietzsche, Schopenhauer holds that the 'character of a human being' is 'individual', which means that 'it is different in everyone' (2009: 68). However, unlike Nietzsche, Schopenhauer argues that each individual character is the 'work of nature itself' (72) and 'constant' across our lives (70). Accordingly, Schopenhauer thinks that we cannot fail to live in accordance with our unique character. As a result, the variations among human beings are not due to human agency, but rather to the inequalities of nature. Schopenhauer thus offers aristocratic judgements quite distinct from Nietzsche's meritocratic view: 'Consider how utterly base the disposition of most people is and how little talent they have, hence how thoroughly common they are' (2014: 393). On this basis, Schopenhauer, unlike Nietzsche's 'great thinker', reveals contempt for 'the plebs of humankind' which form 'an innumerable mass [that] fills and covers everything, like vermin, and is always ready to grab anything indiscriminately and fights its boredom with the help of it, or its lack under different circumstances' (Schopenhauer 2014: 372). Hurka and other aristocratic readers are on stronger ground in attributing the aristocratic reading to Schopenhauer, who argues that 'except for rare strokes of luck, we will find nothing but very deficient specimens of human nature, which are better left untouched' (377). This contrast throws into clearer relief, then, the Kantian meritocratic – as opposed to Schopenhauerian aristocratic – source of Nietzsche's view. It also shows that Nietzsche is no simple student of Schopenhauer in an essay devoted to the man, but is already willing to challenge the teacher.

As we turn to the second and third paragraphs of this opening section, with its call for 'liberation' [*Befreiung*], we can see the parallels with Kant deepen. In these paragraphs, Nietzsche answers the question, why should we live in accordance with our own unique character? We should do so, Nietzsche argues, because we thereby achieve freedom in human life. His argument has three steps. First, he revisits the fundamental question of the value of human existence that emerged in section 1 of 'Utility and Liability', and argues that most of us fail to answer this question, instead evading it by referring to the guidance of nature or human society. Nature cannot provide us with guidance, since nature is becoming – with the attendant image that it is a 'stream' in which all existence is carried along in a purposeless flux – and so nature does not supply a justification for life's value. At the same time, there is no shortage of answers given by societies and states – one's life can be of value in service to them. Yet Nietzsche asks, 'why cling to this clod of earth, to this trade?' Furthermore, 'why heed what your neighbor says? It is so provincial to bind oneself to views that already a few hundred miles away are no longer binding. Orient and Occident are chalk lines drawn before our eyes in order to mock our timidity.' These societies and states provide 'countless paths and bridges' over the stream of becoming, but no answers to the ultimate questions, only fundamentally injunctions to obedience. As such, to accept them would be 'at the price of your self; you would pawn and lose your self' (173). To embrace servitude is to cease asking the question and thereby to abandon our humanity.

For Nietzsche, to abandon oneself to any social, economic, religious or political organisation is in one crucial way no different than abandoning oneself to the becoming of nature and hence to our animality. As he says later in the text,

> The tremendous mobility of human beings on the great earthly desert, their founding of cities and states, their waging of wars, their ceaseless gathering and dispersing, their confused mingling, their imitation of one another, their mutual outwitting and trampling underfoot, their cries in distress and their joyous cheers in victory – all this is a continuation of animality [*Tierheit*]. (210)

What is 'animality'? It is not a biological category, but rather an ontological description of agency. Agency consists at the most abstract level in action towards some aim or good. Animality describes an agent whose aims do not derive from the agent herself, but are given by a force external to the agent. As such, animal agents are functional vehicles for external forces. They are ruled by a higher force, 'shackled by the chains' of these forces (172). For instance, the bird that flies about collecting materials for a nest is following the rule of its instinct. The socialite seeking high status in society follows public opinion's shaping power. The banker seeking wealth obeys the governance of the market's aims. The politician yearning for power is ruled by the state. And indeed, it is easy to 'evade' our 'genius' and become 'all exterior without a kernel', submitting our 'salvation' to 'public opinions' (172). However, animals and these animalistic human beings are engulfed in the ceaseless, purposeless flow of becoming that has no higher aim or purpose to confer value on it. After all, the external forces shaping these human agents – society, market, politics – are themselves shaped by previous causes, and so do not escape the flux of becoming.

The second part of Nietzsche's argument is to develop the contrasting notion of humanity. Human beings are not determined by external forces in the way that animals are determined by instinct. We can inquire into the value of all things, all external forces, and can reflect that it is 'curious' and 'inexplicable' that 'we live precisely today and yet had the infinity of time in which to come into being'. We recognise that we are the necessary result of innumerable causes in the stream of becoming, and yet for all that we are able to peek our heads out of this stream and ask, what is our value? That we can ask this question testifies to our 'freedom', to the fact that we can liberate ourselves from the thrall of all external determination, either natural or social. With this freedom we become 'accountable [*verantworten*] to ourselves for our own existence'. Our freedom demands that we demonstrate that we are not 'a mindless coincidence', not a fungible contingent part of some external force, but rather a necessary part of our own valuable aim. Freedom thereby animates us – in the voice of our 'conscience' – always to ask ourselves 'why and to what purpose [have] we ... come into being precisely at this moment?' In this way, we must become the 'real helmsmen of our existence', in order to live up to our humanity, which, in contrast to animality, refers to agents whose aim comes from our own natures. Humanity, in this sense, is an achievement, not something given by nature.[5] To achieve it, we must govern our lives, surmounting those natural and social forces that would otherwise make us serve them (173).

---

[5] Kaufmann puts the point well: 'individuality, worth, and dignity are – to recall Kant's play on words – not gegeben, i.e. given to us as data by nature, but aufgegeben, i.e., given or assigned to us as a task' (1978: 161).

The third step in Nietzsche's argument, then, argues that freedom as self-determination justifies the value of existence. In this section, Nietzsche speaks of freedom in two senses. In the first, negative sense, he describes the 'liberation' from being enslaved to external forces, such as public opinion. Yet he also has a second, positive sense of our 'true liberation', which promises 'the measure of happiness for which [we are] destined from eternity' (172). This freedom is not a freedom from enslavement, but rather a form of self-determination, in which we 'live according to our own standards and laws' (173). Here, Nietzsche's discussion of uniqueness from the opening paragraph is connected with his view of self-determination. Each of us possesses a cosmic uniqueness, that nothing else in the universe is like us. By acting with 'strict consistency' out of our 'uniqueness', we make ourselves 'beautiful and worthy of contemplation, as novel and incredible as every work of nature' (172). If we adopt this uniqueness as our aim – that is, if we seek to live in accordance with it such that ideally 'each movement of [our] muscles' will testify to ourselves 'alone' – then we become self-determining. We govern our lives in the sense that all our actions are animated not by some external force but by our own laws and aim (171–2). As such, when our conscience asks us, 'What value does our existence have?', we can answer with the principle and aim that we have given ourselves. Our lives are no longer subservient to purposeless becoming, but transcend that flux to aim at human freedom. For this reason, 'no one can build for you the bridge upon which you alone must cross the stream of life' – only self-determination can create that bridge (173).

1B *Freedom requires an education towards culture (pp. 174–5)*

To be self-determining, we must attain self-knowledge. As such, Nietzsche asks, 'How can we find ourselves again? How can the human being get to know himself?' But self-knowledge is not easy to achieve in the modern age. To achieve self-knowledge requires an understanding of what the self is. Despite modernity's critique of ancient myths, we still cling to an understanding of the self as a deep secret locked within ourselves, and that we should 'dig down

into [ourselves]' to find ourselves. Nietzsche rejects this understanding of the self as a myth, as what he will call a 'doer behind
the deed' in *The Genealogy of Morality*. Rather, we begin to gain
self-knowledge not by looking inside, but by examining the innumerable experiences and causes that gave rise to us. Nietzsche
claims that 'everything – our friendships and enmities, our look
and our handshake, our memory and what we forget, our books
and our handwriting – bears witness to our being'. The self is
not forged privately but constituted through our interactions with
others and the world. Indeed, it would be 'agonizing' and 'dangerous' to 'force your way by the shortest route down the shaft of
your own being', since our 'true being does not lie deeply hidden
within' and all we would find is the fundamental contradiction of
our existence (174).

These causes and experiences shape us in decisive ways, in
particular by developing certain dispositions and aims that motivate us. To understand these features of character, Nietzsche asks
the 'young soul' to 'look back on its life with the question: what
have you up to now truly loved, what attracted your soul, what
dominated it while simultaneously making it happy?' Nietzsche
then instructs the young soul to 'place this series of revered
objects before you, and perhaps their nature and their sequence
will reveal to you a law, the fundamental law [*Grundgesetz*] of
your authentic self'. The self, then, is not deep inside me, nor is it
constituted by the conditions that generated me. Rather, it is an
ideal, projected from those experiences, goods and aims that have
shaped me. Our self then is not deep within 'but rather immeasurably high above you, or at least above what you commonly take
to be your ego' (174).

That the self is an ideal projection reveals the freedom at the
heart of Nietzsche's view. Unlike Schopenhauer, Nietzsche does not
think that our self is set in stone by nature, our actions necessarily
flowing from that inner self. Rather, our self is an ideal self-construc-
tion. Indeed, we are shaped by conditions that have come before us,
but we must 'compare these objects' and discern a pattern, a 'stepladder on which until now you have climbed up to yourself'. There
are a tremendous number of 'revered objects' that we can compare,
and so it is up to us to select the salient ones. Furthermore, there are

many ways we can compare these objects, many structural arrange-
ments that our subjectivity can impose on these objects. Finally, we
must decide on 'one' that 'completes, expands, surpasses, transfigures
the others' (174). In any one person, there might be many 'revered'
aims that she has been motivated by. The subject is thus responsible
for affirming one of them, positing the 'unity' of her character amid
the 'amazingly variegated diversity' (171).

This aesthetic self-constitution relates to Nietzsche's earlier
discussion in 'Utility and Liability' on the necessarily constructive character of doing history.[6] For Nietzsche, as for Kant, what
is given to us from the outside does not come to us in intelligible
form, but rather in the form of flux. With our freedom, we construct values and categories to structure what is given, to separate
what is significant from what is insignificant. Just as in the case of
nature and history, so too in our own selves – in deciding what
is most important about ourselves and hence how we are to rank
our dispositions and aims – human subjectivity constructs an ideal
order to make sense of what is given. This ideal is a product of
our freedom. Of course, the ideal will always be in a process of
transformation as we gain more experiences. As such, human life
requires a constant effort to attain self-knowledge and then self-
determination. Insofar as we act towards this ideal – following the
'fundamental law of your authentic self' – we obey a law that we
have made for ourselves and so are autonomous.

Unfortunately, this 'true primordial sense and basic stuff of your
being' is all too often 'bound, paralyzed, and difficult to gain access
to'. It is difficult to attain self-knowledge when public opinion pres-
sures us to understand ourselves as similar to everyone else, and
difficult to achieve self-determination when we abandon ourselves
to some external force. Thus, we need 'true educators and cultivators [*Erzieher und Bildner*]' who can help us gain self-knowledge
and foster our self-determination, and in so doing be our 'liberators
[*Befreier*]' (174). For Nietzsche, 'education [*Erziehung*] is liberation,
removal of all weeds, rubble, and vermin that seek to harm the

[6] Breazeale helpfully classifies Nietzsche's view as a 'blend of "essentialist" and "existential-
ist" elements' – the essentialist element in the form of a single ideal self, while the exis-
tentialist in the form of a self-constructed self (1998: 15).

plant's delicate shoots' (174–5). Education serves to clear those systematic obstacles to our freedom, eliminating the influence of public opinion, for instance.[7] It assists us in our achievement of the telos of our self, satisfying our needs for wholeness and for value. In this way, education plays the role of 'nature' in its 'maternal and merciful disposition'. That is, Nietzsche pictures nature, consistent with the view of modern natural science, as indifferent to human ends, and thus 'cruel and merciless', having a 'stepmotherly disposition and sad lack of understanding' for human needs. Education 'drapes a veil' over nature, 'turns' what is given by nature's indifference 'to good', and thereby redeems nature, allowing it to appear as providential or teleological (175).

2 The exemplar's education of affect

At the end of the first section, Nietzsche transitions from defending basic principles to applying them. Self-knowledge and self-determination are demanding processes that require a good educator. 'Finding oneself' is best achieved by reflecting 'on one's own educators and cultivators'. To illustrate this, Nietzsche presents his own education as a model, particularly under Schopenhauer but also 'subsequently' under 'others' such as Rousseau and Goethe (175). In presenting himself in this way, Nietzsche begins to reflect on and create his own self through the act of writing, a form of philosophical autobiography that he employs in many subsequent works.[8] As in the case of his later works, this self-creation is not incidental but is in fact a necessary feature of his argument. For Nietzsche, abstract, disembodied ethical arguments do not provide a determinate path for oneself or others, nor are any of them successful in justifying moral action. On the contrary, only arguments as embedded within the life of exemplary individuals can accomplish these aims. In light of this, Nietzsche must construct his own self, and lodge the

---

[7] See a note from 1876: 'the purpose of the generation of children is *freer* human beings' (KSA 8.17[28]).

[8] Nietzsche wrote several unpublished autobiographical writings in his youth, prior to this essay, suggesting that he already considered autobiography necessary to philosophy. See Blue 2016.

arguments within his own development, for them to have any determinate guidance, motivating power and ethical justification.

2A *The formation of Nietzsche's early self (pp. 175–9)*

Before he encountered Schopenhauer's works, the young Nietzsche understood nature as 'maternal and merciful'. As such, he 'thought that fate would relieve me of the terrible effort and duty of educating myself', and that 'at exactly the right moment I would find a philosopher to be my educator' (175). His younger self was wrong about this, Nietzsche claims, again highlighting his critique of the notion of a benevolent nature and of fate. The young Nietzsche was wrong because the German educational system contains no genuine educators. His defence of this claim rehashes a number of points he has made already in 'David Strauss' and 'Utility and Liability' (177), in particular the sorry state of the scholar's education, which dehumanises the scholar. Nietzsche compares the 'occupation with scholarship, when it is not guided and limited by any higher educational maxim' to the 'economic doctrine of laissez-faire'. Both are 'pernicious' to the 'morality of entire nations', as they encourage the egoism of the scholar or capitalist rather than subsuming their effort within a broader moral purpose (177).

Indeed, Nietzsche argues that modern education no longer raises moral questions, with the consequence that we have become unable to 'find our moral exemplars and people of distinction, visible embodiments of all creative morality in this age', nor can we even reflect on 'moral questions' that should be the 'occupation of every noble society'. We ignore 'moral education', brand 'virtue' as woefully 'old-fashioned', all the while 'living off the inherited moral capital accumulated by our forefathers' (178). As we saw in 'Utility and Liability', the main preoccupation in modern culture has not been the formation of character but instead the pursuit of truth. The unfettered pursuit of truth has destroyed all premodern communities and has thereby eliminated the systems of value within them, threatening to cast everyone back into egoism. Nietzsche further explains this development here by pointing to the effect of 'Christianity' in surpassing the 'moral systems of antiquity and the naturalness equally prevalent in all of them'

(178). Christianity posited a God who far outstripped nature, and God's son who embraced the meek and humble and recognised the equality of all human beings, so that the natural inequalities and aims of the ancients became morally irrelevant. However, as modern science rendered Christian virtues morally irrelevant as well, no moral principles animated us at all. In this ethical vacuum, Nietzsche argues, we 'desire to find a firm footing somewhere', oscillating between ancient naturalness and Christian virtue, generating a 'confusion in the soul of modern human beings', a 'disquiet' that drives us to long for a new order (179).

The young Nietzsche was wrong about the providential character of nature, but he was prescient about the nature of education. In his youth, there were 'two maxims of education' still 'in vogue today'. Should an educator perfect the pupil's best 'virtue', concentrating 'all his efforts and energies, all his sunshine, on this one spot?' Or should he 'draw on and foster all existing abilities and bring them into a harmonious relationship', that is, foster wholeness (175)? Apparently the precocious Nietzsche had already sketched a synthesis of these two approaches. Namely, he argues that in all individuals, 'everything' in their character – 'all knowledge, desire, love, hate' – already 'strives toward a central point, a root force'. This root is the 'living center' which 'forms a harmonious system' of all our other features of character. Thus, the youthful Nietzsche anticipated the theory he expresses in section 1 of 'Schopenhauer as Educator', that our character should possess a unity of aim or purpose that provides a dynamic structure for the diversity of our traits. As such, the task of education is to help shape each of us into a 'solar and planetary system with its own life and motion and to discover the laws of its higher mechanics' (176). In other words, education should not create individuals according to a general model for some higher purpose. Rather, it should foster their self-determination, to lead pupils to posit their own distinctive unity and to order and perfect their features of character in light of this unity.

2B *The discovery of Schopenhauer (pp. 180–3)*

Modern culture is thoroughly corrupted, and Nietzsche himself confesses to being deeply shaped by it, as we have seen already

(158). It could not be otherwise, of course, since we are all children of our age. Like other youth, Nietzsche found himself 'in such a state of need, distress, and desire' for a teacher. In a culture where everyone is duplicitous and complicated, Nietzsche sought a teacher who could teach him 'to be simple and honest in thought as in life' (179). Schopenhauer fulfilled his need, preparing him to be a 'stepchild' of his age (194).

Nietzsche proceeds to discuss the 'first, as it were, physiological impression that Schopenhauer made' on him. Why is such a physiological description important? For Nietzsche, education cannot be the passive transmission of facts, as is characteristic of modern scientific culture. Rather, education consists in large part in a sympathetic connection between educator and student. The educator models exemplary self-determining activity, and the student shares in this activity by feeling what the educator feels, thinking what he thinks, longing for what he longs for. This sympathetic connection cannot be simply cerebral and abstract – it begins with the embodied, erotic connection among human beings. For instance, Schopenhauer evokes a 'sincere, blunt, good-natured declaration before a listener who listens with love'. Nietzsche praises Schopenhauer's writing here highly because his only encounter with Schopenhauer is through his writing. A good writer, however, can generate this physiological connection. Schopenhauer's honesty in his writing, for instance, expresses a 'powerful well-being' which 'encompasses us at the first sound of his voice . . . we breathe deeply and suddenly have a sense of well-being again' (180). Exemplars such as Schopenhauer draw individuals into the planetary orbit of their selves because they have achieved the self-determination that we all long for.

Nietzsche sympathised with three 'elements' of Schopenhauer's character: 'his honesty, his cheerfulness, and his steadfastness'. First, Nietzsche was looking for an honest voice amid modern dissimulation, and found Schopenhauer's bluntness refreshing. But more broadly, Schopenhauer is 'honest because he speaks and writes to himself and for himself' (183). That is, his aim in writing is not to gain fame in society, or garner wealth or power, but rather to pursue his own thoughts without adornment. Thus he demonstrates the 'naturalness of the sort possessed by people who are at home in themselves', who are true to themselves and demonstrate a wholeness of character. His style reflects this honesty [*Ehrlichkeit*] in its directness and simplicity, and in its rejection of all 'pseudo-Frenchness' and 'courtly grace' (180). Because Schopenhauer attended first of all to himself, he became the 'freest [*freiesten*] . . . of spirits', self-determining, not guided by forces outside him (181). Nietzsche, moreover, shares in this self-determination, as Schopenhauer's honesty makes him feel as if 'he had written expressly for me' (180), and that the 'joy of living on this earth has truly been increased by the fact that such a person wrote'. Schopenhauer's success at finding a 'home' in himself provides a model for all others seeking to 'feel at home on this earth' (181).

Schopenhauer's second 'quality' is a 'genuinely cheering cheerfulness [*Heiterkeit*]', a quality that Nietzsche himself lauds and embodies throughout his career. Cheerfulness, he suggests, has two components – the disposition of the cheerful person and his achievements. First, to be cheerful means to act 'confidently and simply, with courage and strength . . . as a victor', rather than with 'sullen gestures, trembling hands, teary eyes' (179–80). It is a form of self-assertion, an affirmation of the self's place in the world, the confident extension of one's being outside one. In short, it is self-determined activity. Second, one can be cheerful and become a 'victorious god amid all the monsters that he has conquered', or one can merely 'pretend to perceive and fight' monsters. The former is the genuine cheerfulness displayed by Schopenhauer, the latter a false cheerfulness expressed by David Strauss, who claims victory over philosophical problems, but who has only scratched the surface of those problems. Genuine cheerfulness is infectious; it 'cheers us most profoundly' to be 'near one of those victorious people who, because they have thought the most profound things, cannot help but love what is most alive and, because they are wise, ultimately are disposed to what is beautiful'. Around them we 'feel human and natural for once', because we participate in their distinctively human activity (182). They remind us of what it is possible for all of us to accomplish.

Schopenhauer's third quality is his 'steadfastness' [*Beständigkeit*], that he 'cannot be otherwise'. Schopenhauer pursues his aims 'with such firmness and nimbleness, with such inevitability, that

he seems to be propelled by a law of gravity'. His honesty was a
self-determined disposition; his cheerfulness was self-determined
activity; this steadfastness is the internalisation of his self-determination into a second nature, such that his character appears
as if a matter of fate. This internalisation satisfies our two basic
needs, as Schopenhauer's character becomes 'whole', impossible to
divide against itself, but also 'free' (183). It might be surprising for
Nietzsche to describe a nature that 'cannot be otherwise' as 'free',
but this once again reveals the distinctive kind of freedom that he
is concerned with – it is not freedom to act wilfully or arbitrarily, but freedom as being the helmsman of one's own existence.
Indeed, the character who cannot be otherwise is paradoxically
most deeply free because he is unable to be swayed by external forces, unwaveringly committed to acting based on self-given
principles and aims.

3 The exemplar's education of character

Section 2 concerned the exemplar's ability to educate individuals
to self-determination. Section 3 shifts to the exemplar's teaching
on how individuals overcome the main obstacles to self-determination, both universal (A) and particular to modernity (B). As
Nietzsche stresses in this section, all of us share in the frustration
of these dangers, which is why we feel liberated by the life of the
exemplar who illuminates a path through them. Section 3, then,
transitions from the immediate, affective sympathy with the exemplar to a cognitive relationship, from our interpersonal connection
to our engagement with large forces such as society and truth that
require reflection. As in section 2, so too here Nietzsche uses his
own experience as a student to offer a general lesson about education in modern culture.

Section 3 also discusses more clearly the unique features of philosophy and why it is of the highest value for Nietzsche. Thus far
in the *Observations*, he has not specified which type of life is highest for human beings. Many readers assume that 'great individuals'
are 'the conquerors' and 'hereditary rulers', but Nietzsche explicitly argues that this is a 'false idea' of the best life (KSA 7.30[8],
UW 294). By contrast, a sensible conclusion to draw from section

1 of 'Schopenhauer as Educator' is that any type of life is compatible with Nietzsche's ideal, because, after all, some of us are drawn to philosophy, but many, perhaps most of us, are drawn to other callings (Cavell 1990). However, Nietzsche thinks that the 'spiritual' lives of human beings – the artists, saints and philosophers – are highest. Philosophy is distinctive among these in being 'capable of drawing entire nations along behind' it (183). The philosopher has this tremendous shaping power because his 'eye' is 'trained on existence' and 'seeks to establish its value anew'. The 'task of great thinkers' is 'to be legislators of the measure, mint, and weight of things' (193). Philosophers are 'legislators' in the most fundamental sense. They confer value on all things, thereby providing a table of values to an aggregate of individuals, constituting them as a unified people. Statesmen can found a state by coercing the bodies of individuals, but philosophers actually have more far-reaching and greater shaping power, since they found a spiritual community by convincing people to internalise the philosopher's own values, such that the philosopher need not coerce them. They willingly follow his ideas, even die for them. Insofar as the philosopher determines all things, rather than being determined by them, he expresses the highest degree of self-determination, which is why Nietzsche regards him as living the highest life.[9]

3A *Universal 'constitutional dangers' (pp. 183–92)*

The exemplar is someone 'capable of setting an example' of how to lead the best human life. However, the exemplar cannot simply set such an example 'in his books'. Exemplars motivate others most profoundly by embodying their principles in their 'visible life', demonstrating that abstract, self-given laws can shape the otherwise purposeless flux of nature. Ancient philosophers accomplished this very well, as the different schools of philosophy had different 'facial expressions, demeanor, clothing, food, and custom' that flowed from their basic principles (183). These philosophers were 'free and autonomous' in that their 'achieved limitlessness'

---

[9] See Breazeale (1998: 9–13) for a good discussion of the philosopher in 'Schopenhauer as Educator'.

was a form of 'creative self-limitation', in which their lives and actions were determined not by outside forces but by a principle they gave to themselves. By contrast, modern philosophers, especially in Germany, are not whole but divided – their lives do not bear witness to their writings, and vice versa. The German philosophical 'spirit' is 'liberated', but not the 'body'. As such, Kant served as a stunning exemplar of spirit, revolutionising philosophy in the eighteenth and into the nineteenth century (188), but in his humdrum university life, 'his example produced above all university professors', not affecting the general public. German philosophers can learn much from German artists, who 'live more boldly and honestly', above all in the example of Richard Wagner, the focus of the next *Observation* (184).

However, the exemplar faces three 'constitutional dangers [*Constitutionsgefahren*]' in trying to set an example for others (193) – the unreliable recognition of others, the 'despair of truth' (187), and self-doubt. Nietzsche uses Schopenhauer to illustrate these dangers which, he argues, 'threaten us all'. Constitutional dangers are threats implicit in human nature itself, in that contradictory nature that Nietzsche explored in the opening sections of 'Schopenhauer as Educator' and 'Utility and Liability'. Since we share these dangers with the exemplar, we feel kinship with him – the exemplar's contradictions reveal him to be 'all too human' like us, and thus his inner contradiction 'brings us close to him in the most human sense, for we see in him a sufferer and fellow sufferer, and not one who suffers solely in the remote heights of genius' (191–2). This is a strikingly anti-elitist claim on Nietzsche's part – all human beings suffer in the same way as the exemplar, and the exemplar commiserates with us in our shared suffering, but he also shows us how to win victory over these dangers. The exemplar is not an aristocratic figure, far from the demos below, but rather more of a prophet, revealing a hidden but shared truth of benefit to everyone.

The first constitutional danger is that we have to convince others to recognise us as an exemplar. It is a constitutional danger because of the fundamental contradiction between our conscience and our laziness, explored in section 1. Indeed, our conscience speaks to all of us, as 'each of us bears within himself a productive uniqueness as the kernel of his being'. However, 'when he becomes conscious of this uniqueness, a strange aura – the aura of the unusual – surrounds him'. Public opinion, which demands conformity and homogeneity, finds uniqueness 'unbearable', and shuns the aspiring exemplar, leaving him the 'fate of solitude', the 'desert and the cave'. Yet this makes it exceedingly difficult for the exemplar to garner recognition from others, to establish himself as an example. His attempt causes him to 'forfeit almost everything . . . cheerfulness, security, lightness, honor' (192).

Schopenhauer struggled against this imposed solitude. He was unique in German philosophy at the time, not coming from a university background and identifying an unusual problem as foundational to philosophy – the value of existence. As a result, German philosophy at the time subjected Schopenhauer's work to 'inquisitorial censorship' in the form of 'inviolable silence'. His major work, *The World as Will and Representation*, was published in 1818, decades before he would become famous. It was widely ignored by philosophers and the reading public, such that 'the greater part of the first edition of Schopenhauer's chief work had to be pulped'. As a result, he hunted 'for the slightest sign that he had gained recognition', and pathetically triumphed at 'finally being read' (186).

The general danger, then, is that as exemplars 'fle[e] inward for their freedom', away from the conformity of public opinion, they also seethe at the misunderstanding of or indifference to their philosophy (186). Since the self is not deep inside us, but is constituted in part in public, the appearance of ourselves in the eyes of others matters. 'These solitary ones who are free in spirit know' that 'appearance' is 'different from the way they think', and 'they are entangled in a web of misunderstandings', which hampers their own self-determination. As much as they try, they cannot 'prevent a fog of false opinions', and so they 'take revenge for their violent self-concealment, for their coerced constraint', for the distortion of the development of their self. What exemplars most need, then, is 'love', that is, 'companions in whose presence they can be as open and straightforward as they are when they are alone, companions in whose presence the strain of silence and dissemblance can cease' (187). True friends are those who do not seek to impose an external self on their friends, but rather recognise the uniqueness implicit in the friend's self, and assist in fostering this uniqueness. With friends, one need not be solitary, but can gain recognition of one's self-determination.

Schopenhauer does not help us to avoid the first constitutional danger, but he supplies excellent guidance for the second, the despair of truth. The first danger stems from the basic contradiction of human nature, while this second danger arises from our inability to discern the highest truths about the world. Since *The Birth of Tragedy*, Nietzsche had associated this insight with 'Kantian philosophy', particularly with Kant's destruction of metaphysics in the *Critique of Pure Reason*'s Dialectic. For Nietzsche, Kant's destruction of metaphysics has far-reaching moral consequences, because most philosophies and cultures ground claims about justice and morality on knowledge about the structure of the world. These cultures envision nature as having an internal teleological structure. Wisdom involves grasping this structure and then instructing others how to act based on it. Kant's destruction of metaphysics precludes such wisdom and is in this sense part of the broader trend of modern culture towards the dissolution of all pre-modern closed horizons and communities, which throws human beings back upon themselves, with an indifferent nature around them. Kantian philosophy, Nietzsche predicts, will have the same 'popular effect' as the 'deadly truths' of 'Utility and Liability', namely, 'corrosive and disintegrating skepticism and relativism'. Such was the effect on the playwright Heinrich von Kleist, for instance, whose encounter with Kant left him in despair that 'all our efforts to procure [truth] ... that will follow us to the grave are in vain' (188).

Although this danger is less common among the majority of humanity, it still 'is not entirely rare', and will become more common as modern culture demolishes all the old myths (192). Schopenhauer is an excellent 'guide' to lead us 'out of the cave of skeptical disgruntlement or of critical renunciation up to the heights of tragic contemplation' (188–9). Schopenhauer's philosophy begins in the wake of Kant's destructive critique, and his 'greatness' lies in his evaluation of 'life as a whole', not this or that particular facet of life. 'Every great philosophy', Nietzsche claims, offers us a 'picture of life' on the basis of which each of us can 'learn from it the meaning of your life' (189). Schopenhauer defended a tragic understanding of the whole, according to which nature has no overall purpose and human life is ultimately not worth living. Nevertheless, on the basis of this tragic contemplation, we could acquire 'antidotes and consolations' such as the 'sacrifice of the ego', which would lift us out of the 'profound depression over the worthlessness' of existence. This negation of the will in Schopenhauer's philosophy redeems the irrationality of our existence by giving us an escape from the will. Insofar as we can share in Schopenhauer's tragic wisdom, it is 'ultimately for all' (190).

The final constitutional danger is that of self-doubt, which afflicts us all. Each of us discovers 'in himself a limitation – of his talents as well as of his moral will', because each fails to live up to the 'genius within himself' (190). One response to this self-doubt is, of course, to give up, to 'fear' one's 'uniqueness' and the difficulty of achieving it, thus 'abandoning one's self', tearing the 'bond that links him with the ideal', 'hardening' one's soul (192–3), and finally losing one's creativity and 'longing' for self-determination (190). By contrast, the higher response is to embrace 'longing and melan-choly', to submit to one's 'profound yearning for the genius within himself'. This response is higher because it is distinctively human, the 'root of all true culture', as culture's 'aim' is the 'production of genius' (190). However, 'one can just as easily be ruined by this uniqueness as by the fear of this uniqueness' (192). The immense longing for self-determination can tear us apart, between our ideal goal and our actual capacities. Schopenhauer, for instance, had such a 'dangerous duality' – on the one hand, he followed his 'calling with the greatness and dignity of someone who victoriously con-summated himself', confident in his success. On the other hand, 'he experienced a tumultuous yearning', recognising his inability to achieve his goals with grace. Nevertheless, Nietzsche remarks, Schopenhauer possessed an 'inconceivably whole and unbreakable' character, since he was able to hold together such a divided nature in a unity (191).

3B *Dangers of the modern 'age' (pp. 193–5)*

Schopenhauer educates us well only regarding the second consti-tutional danger. Nietzsche suggests that Schopenhauer suffers the first and the third dangers along with the rest of us. Accordingly, Nietzsche continues subtly to indicate the limitations of Schopenhauer, which he first indicated in his implicit critique of Schopenhauer's view of freedom in section 1. In other words, Nietzsche argues that one educator is not enough – other exemplars are necessary in order to complement Schopenhauer's contributions. Before he discusses these other exemplars, however, Nietzsche examines the obstacles to exemplarity not only from our natures, but also from our particular culture or 'age' (191).

The danger of modern culture for the exemplary philosopher is daunting. The philosopher's task is 'to be [legislator] of the measure, mint, and weight of things', to judge the 'value' of the world 'anew'. But to judge the world, we must have some familiarity with it. In this regard, 'the judgment of ancient Greek philosophers about the value of existence says so much more than a modern judgment because the former had life in its sumptuous perfection before and around them' (193). The ancient world, with its closed horizons and tightly knit communities, allowed life to flourish, and individual thinkers had life in front of them to experience. The modern world, by contrast, mediates our relationship to life through knowledge, that 'powerfully hostile star' which has 'shifted' all 'perspectives' back to 'infinity', as we saw in 'Utility and Liability' (108–9). As such, the modern 'thinker' is torn 'between the desire for freedom, beauty, and greatness of life, and the drive for truth that asks only: "Of what value is existence at all?"' The modern world thus confronts us with the contradiction of human nature most forcefully, between our desire for wholeness in life and for perfection that transcends life. It forces the philosopher to choose one side of our natures and so prioritise his role as 'judge of life' before his role as 'reformer' or legislator of life (193). Modern culture and the modern philosopher stand above life, not immersed in it and productive of it.

Schopenhauer's solution to this problem is not to turn back the clock to try to retrieve ancient philosophy. Rather, he finds life in his own 'genius', the 'supreme fruit of life', the 'realm of transfigured physis' (nature) (195). He discovers his genius by removing all the 'impure confusion' of the modern age that covered over his 'true self', becoming a 'stepchild' of his age (194). What remained was his unique self, his genius, that asked 'Of what value is life at all?' On the basis of his genius, then, Schopenhauer could serve as the reformer or legislator of life, since he possessed the fruit of life before him. That is, Schopenhauer did not have to choose either wholeness or perfection, because he located life within his own genius. He could create genuine wholeness out of himself and thus forge a reformed, unified modern culture. In addition, he could satisfy our need for value in life. Schopenhauer's genius is not a return to myth or horizon, but serves to 'justify [*rechtfertigen*] life as such'. For Nietzsche, only the 'marvelous, creative' individual can be the 'advocate' and 'savior' of 'life', which faces 'such grave accusations' and is 'set free' in the self-determination of the exemplar (195).

4 The exemplar's education of culture

Whereas sections 2–3 examined the exemplar's education of individuals, section 4 widens the scope of the exemplar's concern to culture as a whole. In doing so, Nietzsche suggests that personal, individual education is insufficient, since our debased modern culture corrupts the individual soul in the cradle, producing individuals unwilling to heed the call of their conscience. As such, Nietzsche focuses in this section on two fundamental problems of modern culture: atomisation and the apotheosis of the modern state (A). Section 4 builds on the account in 'Utility and Liability' of modern culture's atomisation by expanding on the modern state's counter-movement. He then describes how the exemplar can 'help all of us' by educating culture as a whole (195). These exemplars 'educate [us] against our age' by establishing themselves as the cornerstones of a new modern community (196) (B). This discussion contains some of Nietzsche's most revealing remarks on the ethical justification of exemplary lives.

4A *Atomisation and the apotheosis of the modern state (pp. 195–200)*

In the first half of this section, Nietzsche summarises some of the *Observations'* main criticisms, revisiting the 'David Strauss' critique of German hubris, as well as his 'Utility and Liability' claim that modern culture is steadily dissolving all pre-modern moral community.

What is new here are discussions of two modern counter-movements that seek to redress this atomisation: one that embraces egoism, and one that rejects it. Both of these counter-movements must be resisted, in Nietzsche's view, as they exacerbate, rather than solve, the problems of modern culture. To begin with some context (which Nietzsche offers us only near the end of this first half of section 4): before modernity, 'in the Middle Ages inimical forces were more or less held together and to some extent assimilated to one another by the church and the strong pressure it exerted' (199). As modern culture begins to emerge, 'the floodwaters of religion are receding and leaving behind swamps or stagnant pools' (198). The Reformation further limits the worldly power of the Church, lodging it in the inner life of the individual (199–200). The ultimate result of the decline of traditional religious community is that 'we live in the age of the atom, the age of atomistic chaos' (199). Without a community to draw us out of our egoism, 'almost everything on earth is determined only by the crudest and most evil forces, by the egoism of the moneymakers and by military despots'. Lest the reader think that Nietzsche wants to turn back the clock to the Middle Ages, he declares that this 'atomic revolution . . . cannot possibly be avoided' (200).

However, modernity is not a dreary hell of egoism. Modern culture develops institutions and counter-movements from within itself to address egoism. The first approach is to embrace it, but give it a prudent form by creating institutions that will redound to the self-interest of all. The best example of these institutions is the 'grandly contemptible monetary economy', because it asks so little of the egoist, but promises him so much. Nietzsche also discusses the egoism of 'nations' which 'long to massacre one another'. In addition, the scholarly institutions are patterned on the 'laissez-faire' economy, according to which each scholar can pursue his own interested field, with no sense of responsibility to be 'lighthouses or havens in these agitated seas of secularization' in defence of culture (198). In all these cases, modern life does not implode, because these institutions satisfy the egoists' self-interests.

However, the spiritual life of culture continues to deteriorate as materialistic, egoistic self-interest displaces it.

The most important institution that Nietzsche discusses is the modern state, which he also highlighted in 'Utility and Liability' for developing the notion of a prudent egoism (156). In this section, he goes further in identifying a greater ambition for the state. The modern state does not just promise egoistic satisfaction, but, under the influence of Hegel, seeks to replace culture as the 'highest aim of humanity', such that 'a man can have no higher duty than service to the state' (197). The state fills the vacuum left by religion 'to organize everything anew out of itself and provide a bond that will hold those inimical forces in check'. In exchange, the 'state wants people to worship in it the very same idols they previously worshipped in the church' (200). By worshipping the state, philosophers in Nietzsche's day even claimed that we need no longer inquire into the 'problem of existence', since the victory of the modern state solves it once and for all (197). This counter-movement is pernicious because it obscures this fundamental question that animates culture. For Nietzsche, we must reassert the significance of culture by re-establishing the 'independen[ce]' of culture from the state, and recognising that exemplary individuals' teleology points beyond the well-being of a state' to universal concerns (197).

The second counter-movement repudiates egoism, but 'is only more disquieting' than the first. It is, Nietzsche indicates, a counter to the state's counter-movement, since it consists in the various revolutionary 'radical upheavals' against the 'constitutive force of the so-called nation-state' (199). This revolutionary counter-movement is modern in nature because it radicalises the critical self-consciousness of modern culture, its tendency to challenge all received order and closed horizons. It accelerates the destruction of pre-modern cultures, but also eliminates modern institutions and communities that seek to take their place – the state, commercial society, polite society, and so forth. The adherents of this revolutionary movement long for utopia as a result of their efforts. Nietzsche, considerably more pessimistic about our flawed or contradictory human nature, thinks this revolutionary destruction will undermine all checks on bad behaviour and unleash the 'wild, primal, and completely pitiless forces' in human beings (199).

As a result, in Nietzsche's judgement, the revolutionary movement will usher in the egoistic hell that modern institutions
sought to stave off.[10] Insofar as this movement makes any order
impossible, it is 'more disquieting' than the first movement – at
least the state, the economy, the nation and the scholarly world
all produce some material benefit. The problem of these latter
institutions is that they claim a higher status than they deserve.
They posit themselves as the highest purpose of human life and
society, the ultimate end of all our efforts. By contrast, Nietzsche
thinks, they should be but material means to the higher spiritual
aim of culture and its aim, genius. The education of culture must
therefore effect this re-evaluation of the status of these institutions,
demoting them to means. It must also quell the revolutionary fervour implicit in modern culture.

4B *The modern champions of humanity (pp. 200–7)*

The problem of egoism is not that it is self-destructive. On the
contrary, as Nietzsche recognises here and in his late period,
harrowing, 'Last Man' passage in *Thus Spoke Zarathustra*, egoism
is remarkably resilient. The problem is that egoism dehumanises us. It jettisons the self-given spiritual values and purposes
that distinguish us as human beings, and casts us back upon our
externally given 'bestiality', rendering us a 'selfish worm' with
'bovine fear'. Indeed, Nietzsche argues that we may be reduced
even below the animal, which still has some self-direction. We
may decline into 'robotic automatism', the polar opposite to our
distinctively human self-determination. 'Humanity', in short, is
'imperiled' in modern culture. Nietzsche thereby calls out for
help, asking, 'who, then, will pledge his services as sentinel and
champion of *humanity* [*Menschlichkeit*], to watch over the inalien-
able, sacred treasures [*unantastbaren heiligen Tempelschatze*] amassed

---

[10] In a notebook entry, Nietzsche exclaims, 'by all means revolution', but hastily adds,
'whether it will produce barbarism or something else depends on the intelligence and
humanity of the following generations' (KSA 7.29[207], UW 275). Given that modern
culture has very little of the latter, Nietzsche is pessimistic about revolution's modern
prospects.

by such diverse generations?' (200, original emphasis). Only by keeping humanity alive in the souls of modern individuals will exemplars be capable of liberating us.

Note the similarities and differences between Nietzsche's approach here and in 'Utility and Liability', sections 2–3. In both places, Nietzsche offers a positive account of culture to generate healthy human beings. He seeks to find ways to keep history alive and resonant in the life of a community. Even more particularly, Nietzsche looked to antiquarian history to satisfy our pious need to venerate the 'dignity and sanctity' of our community (103), while here he calls for someone to protect the 'sacred treasures' of the past. Yet the distance between these approaches is equally important. The three forms of history in 'Utility and Liability' fostered the life of pre-modern communities. The antiquarian, for instance, reveres only the history of his community, not everyone's history. By contrast, in 'Schopenhauer as Educator', Nietzsche seeks someone to champion all of humanity, to protect the history of all humanity. The three forms of history worked for pre-modern communities, but modern culture explodes all closed horizons and expands its scope to universal humanity. As such, in themselves, the three forms of history can no longer found a modern community.

Instead, Nietzsche looks to exemplary individuals who 'will erect the *image of the human being* [*Bild des Menschen*]' (200, original emphasis). In his early unpublished essay 'On Truth and Lies in an Extra-Moral Sense', a *Bild* is the artistic schematisation of a chaos of sensations, the creation of something coherent to make the world intelligible (TL 256). Exemplars aim to schematise the chaos of human things and create an ideal image of the human being that we can all share, which can serve as the basis for *Bildung* and the foundation for a new modern community. Through the 'contemplation' of these images, all of us 'mortals' will be driven to 'a transfiguration of [our] lives' (200–1). In this section Nietzsche portrays the ideals, and in sections 5–6 he proceeds to describe this process of our self-transfiguration in light of them.

Although the exemplary individuals replace the three forms of history, there are distinct parallels drawn between them. In the remainder of section 4, Nietzsche examines 'three images of the human being that our modern age has set up' (200). Why three images, rather than five or six? After all, Nietzsche admired other modern individuals such as Schiller, Emerson and Lange. It is not accidental that Nietzsche chooses three images. In my view, each exemplary individual corresponds to a type of history.[11] However, each individual incorporates its corresponding type of history, appropriating it in the context of modernity. As such, just as in 'Utility and Liability', here Nietzsche does not simply return to the pre-modern forms of history nor abandon them, but transforms them in a modern shape.

> 'Rousseau's human being' – Monumental History
> 'Goethe's human being' – Antiquarian History
> 'Schopenhauer's human being' – Critical History

In readings of this section, scholars have argued that the Schopenhauerian human being 'supersedes' the others, which are deficient.[12] This interpretation overlooks, however, the parallel Nietzsche draws with the types of history in 'Utility and Liability'. In my view, just as in the case of the three types of history, all three exemplars have their limitations, and each can check the dangers of the others, making all three complementary and necessary for the health of a new modern culture.

4B.i Rousseau's human being (p. 201)

In comparison with his earlier comments, Nietzsche offers a more nuanced picture of the revolutionary side of modernity by lauding Rousseau as an exemplar of the modern age. Nietzsche sees Rousseau as having 'exerted a force that incited and still incites to violent revolutions', as revolutionaries from Robespierre through the 'socialist upheavals and tremors' cited Rousseau in defence of their activity. In his writings, Rousseau challenged the modern defence of the state, commercial society and polite society, arguing that modern

---

[11] See Zuckert (1976: 75–6) for elaboration on this point.
[12] Schacht 1995: 159. Kaufmann goes so far as to claim that Nietzsche 'generally reviled Rousseau', which is implausible given Nietzsche's inclusion of him as an exemplar (1978: 168).

individuals were 'oppressed and half-crushed by arrogant classes and merciless wealth, ruined by priests and bad education, humiliated in his own eyes by ridiculous customs'. Rousseau thereby draws on the modern impulse to freedom and calls for a return to '"holy nature"', but finds it is inaccessible, since the modern individual 'has sunk so deep into the chaos of the unnatural that nature no longer hears his prayers' (201).

As such, in Nietzsche's reading, Rousseau's ideal is one full of longing, a human being who 'despises himself and yearns to transcend himself'. In this 'mood', the 'soul' can 'make frightful decisions', as he suggested earlier in the section – the revolutionary can destroy all existing orders in search of an impossible utopia (201). Accordingly, this ideal can 'easily become a Catilinarian', that is, a follower of the Roman Lucius Catiline, who supported the plebeians in a plot against the aristocratic senate (203). The lesson of Catiline is that the revolutionary impulse can tear down everything, including essential institutions that preserve a regime's order and stability. However, this immense longing can also lead the soul to 'summon from out of its depths the most noble and rare powers' (201). By following the Rousseauan human being, the modern individual can hear her own conscience calling her to her uniqueness once again beyond the chains of convention. However, convention is so powerful that it requires all our strength to overcome it.

Accordingly, the Rousseauan human being 'possesses the greatest fire', animating our *eros* and driving us to the active life. Furthermore, it attains 'the greatest popular effect' as a genuinely democratic exemplar (201). Rousseau celebrated the wisdom and virtue of the average and humble in contrast to the corruptions of the elite and knowledgeable. With the image of Rousseau, Nietzsche suggests once again that the life of the exemplar can have an effect on everyone, not just the very few. Moreover, Nietzsche draws on Rousseau to underscore his own critique of the moral corruption brought on by modern institutions, as well as the immense self-overcoming required to extricate oneself from them.

The Rousseauan human being is a 'threatening power' to existing order, insofar as it seeks to cast off the old and found a new and just order for all humanity (201). In this way, this first type resembles monumental history which records the deeds of active individuals who sought the 'happiness' of 'all of humanity' by founding new orders (97). Indeed, this human being promises a relief from the meaningless becoming of unjust history through his ideal of the perfect republic. The Rousseauan individual founds this ideal, and so our lives can gain purpose and value by continuously fighting to erect this ideal on earth. At the same time, however, the Rousseauan human being undeniably incorporates critical history, since both Rousseau and critical history involve the critique of ossified institutions. What is distinctive about the Rousseauan ideal is that it combines monumental creativity and striving with critical destruction in a similar fashion to the modern, 'just' individual from section 6 of 'Utility and Liability'. It does so on the basis of the modern revolutionary ideal, which demands justification not on the basis of life, but truth.

4B.ii Goethe's human being (pp. 201–3)

The Rousseauan human being is like Faust from part 1 of Goethe's masterpiece, who is 'oppressed on all sides', the 'authentic religious and demonic genius of revolution' and 'world liberator'. By contrast, the Goethean human being is like Faust from part 2 of that work, the 'world traveler' who moves through all time and space, 'all domains of life and of nature, all past ages, all arts, mythologies, and sciences'. This ideal human gathers 'nourishment' from 'everything great and memorable that ever existed'. The Rousseauan human being leads an 'active' life, founding new modes and orders, striving after his own authentic self. The Goethean human being, by contrast, 'is the contemplative human being in the grand style', who does not intervene in human affairs but rather contemplates the significance of all of it (202).

The Goethean human being is a modern exemplar in his comprehensive scope. He contemplates not this or that community's history, but the vast treasures of all of humankind. This fits him well to be the 'sentinel' over humanity, just as Rousseau served well to 'champion' it (200). However, given its comprehensive scope, very few individuals are capable of living up to this ideal. In fact, this ideal succumbs to a very real danger that Nietzsche spent many pages in the previous *Observations* excoriating – the Goethean human being can degenerate 'into a philistine', since, as we have seen, philistines similarly have an unquenchable thirst for knowledge (203).

In contemplating humanity's great treasures, the Goethean human being is a 'conserving and conciliatory force' (203). As such, he resembles the antiquarian approach to history, which 'seeks to preserve for those who will emerge after him the conditions under which he himself has come into being' (102). However, this human being conserves the past not to preserve a particular community, but rather for culture as a whole. The Goethean human being contemplates the greatness of the past out of the human desire to discover the truth about humanity, expressed in the peaks that humanity displays. Knowledge brings with it its own reward in the contemplation of excellence, since excellence reveals humanity's remarkable ability to escape from the flux of becoming and build a bridge over that stream. Contemplation thereby allows the Goethean human being – and anyone who follows him – to participate in that eternal excellence as a witness. In escaping becoming in this way and experiencing this eternal excellence, we can lead a valuable life.

4B.iii Schopenhauer's human being (pp. 203–7)

Rousseau, then, is the modern exemplar of the active life, and Goethe of the contemplative life. Schopenhauer represents the modern exemplar of the redemptive life, that 'human being' who 'voluntarily takes upon himself the suffering inherent in truthfulness'. The active life creates new orders, and the contemplative life contemplates them. What does the redemptive person do? This individual recognises the injustice of all human things, and thereby gazes into the truth of things, that 'all existence that can be negated deserves to be negated' (203). As we saw in 'Utility and Liability', this judgement arises from the development of modern culture and the destruction of all limited horizons. All pre-modern communities distort the world and are unjust towards it. Schopenhauer radicalises the modern critique of all things by critiquing the value of existence as such. If existence has no value at all, then neither the active nor the contemplative lives have any value either. In this way, the Schopenhauerian individual parallels critical history in seeking justice in the world, rather than love.

Like the 'just' individual, the redemptive Schopenhauerian human being does not act out of 'malice', but rather his 'negating and destroying' are 'nothing other than the outpouring of that powerful longing for sanctification and salvation [*Heiligung und Errettung*]' (203). Schopenhauer does not cause suffering, but rather gets us to recognise the tragic truth of justice, which itself causes suffering. As a secular saint, Schopenhauer takes this suffering on himself, 'always sacrificing himself as the first victim of recognized truth'. Living in accordance with truth means negating all human community and thus sacrificing one's 'earthly happiness', because one must not favour those one 'loves' and one cannot 'spare either human beings or things, even though he suffers with them in their injuries'. In living this way and showing that it is possible to endure the suffering caused by the truth of things, Schopenhauer leads a 'heroic life', as he 'struggles against overwhelming odds for something that in some way will benefit all' (204).

The Schopenhauerian human being strives for 'justice [*Gerechtigkeit*]', which returns us to Nietzsche's discussion of the just individual in section 6 of 'Utility and Liability'. There Nietzsche indicated that there is a positive standard of justice on the basis of which we could justify the value of existence. He develops this standard further here. The Schopenhauerian human being embodies justice, which holds that truth requires that 'all existence that can be negated deserves to be negated'. However, 'to be truthful' also 'means to believe in an existence that could not possibly be negated and that is itself true and without falsehood' (203–4). What kind of existence cannot be negated, that is itself true? Nietzsche answers, that of the 'truthful person', the person whose 'activity is metaphysical', whose activity 'is explicable only by the laws of another, higher life, one that is in the most profound sense affirmative' (204). When Nietzsche uses the term 'metaphysical', he does not mean abstract souls or gods. Rather, he is referring back to his own first section, in which he argued that our unique self is an ideal not present to the senses but a metaphysical projection that we can steadily bring about through our actions. Thus, we can be 'truthful' not by living in accordance with a standard of nature – since nature is in flux and provides no standards – but rather by being true to our own unique ideal self. Human life in general deserves to be negated because it fails to live up to the drive for truth implicit in our distinctively human nature. Yet exemplary life, the life of the truthful person, cannot be negated because it satisfies this drive. The actions of this life are true in that they properly express and realise the ideal self that is the object and normative standard governing all one's efforts.

This standard applies not only to Schopenhauer, but to all of the exemplars, since they all craft selves that are true to their own unique selves. In the last three pages of the section (205–7), Nietzsche extends his discussion beyond Schopenhauer to make two further points on the nature and justification of exemplary individuals.

First, Nietzsche elaborates on the nature of freedom implicit in the exemplary life, and argues against the view that excellence or 'greatness' is a 'gift' from nature. On the latter view – Schopenhauer's view – human excellence is inborn, and thereby 'produced by a mechanism and responded with blind obedience' by the great individual, acting in accordance with 'this inner compulsion'. Since greatness or smallness of soul is a gift from nature, not under our control, then those who 'have not received this gift ... have the same right to be small as the great person has to be great'. Nietzsche attributes this view to those who 'celebrate festivals in memory of great people' (205). These individuals believe this story about the gift of greatness as a way to evade their own conscience calling them to greatness. They tell themselves this story, that greatness is something we are either born with or not, as an excuse not to live freely. For Nietzsche, the many relinquish their self-determination when they submit themselves to the guidance of nature rather than taking up their own call to recognise the exemplar.[13] Indeed, Nietzsche claims in a note to this essay that the 'working classes' could 'easily ... surpass us in matters of education and virtue' (KSA 7.29[216], UW 277).

Furthermore, Nietzsche argues that this view is an 'insult' to the 'great human being', because it entails that these individuals do not merit the praise given to them. Nature is responsi-

---

[13] See Conant (2001: 209f.) for further discussion.

ble for their greatness, and so nature should be praised, not them. As such, the great individual must 'receive gifts or be compelled' by something outside of him. However, 'these are contemptible words with which one tries to escape an inner admonition'. Each individual knows 'how to make his life easy' by accepting the gift of guidance from nature or society. But in doing so, the individual is 'cheat[ed]' out of 'himself' by a 'kind of conspiracy' to 'lure him out of his own cave'. When the individual is determined by nature or society, his own self is extinguished, replaced by the identity and purpose of forces beyond him. As such, the great individual 'resists this, pricks up his ears, and decides: "I want to remain my own person."' Of course, to be self-determining requires descending into the 'depths of existence' and asking the fundamental question of the value of existence (205).

For his second point, Nietzsche deepens his defence of the ethical significance of self-determination. Why be true to ourselves? Why not live for something higher than us? Why not answer the question 'What is the purpose of your life?' with the 'proud answer: "To become a good citizen, or scholar, or statesman"?' Aren't these worthy vocations? The problem with these answers is that they involve making one's life into a 'point in the evolution of a race or a state or a field of knowledge'. Being a good citizen, for instance, means sacrificing oneself for the purposes of the state and its life. But what, then, is the purpose of the state? States come in and out of existence, and have life cycles much like human beings do, desiring self-preservation and seeking to extend themselves into subsequent generations. In this way, the life of states on earth, like the life of animals, is all part of 'becoming', and the good citizen seeks to 'integrate himself completely into' it. Becoming is 'empty, deceitful, flat, and worthy of our contempt' because it never answers our fundamental question of the purpose and value of existence. It only drives us on in a meaningless, purposeless quest. As such, 'eternal becoming is a deceitful puppet play' that 'disperses the individual to the four winds' (206). This quest is deceptive in that it pretends to fill our lives with meaning – politics, society and the market all claim to be valuable – but never answers our fundamental question. Moreover, it 'disperses' us by wrenching us further and further away from ourselves, shaping us to serve an external force and aim.

True heroism, then, 'consists in one day ceasing to be' becoming's 'plaything'. The 'riddle' of the value of our existence 'can be solved only in being, in being what he is and not in being something else, in the immutable' (206). When Nietzsche says that we can only justify our existence through being, not becoming, he is appropriating the Eleatic and Platonic tradition of valuing being over becoming. However, as he did in 'Utility and Liability' with the notion of immortality, Nietzsche humanises being. By 'being', Nietzsche means 'being what [one] is', being my own unique ideal self. My own ideal self is 'being', not 'becoming', because I determine my own fate, unhindered by any external force in the stream of becoming. Of course, all of us are shaped by our particular places and times, but I can liberate myself from the chain of events before me and after me by positing an ideal self outside of this stream of becoming, and then shaping my life in accordance with it. For instance, Schopenhauer lives in immutable 'being', because he constructed an ideal self against his time – the Schopenhauerian human being – which thus becomes an eternal ideal. Any human being at any time can seek to live in accordance with it. Indeed, Schopenhauer himself crafted his life in accordance with it. He legislated for himself his own law, and governed his life with an eternal ideal. By contrast, the good citizen lives in accordance with an ideal image of the citizen, an ideal parochial to this particular state, as such norms of citizenship change from state to state. He gives up his autonomy, accepting a law from an external force, and he governs his life by a transitory ideal.

Although Nietzsche concludes by discussing exemplars in general, it is important to remember that he always discusses several exemplars. There is no comprehensive redemptive figure, no Christ. As such, Nietzsche suggests that every exemplar is limited in some way. No single human being is perfect and wholly complete, because each exemplar perfects only one aspect of a multifaceted humanity. Since human existence is internally contradictory and plastic – capable of being shaped in many ways by our shaping power – humanity can develop in many directions with many perfectible features. As such, only the totality of all exemplars reveals humanity in its wholeness and perfection. As we saw in 'Utility and Liability', the 'republic of genius' reveals humanity in this way, as all exemplars collaborate to realise humanity in a comprehensive project. Moreover, this republic represents the alternative to the 'purely historical' life that Nietzsche explored in 'Utility and Liability', in that these exemplars have achieved a suprahistorical standpoint (KSA 7.34[32], UW 356).

At the same time, Nietzsche also indicates in this section that exemplars do not simply interact and complement one another's strengths. They also check and balance the weaknesses of each other, in much the same way that we saw that the three forms of history did. The Rousseauan individual, for instance, balances the Goethean person by inciting the latter to action. The former prompts the latter to display 'a little more muscle and natural wildness' which makes 'all his virtues . . . greater' (203). On the other hand, the Goethean person balances the Rousseauan individual's weakness by refining his passion – he serves as the 'corrective and sedative for precisely those dangerous excitations to which Rousseau's human being is exposed' (201). Schopenhauer balances both of the others by grounding the active and contemplative life in ultimate significance or value. Rousseau and Goethe balance the Schopenhauerian individual by affirming human existence. What is most needful, then, for modern culture is to combine all three modern ideals in the education of its youth. In doing so, the youth will be presented with the pinnacles of the active, contemplative and redemptive lives for them to model, but also be given the tools to redress the vices in each.

5 Elevating the individual to culture

Thus far in his theory of exemplarity, Nietzsche has discussed the nature of the exemplar as well as how the exemplar motivates us. Since we are free beings, the notion of an exemplar is an acute challenge – if we follow the ideal self of another exemplar, don't we then relinquish our freedom? Indeed, Nietzsche has already pointed out that it is all too easy to fall into hero worship and thus abandon our freedom. How is following an exemplar distinct from hero worship?

In sections 2–3, Nietzsche explained how the exemplar does not coerce the affect and character of the many, but rather liberates them. In section 4, Nietzsche reaches the peak of his account in the exemplar's image of the 'ideal human being', but he has not yet explained how this ideal can motivate anyone without coercing them. Indeed, he ominously warns, this image might be 'nothing but an enrapturing, indeed intoxicating, vision that grants us individual moments only to let us down ... and deliver us over to an even deeper sense of disheartenment' (207). The aim of section 5, then, is to 'demonstrate that this ideal *educates* [*erzieht*]' (207, original emphasis), to show how it can shape us without coercing us and undermining our freedom. Nietzsche's answer is that the exemplary ideal educates because all of us share the same ultimate aim with the exemplar, the redemption of our existence, and exemplars each represent a partial fulfilment of that aim, offering us a glimpse of how we might ourselves succeed.

In sections 1–4, Nietzsche steadily expanded his scope of moral concern. He began in section 1 with the individual's relationship to himself, moved in sections 2–3 to the individual's relationship with an exemplar, and then broadened his attention in section 4 to the individual's relationship to his age. In section 5, Nietzsche makes a new beginning on this broadened foundation. He once again raises many of the points from section 1, the difference between humanity and animality, the concern for the 'stream' in which we are 'submerged' and the need for 'bridges' to escape it (211, 214). What is new here, however, is that the self's aim is no longer itself as in section 1 – Nietzsche now rejects the idea of the 'solitary individual', seeking to forget the 'I'. Instead, Nietzsche looks to integrate individuals 'into a powerful community', namely, 'culture' (213–14). In their readings of 'Schopenhauer as Educator', most commentators have either stressed the individualism of section 1 (Conant 2001; Cavell 1990) or the social perfectionism of sections 5–6 (Hurka 2007). My task in this section and the next will be to argue that individual and community are interdependent in Nietzsche's thought.[14] In sum, my account is this: properly understood, the realisation of my individuality requires

---

[14] See Lemm, who rightly challenges Cavell's and Conant's excessively 'individualistic interpretation of freedom' which is 'too narrow to fully grasp the public dimension of freedom as responsibility' (2007: 5–6). Lemm goes too far, however, in rejecting the perfectionist element in Nietzsche's thought, expressed most clearly in the monumental individuals of 'Utility and Liability' and the exemplars of 'Schopenhauer as Educator'.

my dedication to culture because it is only through culture that I can be an individual at all. We cannot gain self-knowledge nor achieve self-determination through other forms of association.

5A *The nature of obligation (pp. 207–9)*

Nietzsche describes the ideal's motivating power in an interesting way – he states that the 'most difficult task' is to 'derive a new set of duties from this ideal' (207). The task of grounding obligation has long occupied modern ethical thought, given classic form, of course, in Immanuel Kant. The challenge for modern ethical thinkers has been to find a new basis for obligation in the wake of the decline of all pre-modern sources of authority, such as ancestral tradition, nature and religion. Modern thinkers turn inward, to subjectivity, as the source of authority. However, if the subject is not called by something higher than itself but alone places itself under an obligation – on the 'basis of a regulated, self-initiated activity' – then it will not impose duties to drive the individual 'beyond himself'. Modern ethical thinkers thus seem to face a dilemma in Nietzsche's view: either they justify obligation via subjectivity, but then vitiate any self-overcoming, or they ground obligation on pre-modern foundations that draw the subject to higher states of the soul, but then undermine the subject's freedom by imposing a law from an external authority. Nietzsche puts the challenge in this way: 'is it possible to bring that incredibly lofty goal so near to us that it will educate us while drawing us upward?' (208).

As we will see, I think Nietzsche offers a Kantian approach to solving this dilemma, which involves distinguishing our humanity from animality, seeing the source of normative obligation in our humanity, and recognising how far many of us are from realising what seems so close to us, our humanity. At the same time, Nietzsche departs from Kant on the nature of moral obligation. Kant conceives of moral obligation as deriving from the abstract, formal character of pure practical reason. Nietzsche, by contrast, derives obligation from the embodied lives of exemplary human beings. Kant, of course, recognises the importance of exemplars, but only to illustrate and motivate us to act on the moral law. For Nietzsche, the ideal is not abstract but concrete and embodied in its essence. In an unpublished later draft of a preface for a new *Observation*, Nietzsche expressed his similarity to and difference from Kant in this way: he 'resolved to paint portraits of "the philosopher" and "the artist" – to render, as it were, [his] own "categorical imperative"' (qtd Breazeale 1998: 6).

Nevertheless, when we move from the nature to the structure of moral obligation, Kant's view again comes closer to Nietzsche's. In his view of 'imperfect duties', Kant argues that human beings have a standing obligation to perfect themselves and seek the happiness of others. We cannot fulfil these duties all at once, but can only steadily approximate this ideal, for instance by constantly cultivating moral virtue in our character. Similarly, Nietzsche holds that we all have a standing obligation to realise our ideal self. We cannot fulfil this duty all at once, but can only steadily approximate the 'ideal image'. Every successful action shapes our character so that it more closely resembles the ideal, and we thereby fulfil one more link in this 'chain of fulfillable duties'. Thus, we incrementally approach complete self-determination by following this chain.

5B *The telos of nature (pp. 209–11)*

In the remainder of the section, Nietzsche attempts to solve the dilemma of modern ethical thought. The first step in his argument is to return once again to his fundamental principles, reminding us of the basic difference between humanity and animality. Unlike section 1 of 'Utility and Liability', which featured the happy cow, this section features a decidedly bleaker picture of animality. The 'beast of prey' is 'subject to hunger and desires' yet 'driven through the desert by its gnawing torment' and 'seldom satisfied'. The suffering beast's fleeting 'satisfaction turns into agony in the flesh-tearing struggle with other beasts, or from nauseating greediness and oversatiation'. As in 'Utility and Liability', the beast cannot reflect on its own situation nor evaluate it. It clings 'so blindly and madly to life, for no higher reward' and 'far from knowing . . . why one is punished in this way, but instead to thirst with the inanity of a horrible desire'. Accordingly, we human beings meet this 'sight of senseless suffering' with 'profound indignation'. We see nature compelling it through instinct to pursue certain ends but also systematically preventing it from achieving those ends, all the while subjecting it to evils that it cannot avoid or comprehend. Existence itself is contradictory, and animals are the innocent victims of nature's irrationality. As such, Nietzsche points out, many pre-modern cultures developed a myth to justify this suffering, that 'the souls of guilt-laden human beings were trapped inside the bodies of these animals' (209).

'What it means to be an animal', then, is to live without a 'higher reward' or justification for one's activity. This definition of animality follows from Nietzsche's previous account. Animality is agency whose activity is governed by forces outside itself. Accordingly, the animal has no justification for its existence because these external forces have no ultimate justification. As we have seen, this is an unusual, non-biological definition of animality, one that refers pre-eminently to our distinctively human freedom as self-determination. With this definition, however, Nietzsche can ask, 'where does the animal cease', and 'where does the human being begin!' (209). He can claim that the 'greatest part of our lives' is a 'continuation of animality' (210). When we pursue 'happiness' (209), for instance, we do not lift ourselves above the 'horizon of the animal' (210). More broadly,

> the tremendous mobility of human beings on the great earthly desert, their founding of cities and states, their waging of wars, their ceaseless gathering and dispersing, their confused mingling, their imitation of one another, their mutual outwitting and trampling underfoot, their cries in distress and their joyous cheers in victory – all this is a continuation of animality. (210)

We continue to be animals because the forces we serve have no justification for their existence. We accept their authority and their ends and thus relinquish our freedom, casting us back into animality, back into the flux of becoming.

However, we need not give in to our animality, since we are also free – 'there are moments when we understand this', when we recognise that our existence is an injustice and without value (210). This self-reflection gives us insight but also longing for the redemption of our existence. Our self-reflective nature means that we can transcend the endless flux of nature for a moment, lifting 'our heads enough to notice the stream in which we are so deeply submerged' (211). In doing so, we can see how 'we, along with all of nature, are pressing onward toward the human being as toward something that stands high above us'. Nietzsche here and in subsequent pages describes nature in a teleological fashion that runs quite counter to the non-teleological, Darwinian way in which he has been discussing it so far. The introduction of this metaphysical dogmatism is abrupt and is redolent of Schopenhauer's metaphysics. It is strange for Nietzsche to do this, given his critique of Schopenhauerian metaphysics, and the fact that such passages are 'barely intelligible' according to one commentator, and not at all philosophically plausible (Young 2010: 197).

However, there is another way to read these passages that prevents Nietzsche from sliding into implausible dogmatic metaphysics (not to mention creating a puzzle as to why Nietzsche would critique Schopenhauer's metaphysics a few years before this essay, and embrace his metaphysics here). In my view, Nietzsche employs a Kantian strategy here.[15] In the Appendix to the *Critique of Teleological Judgment*, Kant argues that reason drives us to judge our moral perfection as the ultimate end of nature. Yet this judgement is regulative, not constitutive – that is, it does not describe the way that nature is in itself, but is a necessary means to render consistent all of our moral judgements. Similarly, Nietzsche holds that natural existence is in need of justification. Yet nature is indifferent to us and our justifications. As such, we must regard nature as in some sense interested in us, that it aims at our fulfilment. In so doing, when we realise and justify our own natures, we redeem nature as well by conceiving it as the vehicle for our ends. For this reason, Nietzsche describes 'nature' as in 'need' of 'knowledge' (210), and states that 'nature presses onward toward the human being', that

---

[15] See Zuckert: 'the critical powers of the human mind deprive nature of its normative status' (1976: 81). For a contrary view, that Nietzsche held a metaphysical understanding of nature, see Taylor 1997: 36f.; Safranski 2002: 113–14; Ansell-Pearson 2013: 242. Young reads these passages as a 'version of (social) Darwinism' (2010: 198).

'he is necessary for its salvation from animal existence and that in him, finally existence holds before itself a mirror in which life no longer appears senseless but appears, rather, in its metaphysical meaningfulness' (209). In most cases, Nietzsche indicates the regulative status of nature's teleology by emphasising the way nature appears; for instance, that 'life not longer appears senseless'. Of course, on a Darwinian view of nature, it has no purpose. It is senseless. But human beings can conceive of nature as possessing a need, a purpose and a sense of fulfilment in order to make our redemption of natural existence intelligible.

5C *Culture and its aim (pp. 211–14)*

Thus, the first step in the argument – and the first in a chain of duties – is to reveal to us that for the majority of our lives we live like animals, and that living in this way, our lives are not worth living. Fortunately, we can recognise this worthlessness, an insight that makes possible the transcendence of our mere animality and the redemption of our existence. Nietzsche in this way reduplicates the logic of Kant's theodicy of nature in his third *Critique*.

The second step is to identify the 'redeeming human being' and see how we can live up to this high ideal on the basis of our own subjectivity. Nietzsche states quite clearly who the redeeming human beings are – namely, 'those true *human beings, those no-longer-animals, the philosophers, artists, and saints*' (211, original emphasis). Why is it only philosophers, artists and saints who are truly human? Nietzsche states that these exemplars reveal the 'great *enlightenment* about existence', tarrying 'where the fundamental nature of things expresses itself' (212, original emphasis). The vocation of the philosopher, artist and saint is precisely to pursue an answer to the basic question of the value of existence. All other individuals take some answer for granted – the citizen or scholar or capitalist, for instance, take for granted the value of their vocation. The philosopher, artist and saint take nothing for granted but inquire into the condition of the human being as such. Their own reflection on existence can be regarded as a self-reflection of nature itself, nature having given rise to the peak of humanity, capable of calling into question its very existence. In this way, Nietzsche's view of art, religion and philosophy as the self-reflective, self-determining expression of nature resembles Hegel's own view of absolute spirit – art, religion and philosophy as the achieved self-knowledge of being itself.

'Nature needs philosophers for a metaphysical purpose', that is, for 'self-enlightenment', to understand the meaning of existence. Artists, Nietzsche proceeds to argue, serve a similar purpose, which is to provide self-knowledge in a 'pure and finished image', which 'in the tumultuousness of its own becoming, it never has the opportunity to see clearly' (213). Philosophy provides the abstract, cognitive self-knowledge of nature, while art offers the concrete, sensual embodiment of the same. The saint, by contrast, supplies not self-reflection but a shared feeling. In the saint, the 'ego has entirely melted away' such that he has the 'deepest feeling of equality, communion, and oneness with all living things'. The saint takes into himself all the suffering of existence. The philosopher and artist, then, provide a cognitive and imaginative justification for the meaning of existence; the saint offers an affective 'salvation' from all suffering, proving that suffering is not without meaning but has a purpose in the suffering of the saint (214).

At this point, Nietzsche says, he is 'in a position to supply an answer to the question posed earlier', namely, how to escape the dilemma of modern ethical thought. How to 'get in touch with the great ideal of the Schopenhauerian human being on the basis of a regulated, self-initiated activity'. Nietzsche's answer is that our 'duties are not the duties of a solitary individual'. Rather, through these duties

> one is integrated into a powerful community, one that, to be sure, is not held together by external forms and laws, but by a fundamental idea. This is the fundamental idea of culture, insofar as it is capable of charging each of us with one single task: *to foster the production of philosophers, artists, and saints within us and around us, and thereby to work toward the perfection of nature.* (213, original emphasis)

Even though, as we saw in section 1, I am born with an individual and unique destiny, it is only possible for me to realise this destiny in concert with others. The reason is that realising my destiny involves constructing my unique ideal self and determining my life in accordance with it. However, constructing a unique self must occur in concert with others who are doing the same. Otherwise, I will not be able to tell whether or not I am being truly unique. I may unwittingly be rehashing someone else's self, or I may be constructing utter nonsense. Uniqueness is only defined in contrast to others. As such, to realise my own unique destiny, I must at the same time help others realise their unique destiny so as to have contrasts to me. This is all simply to say that I ought to help constitute culture, which is a community devoted to the self-determination of humanity's many unique selves. This is the clearest and deepest substantive definition of culture that Nietzsche gives in the *Observations*. Culture is that community whose aim is the production of exemplary individuals. The formal features of culture that he has discussed thus far – unity amid diversity in its cultural expressions – are in service to this substantive end.

Thus, Nietzsche effects the transition from individual to community. I have a duty not just to myself, but to all humanity, 'to foster the production of philosophers, artists, and saints within us and around us'. Nietzsche claims here that there are potential philosophers, artists and saints within all of us, which challenges the aristocratic reading of 'Schopenhauer as Educator'. At the same time, we must also devote ourselves to developing the same in others in the form of producing culture. The aristocratic reading correctly identifies this emphasis on submitting oneself to the aims of community, but it wrongly implies that the many are coerced to submit to it for the benefit of others. On the contrary, Nietzsche stresses, we need not choose either individual self-determination or community. We must choose both because their aims are mutually constitutive.

This account helps us distinguish between hero worship and commitment to culture. In hero worship, the many are tools for the purposes of the great. In culture, 'all of us are related and connected' to the 'saint, just as we are related to the philosopher and artists'. These exemplars represent the realisation of humanity that everyone longs for. Accordingly, we do not feel resentment for these individuals, nor do they lord their status over us. On the contrary, Nietzsche envisions the relationship as a collaborative endeavour, in which the exemplars 'lift us up', and the many 'continually pave the way for and promote the production of this human being' (214). Our relationship to exemplars is necessarily collaborative because they make possible our own self-determination by fostering the cultural conversation that makes our uniqueness possible. As such, Nietzsche claims, the search for individual self-determination paradoxically results in those 'moments' in which we 'no longer understand the word "I"', in which we recognise something 'beyond our being' and long for a 'bridge connecting the here and the there'. Culture forms the 'bridge' over the stream of becoming, in an image that has recurred throughout the *Observations*. In a draft of this section, Nietzsche states that culture 'lift[s] the individual human being out of the pushing, shoving, and crushing of the historical stream and make[s] him understand that he is not merely a historically limited being, but also an absolutely extrahistorical and infinite being with whom all existence began and will end' (KSA 7.35[12], UW 367). It is precisely through the commitment to the community of humanity's realisation – when I am 'taken up into that most sublime order of philosophers, artists, and saints' – that I receive back my own unique self (214).

Nietzsche thereby solves the dilemma of obligation in the following way. I long to give my existence value by living up to my unique ideal self. Yet the only way to self-knowledge and self-determination is to submit myself to culture, which makes uniqueness possible. The subject's self-given obligation drives the subject to commit himself to a communal order far beyond himself. There are many duties along the way until the subject can receive back his own individuality – Nietzsche envisions a lot of work first in 'discovering what is hostile' to culture's 'development and sweeping it aside' (214). In this way, many individuals will have little time to devote to their own distinctive individuality, but must devote themselves to paving the way for the eventual realisation of culture in which all can realise their individuality. Indeed, in a letter written while he was composing this essay, Nietzsche writes that we are 'so far from this goal' that we must engage primarily in 'negating' in order 'to become free' (KGB 4.362). In the next section, Nietzsche expands on his claim that preparatory labour for culture confers value on existence.

Nietzsche's solution here draws on the tradition in German philosophy that conceives of the individual self as constituted intersubjectively, that is, through community. It finds expression in Fichte's theory of recognition and Hegel's master–slave dialectic, but is more easily grasped in Jean-Jacques Rousseau's *Social Contract*. For Rousseau, human beings outside society possess only 'natural freedom', an independence from the wills of others but a deeper submission to 'physical impulse' and 'appetite'. We can only assume 'obedience to the law [that we have] prescribed to [ourselves]' by joining a society in which we submit ourselves entirely to the general will (Rousseau 2012: 176). By doing so, we regain our individuality from the whole, by becoming 'an indivisible part' of the self-determination of the 'whole' (2012: 173). Similarly, in Nietzsche, individuality is unintelligible outside culture. Only paradoxically by assuming the perspective of the whole of culture can we grasp our own unique contributing part. Moreover, only by helping create that culture can we determine our own unique self.

6 Culture and the value of existence

Section 6 is a continuation of section 5 in that it provides and justifies the 'formula' that Nietzsche promised would 'subsume this new set of duties' (209). This formula amounts to Nietzsche's most direct statement of the value of existence – our existence only has value insofar as we work to produce exemplars. Unfortunately, its directness has led to misunderstanding by prominent Nietzsche scholars, who have read it either as a radically aristocratic or democratic principle. Sections 5–6 together reveal that, for Nietzsche, culture is a collaborative affair. Individuals cannot be forced to belong to culture, but must willingly devote themselves. However, these sections also reveal that a great deal of preparatory work must be done in order for humanity to be realised at all. For Nietzsche, then, many individuals must commit themselves to culture without the expectation that they themselves will become geniuses. The first part of this section, then, examines the formula for the value of existence (A). The second part discusses Nietzsche's derivation of the two main duties or 'sacraments' of culture that all willing subjects bind themselves to (B). The third part analyses the daunting obstacles to fostering culture that make it necessary for many individuals to devote themselves wholly to removing them (C).

6A *The infamous formula (pp. 215–16)*

Nietzsche phrases his formula in two different ways in this section. Its first appearance is objectively stated: 'humanity should work ceaselessly toward producing great individuals – this and only this should be its task' (215). The second appearance is subjectively phrased: you should live 'for the benefit of the rarest and most valuable specimens [*Exemplaren*], not for the benefit of the majority' (216). If we did not have the context of the previous five sections of Nietzsche's text, we might be shocked by such a blatantly elitist statement. Indeed, Hurka (2007) and Ansell-Pearson (2013: 242n) have read these statements as an extension of a kind of naturalistic teleology. In support of their reading, they reasonably point to Nietzsche's exclamation, 'how gladly we would apply to society and its aims a lesson that can be derived from the observation of every single species of animal and plant life, namely, that the only thing that matters is the superior individual specimen'; and 'it is easy to understand that the goal of any species' evolution is that point at which it reaches its limit and begins the transition to a higher species' (215). From these passages, it seems clear that, for Nietzsche, the many are intrinsically worthless, having value only as disposable tools in service to the perfection of the few. We might add to this evidence a notorious claim that Nietzsche made a few years before in his unpublished 'The Greek State': 'every man, with his whole activity, is only dignified to the extent that he is a tool of genius' (Nietzsche 1994: 185).

However, it is difficult to square this interpretation with what we have seen thus far in 'Schopenhauer as Educator'. In sections 1–5 Nietzsche argued that every individual is a unique miracle, and developed a notion of culture that would foster every individual's self-realisation. How could he then turn around and declare that the majority of individuals are thoroughly worthless, only tools of great individuals? Such a blatant contradiction requires that we examine the text more closely. Indeed, Conant's essay aims to untangle this puzzle by attending to the Kantian term *Exemplaren*, translated as 'specimen' in the English edition. For Conant, specimen fails to render this concept properly, because specimens mean 'representative samples of a particular class or genus' (2001: 194). Exemplar, by contrast, is not an instance of a kind, but one of a kind. On this basis, Conant reads this passage in his democratic fashion, that each one of us can live a valuable life in so far as each of us lives for his or her own genius (2001: 226f.). Our own distinctive selves are the exemplars that we seek to foster.

Yet Conant's view, for all its keen insight into the Kantian features of Nietzsche's text, also fails to capture the thrust of what we have seen in 'Schopenhauer as Educator'. In section 1, Nietzsche does stress that each one of us should live up to our own unique selves, but he then proceeds to discuss those exemplars who will help us accomplish this. We then learn in section 5 that the only way to achieve self-determination at all is to engage in a communal project of building culture. Since culture is in such sorry shape, many of us will have to expend immense energy in preparatory work to make it possible at all. Conant, in other words, rightly recognises the individual self-determination at the heart of Nietzsche's project, but misses the communal conditions for the possibility of such self-determination.

However, we are still left with our puzzle: how can Nietzsche affirm the uniqueness of all individuals and the collaborative nature of culture, while at the same time affirming the worthlessness of the majority of individuals? We can solve this puzzle by looking carefully at the way that Nietzsche presents the analogy with natural specimens. Note that he nowhere justifies the formula with reference to natural teleology. Rather, the references to natural teleology are rhetorical means that Nietzsche employs to challenge the widespread 'delusions' that prevent us from 'conced[ing]' the formula. He begins the section not with a justification of the formula, but with frustration at the resistance to it: 'at times it is harder to concede something than it is to understand it'. To address this resistance, Nietzsche states that he would 'gladly ... apply to society and its aims a lesson that can be derived from the observation of every single species of animal and plant life, namely, that the only thing that matters is the superior animal specimen'.

Note that he does not say that this lesson justifies the formula, only that he would 'gladly ... apply' it. He would do so because 'it is easy to understand that the goal of any species' evolution' is the higher individuals, not because this claim is true.

Why, then, would Nietzsche engage in this rhetorical activity? Society puts up 'stubborn resistance' to the formula, so a regulative judgement about natural teleology would help us make sense of our life in the grand scheme of the cosmos, not just our particular lives and history (215). Indeed, Nietzsche describes the 'attitude' that should be 'cultivated in every young person', which is to regard oneself as completing nature's failed efforts: 'I shall pay tribute to [nature's] great intention by being at its service so that it might someday be more successful' (216). That is, it is easier for a young person to 'concede' the formula if we claim that all of the cosmos inclines him in this direction, rather than that humanity must make its own way in an indifferent universe.

As such, Nietzsche does not justify the formula with regard to natural teleology, and so does not contradict his earlier claims. Instead, he justifies it by once again asking the fundamental question, 'how can your life, the life of the individual, obtain the highest value, the deepest significance?' (216). The answers common in Nietzsche's day were that 'that ultimate aim is supposed to lie in the happiness of all or of the majority; others think that it is to be found in the development of great communities' (215). Yet as Nietzsche has argued, if one commits one's life to the majority or to the state, one does not confer value on one's existence, because these entities themselves do not have intrinsic justification or value. Rather, the only thing that can confer value on existence is self-justifying or 'true human beings' (218). Even if I do not myself become such a true human being, I can participate in the genesis of such a being by preparing the conditions for his or her emergence. Doing so does not make me a fungible tool of genius, however. The exemplary individual's self is shaped by all the conditions that contributed to its emergence, including me and the culture that brought this individual into being. As such, my own distinctive individuality, my own work, will be taken up in the self-determination of this individual. In this sense, my individuality is entirely unlike those many plants and animals that are

disposable specimens; on the contrary, my individuality is a necessary contributing part of a self-justifying whole, one that will be
immortalised as a part of the ideal self of the exemplar.

6B *The two sacraments of culture (pp. 216–18)*

Nietzsche's commitment to the ethical value of freedom means
that he cannot defend a natural teleology. To do so would cast
him back to pre-Kantian metaphysics, which held that individuals
should commit themselves to a metaphysical, teleological structure outside themselves. That he instead develops a post-Kantian
philosophy of freedom – that I obey my own subjectivity in committing myself to realising humanity – is evident from the two
sacraments of culture that Nietzsche derives from the formula.

The formula holds that human beings commit themselves to
the realisation of humanity, especially its peaks. This realisation
occurs in 'culture' (216). Culture is a community, and so individuals must earn membership in that community. Nietzsche compares
the spiritual community of culture to that of religion by enumerat-
ing two sacraments that individuals undertake to merit admission.
Indeed, the comparison is not accidental, because 'Christianity is
certainly one of the purest manifestations of that drive for culture',
particularly for the 'production of the saint' (220). The first sacrament of culture involves a profession of 'faith in culture'. This profession involves two parts. First, it consists of a 'dissatisfaction with'
oneself, a 'contemptuous perspective' on oneself, to be 'ashamed
of oneself', to display 'hatred of one's own shriveled narrowness'.
That is, to undertake the first sacrament requires that we recognise
our failure to live up to the call of our own conscience, our wilful
embrace of our animality, and that we condemn this evasion of
our conscience. Accordingly, Nietzsche does not claim that anyone – the state, a great individual – compels us into service, but
rather that each and every one of us ought to 'place himself within
the circle of culture' (216).[16]

---

[16] See Taylor, who offers a similar point about this passage. Nietzsche did not believe 'that
those of modest abilities should slavishly subject themselves to the interests of the truly
distinguished' (1997: 156).

The second part of the first sacrament is a commitment to the realisation of humanity, that 'I see something beyond myself that is loftier and more human than I am'. This commitment comes from our 'love' of our 'higher self that lies hidden somewhere'. As we saw in section 1, we have an erotic drive to realise the ideal self that we construct, and Nietzsche returns to this idea here, employing it to fuel our commitment to culture as a necessary condition for creating this higher self. Our love cannot be taught, but is fueled by our 'sympathy with the genius' whom we encounter in culture – Goethe, Rousseau or Schopenhauer – who provides a model for self-determination and justifies our profession of faith in culture. The exemplar realised by culture – that which we are professing our faith in – is a 'human being' who 'senses himself to be full and infinite in knowledge and love' (216). This individual achieves wholeness – he 'put[s] together what belongs together', answering our call to 'complete us!' and our 'immeasurable longing to become whole' (217) – by forging a self-related unity of character, a product of culture that unifies culture in return. This individual is also 'infinite in knowledge', thereby perfecting what is distinctively human in us (216). The exemplar does not literally know all the facts, but demonstrates infinite self-knowledge, that is, an ability to 'use his own struggles and longing as the alphabet with which he can now spell out the aspirations of human beings' (217). The exemplary individual realises a facet of humanity, and understands himself to be a representative of a type of human being.

The second sacrament of culture involves external 'action', not just an inner transformation; works, not just faith. Nietzsche admits that this second sacrament is 'more difficult' and hence more rare. It is more difficult because we must 'fight for culture and oppose those influences, habits, laws, and institutions in which [we do] not recognize [our] goal: the production of genius'. As we will see, these obstacles to culture are forbidding, and overcoming them requires great risk on the part of individuals. It is one thing to consecrate oneself to culture; it is another thing to transform the 'great, turbulent world' so that it accommodates culture (217). The first sacrament can confer meaning on my existence because I am at the very least transforming one part of the world so as to produce genius – namely, my empirical character. The second sacrament confers more meaning on my existence, however, because I can extend my subjectivity beyond myself into the world, shaping the world in accordance with the aim of culture, such that it reflects culture's shaping power and – insofar as I am part of culture – me. As we become an ever more significant part of culture, giving rise to self-determining geniuses, my life gains ever more value. The less significant the part I play – and indeed the more I turn away from my conscience and ally myself with the obstacles to culture – the less value my existence has.

6C *The obstacles to culture (pp. 218–34)*

In a lengthy final part of this section, Nietzsche discusses the main obstacles to culture that exist in human societies, and in particularly acute form in modern societies. He does so to flesh out the tasks of the second sacrament – what are those obstacles that prevent so many of us now from achieving self-determination? But he also does it in order to justify his claim that only a few human beings ever achieve complete self-realisation. It is important to justify this claim because otherwise it would seem quite unfair to those of us who fail to achieve self-realisation. Nietzsche's claim in what follows is that we prevent ourselves from achieving self-realisation – it is not due to some deficiency of nature. As Kant says in 'What is Enlightenment?', our failure to be free is 'self-incurred'.

Nietzsche also discusses these obstacles here in order to continue to challenge the idea that nature produces exemplary individuals. Indeed, he expressly denies the natural teleology that Hurka's and Ansell-Pearson's aristocratic reading attributes to him. Some in Nietzsche's day argued that there is an 'unconscious purposiveness in nature' that works through human beings to produce a natural end. Nietzsche rejects this natural teleology, seeing all around him evidence of nature's failure to achieve any purpose. The most important evidence is that modernity systematically prevents the emergence of geniuses, treating the latter as if they were engaged in 'incessant cruelty to animals' (218). In his criticism, Nietzsche describes nature as a 'dark, driving, insatiable power', a description that closely resembles his own definition of life in 'Utility and Liability' (106). In denying that nature has any purpose, but that it is in fact indifferent to us, he thereby also denies that life has any normative relevance. In other words, these reflections help us see that the basis of Nietzsche's normative ethics is not in nature or life, as many commentators have held.[17] Nature provides us with no guidance, so we must instead formulate a 'conscious intention' to 'take the place of that "dark drive"' (218). Once again, then, Nietzsche announces the foundation of his ethics in human freedom.

Nietzsche identifies four obstacles to culture. He already mentioned them in section 5, in which he pointed out 'how we hasten to sell our soul to the state, to moneymaking, to social life, or to scholarship' (210). These obstacles to culture are all modern in nature, as Nietzsche is discussing 'those powers' of 'today', those powers that have sought to fill the void of community after the decline of pre-modern traditions and religions. These four obstacles share in common the fact that they do not openly oppose culture, as in the case of barbarism, the contrast to culture that Nietzsche drew in 'David Strauss'. Instead, like the cultural philistines of 'David Strauss', these obstacles 'exploit' culture and end up subverting it. They produce an anti-culture, a false culture masquerading as the genuine thing, thereby preventing its emergence. These powers 'most actively promote culture' while also having 'ulterior motives' (218). They broach no goal 'higher than [their] own welfare and existence' (230–1). In this way, they are doubly nefarious – first, they tempt individuals to evade the call of their conscience and commit their lives to a valueless external force; second, they harness culture and its existential capital, fooling individuals into thinking that they have found a community that can justify their lives. In general, what these powers do is replace the end of culture – the production of genius – with their own end, and press culture into service towards it. This allows culture to flourish to a degree, though it ends up distorted since it serves an external master.

---

[17] See, for instance, Taylor 1997: 91.

1. *The Market*: commercial society takes as its aim 'earthly happiness' for all, and contends that market mechanisms are the best instruments to achieve this happiness (219). The true believers in the market want to reorganise society so as to create 'maximum profit and pleasure', and produce the greatest increase in wealth. The market hence presses culture into service to this end. It uses culture to cultivate 'knowledge and education' in workers so that they can maximise the efficiency of the market (218). Culture serves the market by turning human beings into efficient cogs in the machine of the market. Culture's overall aim, the liberation of human beings, is thereby subverted, producing instead 'refined egoism'. Of course, the market encourages liberated minds of a sort, as it needs smart individuals in order to produce innovative products. However, the type of education it demands must be justified with reference to the market. There is little room for 'general education', but rather 'intelligence and property' must be closely allied (219).

2. *The State*: as we saw in section 4, the state also seeks to hijack culture to serve its self-aggrandising end. The state, like the market, needs intelligent individuals to serve it, and so liberates 'the intellectual energies of a generation to the extent – but only to that extent – that they can serve and be of use to existing institutions'. In this way, culture no longer liberates individuals to self-determination, and it narrows the scope of education only to that knowledge of benefit to the purposes of the state. As such, 'this liberating is at the same time, and to a greater degree, a shackling' (220).

3. *Society*: Nietzsche synthesises some of his discussion from 'David Strauss' and 'Utility and Liability' here. He points out that the desire for social recognition also appropriates culture. In modern culture, we all possess an 'ugly or boring content' to our character (222), developed either from the 'selfishness' of the market, the state, or the chaotic aimlessness of the scholar (224). As such, when we encounter one another in civil society, we need a way to rank one another's excellence. Instead of transforming the content of our character, we 'disguise it behind what is called "beautiful form"'. That is, we put on a beautiful exterior to our character by demonstrating competence with 'piquant

and spicy dishes' from the 'Orient and the Occident' (220), or knowledge of the latest fashion and architecture from France (221). This exterior beauty and the social status that comes with it become ends in themselves, and thus society compels culture into service to it. It demands that education produce individuals who can impress others at dinner parties, not letting 'others notice how wretched and base one is, how predatory in striving, how insatiable in acquiring, how selfish and shameless in enjoying' (223). Nietzsche offers German society after the Franco-Prussian war as a prime example, which has sought to 'escape those ancient obligations imposed upon' German culture 'by his wonderful talent, his peculiar natural inclination for seriousness and profundity' (222). Cultures, like individuals, have a conscience as well that calls them to their own distinctive identity, but these same cultures can evade this call of conscience and give themselves over to the animal pursuit of social recognition.

4. *Scholarship*: Nietzsche devotes a lengthy section (224–30) to scholarship as an obstacle to culture. Scholarship sets as its goal the achievement of knowledge and truth. In some ways, this might seem congenial to culture, but as Nietzsche argued at great length in 'Utility and Liability', modern scientific scholarship undermines, rather than promotes, the conditions for culture. In this section, Nietzsche emphasises the fact that scholarship fails to address the basic phenomenon that drives individuals to culture, 'suffering'. Scholars regard suffering as 'something irrelevant and incomprehensible', not as the basic challenge to existence that must be addressed by culture (224). Furthermore, Nietzsche proceeds to enumerate the many character traits of scholars that drive them to scholarship. It is not the pure pursuit of knowledge, but a sense of curiosity, or loyalty to teachers, and so forth. However, their ultimate pursuit of 'passionless knowledge' prevents them from elevating their character into genius that can be creative, that can 'augment nature with new living nature'. Instead, scholars are 'unfruitful' and 'seek to kill nature, to dissect and understand it' (230). Scholarship prevents culture from achieving its end and producing genius.

In the last few pages, Nietzsche calls for a reform of our educational system such that it takes as its final aim not the end of one of these four powers, but rather the end of culture itself. We must 'replace the fundamental principles of our present educational system – which has its roots in the Middle Ages and imagines the medieval scholar as the goal of perfected education'. In its place we must create a 'new fundamental principle', that of the new modern cultural community. However, the creation of this new culture will not be easy. The call to displace these four powers amounts to a threat to their welfare and existence, and so they will fight to retain their status. Indeed, the very universality of genuine culture and its universal critique of all dogmatic claims threaten the legitimacy of these institutions, challenging the value of their existence. Thus these four powers use the educational system to create 'ranks' of soldiers who 'treat all those who refuse to join the rank and file as enemies' (232). They employ the power of the demos to create social pressure, preventing the emergence of any cultural figure in the first place. This kind of all-encompassing power is even more pernicious than the ancient Athenian authorities who called Socrates to trial. Nietzsche concludes that our 'aversion to originality has increased to such an extent that Socrates would not have been able to live among us and, in any case, would not have reached the age of seventy' (231). Our modern educational system would have squashed the development of the Socratic impulse, killing Socrates effectively in the cradle, not even allowing him to live out 70 years, as Athens did.

7 Modern conditions for fostering genius

After a lengthy discussion of the obstacles to cultivating exemplary individuals, Nietzsche leaves the reader distraught. How could it even be possible to create this new culture? Longing for such a 'distant future' is pointless if these obstacles are so immense. In the final two sections of 'Schopenhauer as Educator', Nietzsche shifts to discuss the 'present conditions' that 'provide for an emerging philosopher so as to make it possible for him to breathe at all'. Nietzsche stresses that now his 'observations [*Betrachtung*] move in the direction of practical and objectionable matters' (234). In particular, Nietzsche reflects most extensively on the modern political conditions that can foster genius.

After his initial promise of 'practical' matters, however, Nietzsche dives in to a long discussion of natural teleology once again. As I argued above, Nietzsche's own commitment to Darwinian natural science renders any such appeal to natural teleology suspect. On the Darwinian view, nature does not have any aims, but rather is indifferent to our fate. Furthermore, it is hard to make sense of Nietzsche's claim that 'the artist and philosopher bear witness against the purposiveness of nature in its means, despite the fact that they provide the most splendid evidence for the wisdom of nature's purposes'. Indeed, if we observe that geniuses are rare in society and have very little 'effect' on it, and instead appear despite obstacles, it seems better to conclude that genius appears 'by chance', not according to the intention of nature (235–6). Moreover, it is not clear what would constitute empirical evidence of the 'wisdom of nature's purposes' if everything seems stacked against the genius. Nevertheless, in a Kantian spirit, we can still regard nature as having aims in order to make sense of our fate in the cosmos. Moreover, this natural teleology can be a heuristic to grasp how we should arrange social and political institutions to foster genius. In my view, section 7's discussion of teleology should be understood in service to this latter purpose.

Nietzsche's heuristic is the following: 'nature always seeks to work for the common good, but it does not know how to find the best and most skillful ways and means to accomplish this purpose: this is nature's great sorrow, the cause of its melancholia' (234). This highly anthropomorphised description casts doubt on the constitutive nature of this natural teleology. However, it serves a useful regulative role in helping us understand our challenge. In Nietzsche's image, nature produces genius, 'expending much too much energy' on it, such that it does not have enough energy to expend on a populace that will properly appreciate the genius. The 'artist' to his 'fans', then, is like 'heavy artillery to a flock of sparrows'. It would be more 'sensible' if nature had cut 'expenditures' on the genius and instead invested it in the populace (235). In this case, a more 'responsive audience composed of people who are stronger and more powerful than the artists themselves'

would have extended the effect of the artwork (236). Or, to put
Nietzsche's heuristic in different terms: human nature is contradictory. On the one hand, our consciences call us to our uniqueness, and on the other public opinion tempts us away from it. This
contradictory nature makes it very difficult for exemplary individuals to shape public opinion. Although our nature evolved in
this way, we can indeed conceive that our nature may have turned
out differently – it may have been the case that the temptations
to ignore our conscience were not quite so strong, such that the
exemplary individual might have an easier time enjoining individuals to follow him according to their own consciences.

However, given nature's 'inexperience', it is crucial for us to
supplement it with wisdom (234–5). Or, in non-anthropomorphic
terms, it is up to us to heal the contradiction of human nature.
We need to find and support social conditions that would heal
this contradiction. However, Nietzsche notes that nature 'evinces'
its 'ineptitude … once again today'. That is, modern conditions
exacerbate the problem of nature's contradiction – the institutions of the state, market, society and scholarship strengthen public
opinion and thus more powerfully tempt us away from our conscience. Nietzsche examines Schopenhauer to find that there are
nevertheless modern conditions that redress this contradiction of
human nature. These conditions do so by helping individuals resist
the temptations of state, market, society and scholarship, or the
'fashionable perversity of the times'. Nietzsche discusses two of
these conditions: 'republicanism' and commerce (238).

The paragraph on pp. 238–9 provides one of the clearest
expressions of Nietzsche's own early political commitments.[18]
Casual readers of Nietzsche's later work might be surprised to
see him approve of the 'proud and free republicanism' expressed
through Schopenhauer's father, which balanced the 'vain aesthete'
character of his mother (238). Republicanism is a broad and multifaceted term in the history of political thought. In this context,
Nietzsche is drawing on the ancient 'Greek' and Roman sense

---

[18] The other clear statement is in the unpublished 'The Greek State'. But see Church
(2015a: ch. 8), for complications of the usual reading of that text.

of republicanism (241), where the republican citizen is characterised by 'unbending and rugged manliness' and self-sufficiency.
Unlike subjects in a monarchy who, like children, depend on their
patriarch, the republican citizen governs himself. The republican
citizen is sceptical of government which can, like a monarch,
take away his liberty. In this regard, Schopenhauer's father was
'numbed' to 'national limitations' and 'did not consider it an honor
to have been born a German'. Nationalism is an important way in
which modern governments accumulate more power over their
citizens. For the republican citizen, the role of government should
be extremely limited: 'the only purpose of the state was to provide protection from internal enemies, protection from external
enemies, and protection from the protectors, and that to ascribe to
the state any purpose other than protection could easily endanger
its true purpose' (238). Political activity by its nature is contrary to
the liberty of the mind, as it forces one to 'serv[e] in a party' and
fight for a faction, not for humanity. As such, the republican citizen recognises the tension between culture and politics, such that
'anyone who has the *furor philosophicus* will have no time whatsoever for the *furor politicus* and will wisely refrain from reading the
newspapers every day' (239). Although the state should be limited,
it nonetheless plays an important role, such that Schopenhauer's
father 'bequeathed his entire fortune to the widows of those Prus-
sian soldiers who had fallen in 1848 in the struggle to maintain
order' (238–9). The citizen will not 'hesitate for a single moment
to take up his position if his fatherland is threatened by a real
danger' (239).

Where does this place Nietzsche's politics? In this paragraph,
he approves of Schopenhauer's liberal republicanism. He approves
of the 'free' self-government of republicanism because it reflects
and fosters the deeper freedom as self-determination in one's
character (238). His admiration of republicanism also helps make
sense of Nietzsche's inclusion of Rousseau as an exemplary individual who modern culture should embrace. Accordingly, his
republicanism certainly entails that he is not a radical aristocrat
aiming to establish a rigid caste system. However, he also approves
of Schopenhauer's support for Prussia against the progressive 'so-
called liberals' in the wake of the revolutions of 1848. In this way,

Nietzsche could not be a radical democrat either. Nor is he anti-political, as several commentators since Walter Kaufmann have argued (Bergmann 1987; Shaw 2007). We might expect Nietzsche to adopt an anti-political stance, since he sharply distinguishes the drive for philosophy from the drive for politics. Nevertheless, he envisions a crucial role for politics in the life of the republican citizen, namely, for bodily protection, a basic precondition for any higher life of culture. Yet he emphatically sees politics as instrumental to the higher aim of culture, not a worthy life in itself – a 'nobler form of humanity is the aim of the state, its purpose lies outside of itself, it is merely the means' (KSA 7.30[8], UW 294).[19] In this way, the early Nietzsche is best understood as a moderate liberal, given his extreme scepticism of a powerful state and his affirmation of republican self-government.

The second beneficial modern condition is equally surprising for Nietzsche readers: commerce. Schopenhauer did not make a living as a young man in the scholarly world and so did not deaden his sensibilities like Kant, who was a 'great thinker' but not a 'genuine human being'. Scholars allow 'concepts, opinions, past events, or books' to 'come between' themselves and the world. Schopenhauer, by contrast, had a more immediate connection to the world as a merchant, where he 'breathed the freer air of a large trading house'. To be self-determining, Nietzsche argues, an individual must 'draw most of his own instruction from out of himself' (239). The freedom from the stifling scholarly world afforded by commerce allowed Schopenhauer to do just this, and he did so by admiring the genius of Goethe, who gave him a 'glimpse' of a 'free and strong human being' (240). Nietzsche does not discuss at any length how commerce can benefit human beings, which is unfortunate given his earlier critique of the cultural corrosion caused by commercial society. It seems, however, that commerce can at least have negative utility in liberating the mind from stultifying scholarly education, as well as providing 'freedom from the narrowness of patriotism' and 'no ties with the state' (241). That is,

---

[19] See Taylor, who claims that 'Nietzsche was not entirely "anti-political"', but saw an important instrumental role for the state (1997: 27).

commerce, though perhaps corrupting in itself, can also serve as a check on state and scholarly corruptions.

8 The independence of culture from politics

Republicanism and commerce help promote genius because they provide what is most needful: 'freedom and nothing but freedom' from the obstacles of state, society and scholarship (241). In this final section, Nietzsche continues his practical observations by examining the role of politics. His observations are not encouraging. He argues not only that the state exists in a perennial conflict with philosophy, but also that the modern state has co-opted philosophy and thereby corrupted it. Politics can do little to advance culture, but rather should stay out of the way.[20] For Nietzsche, it is up to philosophers themselves to create cultural organisations that can demonstrate the value of an independent culture.

What is the role of politics in culture? According to most scholarly readings, Nietzsche follows Plato in arguing that a philosopher-king figure should rule an ideal polity. Section 8 reveals why this interpretation cannot be correct – Nietzsche himself challenges Plato and his 'entirely new state'. The reason is that Plato has been successful in one way, but in another, more important way, not. Plato was successful in convincing thinkers in the Middle Ages and in modernity that we ought to produce 'a system' that 'essentially conformed to his proposals', namely, a state that would let the wise rule. However, Plato was unsuccessful in that every time actual states carried out his aim, the ideal state became a 'hobgoblin'. The 'priestly state' of the Middle Ages and the scholarly state of modernity generate rulers quite opposed to Plato's philosopher. Accordingly, 'experience teaches us better', that politics cannot promote but always subverts the aim of philosophy (242).

---

[20] Based on sections 7–8, I disagree with Lemm's contention that Nietzsche held a view of culture 'as thoroughly public and political' (2007: 13–14). Public, yes, but Nietzsche sharply distinguishes the philosophical from political 'furor'.

Nietzsche does not support the utopian aims of *The Republic*, but he is a follower of Plato on a subtler reading of him. On this reading, Plato identifies a perennial conflict between politics and philosophy, expressed most clearly in *The Apology* (Strauss 1964). The source of the conflict is that the fundamental aims of politics and philosophy – order and truth, respectively – come into conflict with one another. The purpose of politics is to 'provide protection' for our material lives and goods from internal and external enemies (238). To accomplish this aim, however, the state has to ensure that citizens obey the law. The state can ensure this in part through fear, but must also do so by cultivating loyalty. Doing so requires that the state regulate 'religion', banishing and treating 'as an enemy any religion that sets itself above the state and wants to act as its judge' (244). As Rousseau argued in the *Social Contract*, politics requires a civic religion to attach individuals to the laws (2012: 271–2).

The purpose of philosophy, by contrast, is the 'love of truth' and the pursuit of it at all costs (255). As such, the philosopher 'measure[s] everything, including the state, by the standard of truth' (244). Since the state uses myth and religion and other closed horizons – all of which, in Nietzsche's view, do an injustice to the world and hence are untrue – the philosopher's critical eye turns on the state as well, potentially undermining the state's ideological support structure and the basis for the loyalty of the citizenry. The state cannot compel nor bribe the philosopher into service, because 'it is part of truth's very nature never to serve, never to take payment' (251). Accordingly, the 'state is afraid of philosophy as such' (244). This tension between politics and philosophy reduplicates the conflict between love and justice that we saw in 'Utility and Liability' – politics requires erotic commitment to its aims, which entails forgetting the flaws of and alternatives to one's beloved. Philosophy by contrast, seeks truth and so reveals these flaws and alternatives, vitiating the erotic commitment to the state.

For Nietzsche, both politics and philosophy have legitimate claims. Politics must maintain order for philosophy to be possible at all, and philosophy seeks truth in order to perfect our distinctively human natures. Thus, Nietzsche claims that the state is 'justified [*im Recht*] in banishing such a person and treating him as an enemy' if the philosopher threatens the state's aims (244). It appears, then, that we have a tragic conflict, because the conflict involves irreconcilable yet legitimate goods.

How then does this conflict get resolved? Nietzsche argues that ancient and modern states strike a bargain with philosophers. They secure 'freedom' for them to engage in their activity without civic obligation, but they expect something in return, namely, the production of culture. Of course, since the state exempts the philosopher from civic duties, 'every ordinary son of the earth has the right to look with resentment upon someone who is privileged in this way'. The philosopher is thus saddled with the age-old caricature that he is a malingering leech on society. However, the philosopher's 'freedom is really a heavy burden of guilt, and it can only be atoned for by great deeds' in service to the state. It is a 'terrible obligation', because, as we have seen, to discharge one's obligation as an exemplary individual is extremely difficult (241).

The modern state adopts a distinct strategy towards the philosopher. It does so because modern culture has become sceptical of the capacity of myths and religions to secure citizens' loyalty. Modern culture demands instead a rational 'legitimation' of the state (251; cf. Shaw 2007). This legitimation cannot be provided by artists or priests, but rather only by philosophers. The modern state thus purchases philosophers, providing them with a secure income and a position of power. In exchange, the state expects the philosopher to confer 'legitimation and sanctification [on] the state'. The state in this way acts like the 'medieval prince' who 'wanted to be crowned by the pope but could not attain papal assent' and so 'appointed an antipope to perform this service'. State-hired philosophy becomes 'anti-philosophy' (251). Nietzsche employs as the most important example the German universities of his day, in which professorships were state-appointed positions, allowing the 'state' to select 'its own philosophical servants', and 'force' the philosopher to teach certain subjects that legitimised it. The German state defanged philosophy by enjoining it to teach only the 'history of philosophy' rather than philosophy itself (245). The university hence 'crams' the youthful mind with 'fifty systems' and 'fifty critiques of these systems', without any notion of how this philosophy can be connected to life, to 'see if one can live by this philosophy' (246).

By using philosophers in this way, the state not only purchases an ideological legitimation for itself, but also addresses the perennial conflict between politics and philosophy. It does so, however, only by twisting philosophy into its opposite, in which the philosopher is robbed 'of his most glorious freedom, the freedom to follow his genius whenever and wherever it calls him' (245). The state cultivates philosophy not for the 'production of philosophical genius', but rather for the advancement of its own aims. As such, strictly speaking, it does not solve the conflict between politics and philosophy so much as insidiously masquerade false philosophy as true philosophy, pretending that it fosters culture while its 'real goal [is] the prevention of its production' (247). Nietzsche here returns to his 'David Strauss' claim that German culture has become not barbarism but anti-culture, unified only in its aim of suppressing genuine culture. He reads many of the developments in neo-Kantian philosophy as evidence of this anti-philosophy and anti-culture: 'recently' neo-Kantians 'have begun to take pleasure in maintaining that they are actually only the border guards and watchmen of the learned disciplines; to this end they are served especially well by Kantian doctrine, which they are intent on making an idle skepticism to which soon no one will even pay attention' (248).

This 'swarm of bad philosophers', mercenaries of the intellect, are 'ridiculous'. However, Nietzsche worries that they are also 'harmful', because they make 'philosophy' in general 'into something ridiculous' (250). Human beings in general cannot distinguish true from false philosophy, and so defer to the state's judgement. What they find is a highly technical discipline divorced from the concerns of life. Far from being the unsettling danger to political and social order that Socrates represented, philosophy appears utterly useless. However, this general judgement is harmful because it makes the retrieval of genuine culture and philosophy much more difficult. Who among the youth will dream of becoming a philosopher?

At the same time, Nietzsche suggests, the impotence of modern philosophy may represent an opportunity for the rebirth of culture. First, because of philosophy's ridiculousness, the 'state no longer needs to be sanctioned by philosophy; as a result, philosophy has become dispensable for the state'. Given the great monetary expense of the university, Nietzsche counsels the modern state that it would be in its best interest to 'cease to maintain its professorships' (252). If the state removes itself from the business of philosophy, this would reintroduce the independence necessary for culture, meeting the 'requirement of culture that it eliminate from philosophy every form of state and academic recognition' (250).

Second and more importantly, the current impotence of philosophy gives genuine philosophers an opportunity to demonstrate the difference between true and false philosophy, to remind the public once again what true culture is and what is its value. This is no easy task, for all the reasons we have seen thus far, such that the 'dignity of philosophy has been trampled under foot'. The task of philosophy's 'true friends' must be to 'testify against this confusion' between true and false philosophy and 'at the very least to demonstrate that it is only those false servants and undignitaries of philosophy who are ridiculous or irrelevant'. These friends should establish a 'higher tribunal' that is 'outside the universities', dedicated to overseeing and judging current universities 'with regard to the education they promote' (253). This will allow university philosophy no longer to be a handmaid to the state, but rather to be committed to preparing the way for culture. Once again, Nietzsche argues that much of the task for the free spirit will be preparatory work, clearing the ground of the obstacles to genuine culture.

However, philosophers must nevertheless 'prove through their actions that love of truth is something terrible and powerful', as Schopenhauer did. In its essence, philosophy legislates a new system of values for a people, giving them a new way of understanding the value and significance of their lives. Nietzsche quotes Ralph Waldo Emerson's essay 'Circles' to the effect that true philosophy is thus powerful and even revolutionary, as it 'would instantly revolutionize the entire system of human pursuits'. Nietzsche emphasises here the power and terror and 'dangerous' character of the philosophers, but it is crucial to remember that these philosophers act fundamentally out of the debt that they owe to the community for making their activity possible (255). The philosopher does not remake the world solely for his own good, or at the expense of us. On the contrary, he remakes the moral world so as to create a genuine culture that will redeem our lives, grounding the value of existence. As Nietzsche puts it in a draft of section 7, the aim of the philosopher is the 'well-being of a people and an age, perhaps also . . . all peoples and all ages' (KSA 7.29[218], UW 278).

However, at the same time the terror and danger of the future philosopher revive once again the conflict between politics and philosophy suppressed by the modern state. Nietzsche ultimately suggests that this tragic conflict is insurmountable. Indeed, he insists that 'if philosophy becomes aggressive and dangerous' to the state, then 'the state may persecute it' (251). Furthermore, it might be good for philosophers to once again be persecuted, because then they will re-commit themselves to their vocation and 'you will behold miracles!' (250). Nevertheless, the fact that Nietzsche castigates the scholarly world, university philosophy and the ideologues in support of the state, but not the policies of Prussia and Otto von Bismarck as he does in his letters, indicates that he recognises the importance of prudence on the part of the philosopher. The philosopher, after all, can only successfully revalue all values if he is alive, not tortured or executed by state officials. The philosopher may have to cloak his true views of the state under the guise of a critique of the state's lackeys, for instance. The philosopher can also pay his debt to the state and so appease it by fostering a unique national cultural excellence, allowing the state to take pride in its culture. More generally, culture must cater to the spiritual health of the people in such a way that it maintains its independence from state concerns, not infringing on the state's territory such that the state's efforts are undermined. In this way, Nietzsche's vision of culture is not that of free-wheeling freedom of expression and 'experiments in living' à la John Stuart Mill, but one that prudently maintains the separation of politics from philosophy.

5
Richard Wagner in Bayreuth

The fourth part of the *Observations*, like the first, remains largely neglected among Nietzsche scholars. The primary scholarly focus on this essay has been biographical – namely, scholars have analysed it for clues as to Nietzsche's changing relationship with Wagner. As I pointed out in the Introduction, from 1874 onward Nietzsche became increasingly ambivalent about Wagner, and this essay is a product of 1875–76. In his *Nachlass* from 1874, for instance, Nietzsche makes celebratory comments about Wagner – for instance, he has a 'legislative nature' (KSA 7.32[10], UW 315), he 'has a sense for unity in diversity – that is why I consider him a bearer of culture' (KSA 7.32[12], UW 316). All these claims reappear in the published essay. On the other hand, Nietzsche critiques Wagner for his 'lack of restraint', and he expresses 'doubts about whether Wagner has musical talent' (KSA 7.32[15], UW 317–8); Wagner is 'incapable of any charm, delicacy, and dialectical rigor' (KSA 7.32[30], UW 322). These critical comments do not find their way into the *Observations*.

Our main concern here, however, is not with Nietzsche's biography but with his philosophy. In the latter context, 'Richard Wagner' represents, I will argue, the culmination of Nietzsche's positive argument. 'Schopenhauer as Educator' served to establish the positive condition for a renewal of culture, and so 'Richard Wagner' describes the exemplary individual – Wagner himself – who fosters an improved German culture and provides hope for humanity's redemption. Wagner's character was formed by the corrupt modern culture around him, as was Nietzsche's own character, as he himself confesses (158). What is most amazing about Wagner is that he demonstrates an ability to transcend this culture despite its many obstacles. Modernity provides Wagner with a depth and breadth of work and character unparalleled in the history of art.

Structural overview

1   The tasks of the audience
2–3   Wagner's character (his 'becoming', according to Nietzsche's outline (KSA 8.11[47))
4–7   Wagner's freedom (his 'being and the expression of his power' (KSA 8.11[47])
8–10   Wagner's life, art and influence (his 'future' (KSA 8.11[47])
11   Exhortation to audience

1 The tasks of the unfashionable audience

In the previous chapter, I discussed how the opening sections of 'Utility and Liability' and 'Schopenhauer as Educator' reflected one another. The first section of 'Richard Wagner' also reflects 'David Strauss', as we would expect, given the mirrored structure of the overall work. The topic of the opening section of 'David Strauss' was a political event in 1871 that strengthened the cultivated philistines and corrupted German culture. The opening section of 'Richard Wagner' concerns a cultural event in 1872 – the founding of the Bayreuth Festival – that justifies 'faith' in a better, indeed, 'great future' in which the 'cultivated' [*Gebildete*] are soundly defeated (260–2). David Strauss represents for Nietzsche the champion of the ascendant anti-culture, while Richard Wagner is the 'prophetic' figure for the promise of 'resurrected art' and culture (261).

The main difference between this first section of 'Richard Wagner' and the previous *Observations* is that Nietzsche broadens the scope of who is 'unfashionable' from Nietzsche himself to 'all those who attend the Bayreuth Festival' (260). In this way, *Unfashionable Observations* shifts from Nietzsche's solitary reflections to a growing community of like-minded critics, a shift from the 'I' to the 'we' that makes the *Observations* a hopeful book. Indeed, the *Observations* portrays a maturation process in its audience – in 'David Strauss', Nietzsche announces his withdrawal from fashionable culture, and in 'Utility and Liability' he reaches out to the youth as his audience and as the future of culture. 'Schopenhauer as Educator' describes the education that the youth would require to become consecrated to the tasks of culture. Finally, 'Richard Wagner' opens with the maturation of that youth, who are ready to fight with Nietzsche for the future of culture. Now they need a particular focus and direction.

The first section, then, is a call to action for his sympathetic audience to assist in the advancement of culture. As we saw in 'Utility and Liability', Nietzsche rejects the Hegelian idea that history has a necessary purpose, and so human beings are capable of changing their fate. Indeed, even a few 'hundred' can do the trick (131). Furthermore, Nietzsche also rejects here and elsewhere a 'great man' view of history, according to which individuals alone direct history. He announces at the beginning that, 'for an event to be great, two things must come together: the great sensibility [*Sinn*] of those who create it, and the great sensibility of those who experience it'. The monumental founder who Nietzsche introduced in section 2 of 'Utility and Liability' effects great deeds. However, the people who receive these deeds must also be 'worthy' [*würdig*] of them. Otherwise, even if 'vast states are founded', the 'breath of history' will blow them away, as no one will exist to transmit the deeds of the cultural founder (259).

Nietzsche is quite clear here, then, that the people matter just as much as the great individuals, contradicting many scholars who have concluded that, for Nietzsche, the lives of nobody except the exemplar matter. There must be a 'correspondence between an action and its reception'. One condition for greatness, Nietzsche suggests here, is that the founding individual understands and creates an audience. He knows not just how to act, but when to act, when the 'necessary' moment is (259). In this way, the exemplary individual cannot be monomaniacally and selfishly devoted only to his own greatness, as is suggested by some readings of Nietzsche. Furthermore, the people can also be 'great' in possessing a 'great sensibility', a properly honed judgement to distinguish between the truly exemplary and the hollowness of the philistine

(260). Wagner had 'faith' not only in the 'greatness of his action' but also in the 'great sensibility' of those he chose to be at the founding moment of the Bayreuth Festival on 22 May 1872 (260). This group of people, Nietzsche claims, should 'feel pride' in their greatness, in the fact that a great individual needs 'their support' and 'sympathy' (260). Indeed, he proceeds to argue, the 'spectator is a spectacle worth seeing', not just the works of the great man. This group of 'unfashionable people' are like a 'warm current . . . rising up from other, from deeper sources' that provides cultural support for Wagner's great art (260).

In the last two pages of the section, Nietzsche discusses two ways in which Wagner needs help. First, there are many powerful people hostile to Wagner's project, a group we were introduced to in 'David Strauss' – the 'cultivated person[s]' [*Gebildete*]. Thus far, in large part, these philistines – the 'jeering journalists' – have engaged in a 'parody' of Wagner's work. Nietzsche hopes that this 'levity and laughter go on yet for a little while', because parody is harmless to the prospects of Wagner's cultural success. However, this ridicule hides a 'spirit of alienation [*Entfremdung*] and hostility [*Feindseligkeit*]' that the philistines feel just below the surface, a spirit that Nietzsche hopes will stay buried. This spirit stems from the democratic sensibility of the philistines that we explored in 'David Strauss', which objects to the rule of a single genius. Here, this sensibility manifests itself in the desire for a 'gradual development' in the arts, which is radically challenged by Wagner's revolutionary artistic innovations, which threaten to devalue all previous modern art as mere 'luxury items', and are 'prophetic' of the 'imminent demise of the arts' (261).

In response to ridicule, the 'disciples of resurrected art' should not publicly defend Wagner, lest the parody turns serious (261). Instead, Wagner's unfashionable supporters should maintain 'silence' and 'purify' themselves of the 'repulsive idolatry of modern cultivation'. Instead of defeating the philistines in public, they should defeat philistinism in themselves by devoting their energies to a deeper understanding of Wagner's artistic significance and the 'great future' that his work promises (262).

Wagner's first need, then, is a negative one, an inner purging of the corrupt features of modern culture that Nietzsche has been discussing in the *Observations*. The second is positive, and indeed motivates the work as a whole. For Nietzsche, the audience must come to understand the 'greatness of his deed', namely, the founding of the Bayreuth Festival. To grasp its greatness, the audience must see how it is a focal point of Wagner's life – which Nietzsche compares to a similar moment in the life of another founder, Alexander the Great – in which it becomes clear 'how he had become what he is, what he will be'. Indeed, this is the task of the essay, to trace the genesis and development of Wagner's character to the present, in order to comprehend its exemplary significance. With this understanding of Wagner's founding moment, the unfashionable audience can 'vouch for its fruitfulness [*Fruchtbarkeit*]' (262). This attesting to his significance is Wagner's second need. That is, Wagner requires a group to recognise the greatness of his work and transmit it to a new generation. If the first need was to clear the ground, this second need consists in the planting of the seed for a new culture.

2 Wagner's two drives

Nietzsche begins his discussion of Wagner's development with a general theory about the character of exemplary individuals, those with 'outstanding talent' (262). Namely, the lives of these individuals will possess a pervasive unity or wholeness, a claim that we have seen in previous essays. Their 'life' will become 'the reflection of their character, but also above all the reflection of their intellect and their own particular abilities. The life of the epic poet will have something of an epic quality' (262–3). By contrast, ordinary individuals will lead lives riven by many different influences and fragmented by many features, and so they will not demonstrate this unity. Throughout the *Observations*, Nietzsche argues that this unity is normatively valuable because it expresses free self-determination, whereas fragmentation reveals heteronomy. The same is true here, as Wagner is described as 'free' (266).

However, Wagner's 'childhood and youth' did not demonstrate this unity of character (263). Rather, Nietzsche argues that Wagner was a product of the same modern culture that he describes in 'Utility and Liability'. He was born and raised in a 'university town' in which he merely 'toyed with intellectual pursuits' and so 'his feelings were easily aroused, but remained satisfied only in shallow ways'. The 'diversity of modern life' afflicted Wagner, along with all modern people, with a 'restless, irritable spirit, a nervous haste in seizing upon a hundred different things' (263–4). The fragmentation of modern culture was like a 'violent childhood illness' in him, such that he could not experience the simplicity or 'naiveté' of childhood (264). As Nietzsche points out in 'Utility and Liability', modern culture's reflectiveness and fragmentation generate individuals who are born into old age. They have no wonder, no immersion in the natural world, and indeed this naiveté has to be achieved 'only late in life' (264).

Wagner's impressive achievement was to do what seemed impossible in 'Utility and Liability', to forge a unity of character out of his fragmented inheritance from modern culture. Wagner 'achieves his intellectual and moral [*geistige und sittliche*] manhood', Nietzsche claims, when a single 'ruling passion [*Leidenschaft*] attains self-awareness and takes possession of his entire being' (263–4). At this point, the 'often quixotic trajectory of his plans is now governed by a single inner law [*Gesetzlichkeit*], a will that makes them explicable' (263). Nietzsche does not identify this passion that follows an inner law, but it becomes clear by the end of the section that Wagner's distinctive longing is for 'purification' (265).

To understand Nietzsche's account of Wagner's character, we must first recognise the type of exemplary character that Wagner represents. He writes music dramas, and so 'the life of the dramatist will take dramatic form' (263). The dramatic form of Wagner's life is that his character is 'simplified in a terrible way, torn between two drives [*Triebe*] or two sides [*Sphären*]' (264). The drama hence consists in the conflict and the attempt at a reconciliation of these two drives.

The first drive comes from 'below', where 'there rages the rapid current of a violent will that seeks out, as it were, all paths, crevices, and ravines to bring itself to light and that desires power [*Macht*]'. It is a 'limitless, tyrannical desire' (264). This drive resembles the 'shaping power' from 'Utility and Liability' in that both seek to rule or to govern the world by reshaping it in one's own image. However, Wagner's drive for 'power' is distinct in that it is hidden from sight and aims to manifest itself, and it is inexhaustible. As scholars have recognised, Wagner's drive for power prefigures Nietzsche's late period theory of the will to power (Hollingdale 1999: 105).

The second drive 'descended upon Wagner' from above and 'consolingly covered him with its wings; it showed him the way'. This 'spirit' [*Geist*] is 'full of love' and is characterised as a drive towards 'free, selfless love', or the 'creative, innocent, bright side' of his nature (265–6). In 'Utility and Liability', we saw that Nietzsche understood love to be the desire for wholeness, to submit one's will to a partnership in common with others – whether a lover, or friend, or community member. By connecting Wagner's second drive back to Nietzsche's theory of love, we can also then pair Wagner's first drive with Nietzsche's theory of perfection and justice. For Nietzsche, what is distinctive to human beings is our capacity for our will to transcend any given order, not to submit to anything, but to subject everything to ruthless criticism. The division in Wagner's character thus represents in a dramatic way the basic contradiction of human nature that Nietzsche has been exploring thus far. In addition, Wagner's drive for power also helps explain the genesis of the desire for perfection and justice, thus connecting the dark drive of life with the distinctively human in a way that Nietzsche has up to now left unclear.

How can these two drives be reconciled? Most individuals are not able to reconcile the drive for power and for love. Most of us 'direct' the drive for power in 'narrow' and unsuccessful ways, and so this frustrated drive leads us to become 'embittered' or to blame others, and even 'turn savage' (264–5). Wagner, by contrast, succeeds by turning this drive for power inward, akin to those 'hermits and monks' who chased 'after their own moral purification'. That is, Wagner's drive for power is satisfied through tyrannising himself, by submitting himself to a difficult law and 'moral nobility'. Nietzsche describes this as the 'process of purification', according to which Wagner moves progressively from tyranny over the outside world to control over his inner world. According to Nietzsche, this dramatic sublimation of his tyrannical drive is reflected in the characters of his music dramas. From 'Rienzi' through finally 'Wotan', we see an 'underground stream of moral nobility and grandeur that progressively flows ever clearer and purer' (265). At first, the characters start 'in darkness and restlessness', and seek 'satisfaction' by tyrannising the outside world with 'power and intoxicating pleasure'. The frustration of this narrow drive for external power eventually leads to the attempt to 'throw off his burden ... to forget, deny, renounce', that is, to exert tyrannical control over the desire for tyranny. At the pinnacle of this development, Nietzsche contends, Wagner and his characters submit themselves to their own law of 'fidelity, selfless fidelity [*Treue*]' (266).

Nietzsche's word here – *Treue*, translated as 'fidelity' – means literally to be true [*treu*] to someone. Accordingly, by using fidelity, Nietzsche connects his discussion back to the will to truth in 'Utility and Liability' which is so hard to control in modern culture. The desire for truth is a distinctively human feature and expresses our desire for perfection and justice. In this way, Nietzsche does not seek to reject this drive and suggest that we wilfully blind ourselves, since doing so would sacrifice our humanity. As we have seen, in the *Observations*, Nietzsche finds different ways to satisfy our desire for perfection. Wagner here provides another ethical model. Wagner constructs particular roles that require self-sacrifice, such as 'brother to sister, friend to friend, servant to master', and then dramatises characters who remain unconditionally true to the law guiding these actions. They exert tyrannical control over any attempt to evade duty or rationalise away self-sacrifice, which confers on them the 'sublime' character of soaring above any danger and all-too-human temptation to think of themselves first (266). In this way once again, Nietzsche adopts a Kantian turn in his ethics, arguing that the highest truths can be obtained not through theoretical metaphysics, but through practical autonomy, by being true to the law we have created for ourselves.

The sublimation of the tyrannical drive does not simply reconcile it with Wagner's drive for 'free, selfless love'. The two drives become ultimately identified, as fidelity to spouse or friend or master merges with love of the spouse or friend or master. Love and justice, wholeness and perfection are unified. Love, however, also confers on self-mastery a grace, as Schiller held eighty years before in 'On Grace and Dignity'. The 'creative, innocent, bright side' of Wagner's character could express the 'fullness of his gratitude' to his nature for achieving this self-mastery. It does so by 'giving', that is, by making self-mastery appear not as a hellish prison, but as something freely obtained and freely given to the audience. In this way, the free spirit ultimately becomes the governing law in Wagner's character – Nietzsche mentions the 'submission' of the dark drive to the free drive at the beginning of the next section – since the free drive exemplifies the moral nobility achieved through self-mastery (267). At the same time, this free spirit 'remained faithful to the dark, uncontrollable, and tyrannical one' (266).

Nietzsche describes this sublimation of the tyrannical drive with a spatial metaphor – from low to high – familiar already from 'Schopenhauer as Educator'. Recall that in the first section of that essay Nietzsche envisioned the development of the self to be one from our dark inner nature to 'immeasurably high above you' (174). We now see more clearly how Nietzsche justifies the normative distinction between high and low, or noble and base. Namely, it concerns the degree to which we internalise our drive to shape and control the world. As we internalise this drive, we expand our inner world, because we construct an ideal subject to dominate our animalistic drive to dominate others. The conflict between our ideal drive for self-control and our animal drive for control over others deepens and enriches our self.

This dynamic process also helps us to understand Nietzsche's Kantian use of the terms sublime [*Erhabene*] here in 'Richard Wagner' and throughout the *Observations*.[1] The sublime, for Kant, consists in our awareness of practical reason's ability to transcend all dangers and temptations of nature (CJ 5:264). Wagner's ascent to 'moral nobility' places him even higher, such that 'even the sublime, lie[s] far below' (266). Earlier in the *Observations*, Nietzsche employs the sublime to describe our feeling about the human capacity to transcend and obey laws of our own making. In the discussion of the monumental individual in 'Utility and Liability', Nietzsche discusses the 'sublime derision' of the great individual towards those who regard this animal 'span of time with such greed

---

[1] See Ansell-Pearson (2013) for a thorough analysis of Nietzsche's use of the sublime in the *Observations*.

and gloomy earnest' (98). Nietzsche bemoans modern individuals who cannot 'hold on to the sublime', since the 'greatest and most wonderful things' cannot be transmitted to the next generation (116). In 'Schopenhauer as Educator', Nietzsche describes that 'most sublime order of philosophers, artists, and saints', who have transcended animality and lead true human lives (214). Nietzsche's use of the notion of sublime throughout the *Observations* reveals a further debt to Kant.

3 Wagner's struggle with modern culture

In the previous section we saw that Wagner was a product of our diseased modern culture. In this section, Nietzsche examines Wagner's struggle with modern culture as he tried to remain 'faithful to his higher self' (273). He focuses on two features of modern culture: first, its diverse temptations for power and pleasure, and second, its deadening, encyclopaedic approach to history and philosophy.

First, Nietzsche adumbrates some moments from Wagner's early career to discuss the 'temptations' of the modern state, economy and society for him. To make ends meet, Wagner had to assume an 'official position' in a 'post' as 'concertmaster in city and court theaters', as, for instance he did in Dresden as the Royal Saxon Court conductor from 1843 until his exile after the 1848 revolution. These positions, Nietzsche claims, drove Wagner to seek to 'achieve honor and power' through them (267). However, these 'modern institutions' are 'principally structured around frivolity and demand frivolity', and so 'disgust overtakes him and he seeks to flee' as he did to Switzerland after Dresden (268). He then seeks a new position and the cycle repeats itself. The general problem, then, is that Wagner's two drives 'strove to reach the immeasurable', and modern culture provided many more temptations for these drives than any previous culture. The drive for power could find a multitude of outlets in state, economy and society, and the desire for love could find 'self-seeking contentment characteristic of contemporary human beings' anywhere. Under these conditions, it was difficult to 'remain faithful' to his ability 'to remain whole' and true to himself (267).

Nevertheless, Wagner turned this feature of modern culture to his advantage. He dramatised this struggle for wholeness and modernity's many temptations in *Tannhäuser* (267). Furthermore, his inability to achieve victory over these modern conditions 'tortured him like thorns'. It drove his 'imagination' to expand itself capaciously in order to master the breadth of modern culture. Thus, as his 'life became ever more complex', he developed 'bolder, more inventive ... dramatic makeshifts' in order to govern this complexity (268).

Second, Wagner read voraciously in history and philosophy. History was a 'danger' for Wagner, as we saw in the second *Observation*, as modern historians value the accumulation of facts over the purposes of life. However, Wagner's work did not succumb to this danger, even as he learned more and more about German history to incorporate into his music dramas. On the contrary, even as the accumulation of historical knowledge made the 'edifice' of his thought 'larger and heavier', it did not collapse, but rather 'the greater becomes the tension on the arch of his ordering and dominating thought' (269). He was able to incorporate the immense historical knowledge of modernity by adopting the 'relationship the Greeks had to myth'. That is, 'history becomes malleable clay in his hands', and he 'shapes or poeticizes' history. Nietzsche does not mean here that Wagner falsifies history, but rather that he adopts a suprahistorical point of view, according to which 'he can poetically infuse the individual event with the typical aspects of entire ages and thereby achieve in his representation a truth that the historian can never achieve' (270). As we saw in 'Utility and Liability', the suprahistorical individual synthesises broad patterns or types out of the myriad data of history. This synthetic activity Nietzsche sees as an artistic activity, as he argued in section 6 of 'Utility and Liability'. There, Nietzsche longed for a true historian who would be up to the task of synthesising the wealth of history that modernity has provided. Wagner represents the best example for the early Nietzsche of the individual who is up to this challenge.

In his final few pages on Wagner's reading of philosophy, Nietzsche builds on his critique of the Hegelian spirit from 'Utility and Liability'. The problem with Hegelian philosophy is that it is a 'disguised Christian theodicy', celebrating the achievements of the present and thus serving as an 'opiate against everything subversive and revitalizing' (272). Nietzsche builds on his critique by pointing out that this Hegelian philosophy makes the German people susceptible to 'enervation' and to 'regression and weakness, so that they then are dangerously vulnerable to every fever to which they are exposed, for instance, to the political fever' (271). Anyone claiming to represent the rationality of the actual will gain unquestioning, passive devotion. What Wagner does – and what Nietzsche agrees with – is to reject the Hegelian account of the necessary development of history, and so make possible and arouse human agency. As such, Wagner turns to philosophy to distinguish between what is necessary – 'which things possess an unalterable nature and form' – and what is contingent, so that 'we' – Wagner, Nietzsche and his unfashionable audience – can 'with relentless courage set about the *improvement of that aspect of the world recognized as being alterable*' (272, original emphasis).

4 Art and the tragic justification of existence

Having discussed Wagner's 'becoming' in the previous two sections (KSA 8.11[47]), Nietzsche now begins to take stock of his significance, and in doing so reminds his audience of its role. In the first part of this section, Nietzsche locates Wagner's significance within the broad 'development of culture since the Greeks'. Nietzsche's philosophy of history is, as we have seen in 'Utility and Liability', explicitly anti-Hegelian. He rejects Hegel's claim that history necessarily progresses in one direction, claiming instead that history is shot through with contingency and retrogression. He adds here some substance to that philosophy of history. According to Nietzsche, there have been two great cultural forces at work in the world in the past 2,500 years, the 'Hellenic' and the 'Oriental'. He understands the 'task of Alexander the Great' to have been the 'Hellenization of the world'. In carrying out this first task, however, Alexander brought back influences from the East and so effected the 'Orientalization of the Hellenic'. These two forces have struggled over culture in the past several millennia. At first, the Hellenic was victorious, but eventually the 'Oriental' won by transforming itself into 'Christianity', which brought the former 'to its logical conclusion'. Like several of his contemporaries, the early Nietzsche understood Christianity's other-worldliness to stem from Plato's prioritising of ideal forms, which in turn came from the influence on Plato from the East. With the 'waning' of Christianity in modernity, we are beginning to see the re-emergence of the Hellenic, such that 'there are such affinities and kinships between Kant and the Eleatics, between Schopenhauer and Empedocles, between Aeschylus and Richard Wagner'. Rather than moving inexorably in one direction, history is like a 'pendulum' that moves between these cultural forces (273).

Unfortunately, the struggle of the Hellenic and the 'Oriental' is not the only battle that has characterised Western culture. As Nietzsche has discussed, we have also seen the rise of modernity in culture, which means that all features of culture are 'infinitely dispersed in our present-day world'. There is no centre or unity to modern culture, but it is fragmented, weak and 'ghostly'. What is most needful, then, is for someone to 'bring together the most manifold and distant points of knowledge', to unify our culture's Hellenic and 'Oriental' forces. Wagner is this figure, for Nietzsche. Unlike Alexander, who dispersed these cultural forces to the far reaches of the earth, we now need a 'counter-Alexander' to 'consolidate and connect, to pull together the most distant threads and prevent the fabric from fraying' (274). As an Alexander figure, Wagner is not simply an exemplar to bind together German culture. His character has a much more comprehensive reach. In this way, he resembles the modern exemplars of 'Schopenhauer as Educator', namely, Rousseau, Goethe and Schopenhauer, whose cosmopolitan exemplarity was made necessary and possible by the universal scope of modernity.

For Nietzsche, Wagner unifies modern culture because he is a 'simplifier of the world', drawing together in his music dramas myth, history, religion and philosophy, all within a self-enclosed artistic whole, his famous *Gesamtkunstwerk*, or the complete work of art that synthesises all genres of art into one. To illustrate Wagner's unifying effort, Nietzsche focuses on a particular example, Wagner's 'reformation of the theater' (274). He paints a rather depressing picture of the modern theatre, whose purpose seems wholly for 'amusement, for entertainment at any price, pedantic considerations, pomposity ... brutal greed for profit', all for a 'society that attends theater performances and concerts without ever being reminded of its obligations' (275). In contrast to the modern theatre, Nietzsche offers the example of the 'Greek theater' whose function was to elevate and educate the audience, and remind them of their civic obligations. Bayreuth promises the retrieval of the Greek model of theatre (276).

In the remainder of the section, Nietzsche pivots to address the unfashionable audience once again. He repeats his call for this audience to assist Wagner in combating the modern theatre and its 'cultivated' defenders, and to usher in Wagner's transformation. Fortunately, Nietzsche points out to his audience, there is reason for hope. The cultivated philistines have not defeated Wagner and instead have 'revealed that they are weak'. The 'edifice of education' supporting modern culture 'has been found to be rotting', indeed by Nietzsche himself in his previous *Observations*. Even the 'spheres of violence and injustice, state and society' are 'weak and exhausted'. These features all suggest that modern culture is crumbling and that 'the time is rife for those who wish to conquer and to triumph powerfully' (277).

However, just because modern culture is diseased does not mean his audience should support Wagner and Nietzsche. In the last two pages, Nietzsche discusses once again the justification of human existence, and argues that the 'morning consecration' to Wagner's art on this 'day of battle' is a valuable life (277). As with Nietzsche's previous justifications of existence, this one begins with the challenge to natural existence. 'Everywhere', Nietzsche claims, the 'individual finds only his personal inadequacy, his partial or complete incapacity'. This inadequacy means that we are susceptible to the 'great suffering that exists for the individual', caused by 'the lack of a knowledge shared by all human beings, the lack of certainty in ultimate insights, and the disparity in abilities'. Nietzsche connects this critique of existence back to his earlier one in 'Utility and Liability', that natural existence prevents us from satisfying our needs for wholeness and perfection, or 'love and justice'. First, 'we cannot be happy' or whole because 'everything around us is suffering'. Second, 'we cannot be moral' or

perfect our natures 'as long as the course of human events is determined by violence, deceit, and injustice'. Finally, 'we cannot even
be wise' and find a path to reconcile our divided nature, since
'humanity has not entered the competition for wisdom' in the
form of exemplary individuals (278).

Just as in section 6 of 'Schopenhauer as Educator', here too
Nietzsche argues that to meet this challenge, the individual has to
be 'consecrated to something suprapersonal' (278–9). Also as in that
section, Nietzsche here argues that all individuals can accomplish
this consecration – it is not just for the few. In this section, however,
he develops his account by claiming that this consecration amounts
to adopting a 'tragic disposition'. This consecration is tragic because
it involves self-sacrifice and even perhaps the death of one's bodily
frame. However, tragedy 'compensates' us for the 'terrible anxiety
that death and time' or becoming 'cause' us, in that through our
consecration we 'can encounter something sacred'. Indeed, tragedy
helps the human race as a whole come to grips with the possibility
that 'all of humanity should have to perish', which is possible in the
passing away of all things. As such, this tragic consecration is not
simply for oneself, but for the 'goal of growing together into oneness and commonality so that it can confront its impending doom
as a whole and with a tragic disposition' (279). Indeed, if we lost
this tragic consecration, it would be the 'bleakest picture imagina-
ble to a friend of humanity', since the value of humanity's existence
relies on such consecration (280). We must, Nietzsche exclaims,
'prevent the tragic disposition from dying out' (280, original emphasis).

What is the 'sacred' that this tragic disposition celebrates, and
how does it justify existence? We have already seen in 'Schopenhauer as Educator' Nietzsche's account of the sacred character of
the philosopher's exemplary personality. In this section, he discusses instead the sacred character and role of art. Art does not
have an immediate utility or educate for 'immediate action'. Nor,
however, does it portray 'objects' that are 'worth striving for in and
of themselves'. Strikingly, Nietzsche argues that 'in real life' the
objects pursued by characters in artistic works 'are rarely deserving
of the same value and effort'. Art, in short, serves no didactic role,
but is a kind of 'dream', in which we 'feel transfixed by the spell of
art' and the 'value of things is altered'. Most importantly, art offers

a '*semblance* [*Schein*] of a simpler world, of an easier solution to the riddles of life'. In this sense, art's 'greatness' and sacredness consist in the fact that it is a creation of the freedom of human beings in which we simplify the world, and create an eternal artificial world outside the 'real world' that human beings in all times and places can appreciate (279).

Yet if art does not serve a purpose in the real world, what does it do? Nietzsche argues that art serves as a kind of respite from the toils of the real world – 'no one who suffers from life can do without this semblance, just as no one can do without sleep'. We need this respite because the 'more difficult our knowledge of the laws of life becomes, the more ardently we desire that semblance of simplification'. We need this simplification, in other words, to ease the 'tension between the universal knowledge of things and the intellectual-moral capacity of the individual. Art exists *so that the bow does not break*' (279, original emphasis). In a way, Nietzsche is thinking about the function of art as Aristotle conceived of leisure, which is to serve as a respite from the toils of life. Unlike Aristotelian leisure, which is private and subjective, Nietzsche envisions art as conferring a 'suprapersonal and universal pleasure'. This pleasure allows us to share in the 'rejoicing of humanity at the guaranteed cohesion and continuation of all that is fundamentally human' (280). In other words, the respite that artworks provide us with also gives us a glimpse of the sacred human freedom, our species' capacity to transcend nature and becoming and tarry with something eternal.

This section on the 'semblance' of artwork has garnered interest from some commentators, who see it as evidence of Nietzsche's changing assessment of the value of myth and illusion. Indeed, 'Richard Wagner' is the last piece of writing from his early period, and so scholars see it as a transitional work to his middle period positivism and naturalism. For instance, Julian Young argues that in the essay, Nietzsche undergoes a 'profound shift' in his assessment of illusion or *Wahn* that is so central to Wagner's thought. Before this essay, Nietzsche insisted on the importance of myth and illusion, and in this essay he reveals illusion for what it is, claiming that there is 'no metaphysical domain beyond the everyday world of individuals' (2010: 221).

However, as we have seen in the *Observations*, Nietzsche does not celebrate myth and illusion. On the contrary, in 'Utility and Liability' Nietzsche holds that illusions can no longer serve the salutary purpose they once did, because all myths have been revealed to be groundless. In this way, the *Observations* has a consistent view of illusion, not an evolving one. Moreover, it is important to recognise the distinctive context here in which Nietzsche discusses illusion, namely, the context of the function of the work of art. He does not employ Wagner's favoured term – *Wahn* or 'delusion' – but rather Schiller's term *Schein* or 'illusion'. Illusion is in a way a bad translation of Schiller's concept, because it implies that there is a reality that the illusion is masking. On the contrary, for Schiller as for Nietzsche, the work of art creates a self-standing world in which human beings can immerse themselves, which is not meant to apply to or represent the real world outside it. Even in this sense, then, we do not see Nietzsche adopting a more hostile or even ambivalent assessment of illusion. On the contrary, he celebrates illusion, and is also clear-eyed that we should not replace truth with illusion (as if that were possible). In both these ways, Nietzsche remains consistent throughout this work. A contrast with the role of philosophy is instructive here – for Nietzsche, art uses myth but does not pass it off as truth; philosophy does not use myth and seeks to legislate value based on the true personality of an exemplar.

5–6 Wagner's redemption of modern culture

In the previous section, Nietzsche identified the significance of Wagner's art in justifying the value of existence. In sections 5–6, he discusses the significance of Wagner in the development of modern culture, which can guide the audience's efforts in assisting Wagner to live up to his role. As we have seen, Nietzsche rejects the Hegelian philosophy of history, according to which history necessarily moves in one direction. However, he also argues that exemplars ought to fit their efforts within the developments of their culture, and thus construct the appearance of progress in history. These exemplars should work within rather than against the currents of culture so as to increase their chances of success, but, more importantly, so as to redeem the existing culture. If an exemplar comes along and smashes a culture and then tyrannically puts it back together in his own image, all the previous efforts of that culture are without purpose. All those lives become meaningless. Instead, the exemplar must appear to be a 'transfiguring and legitimizing necessity', creating the image of a necessary development of a culture (290). In this case, the efforts of culture appear as necessary contributions to the genesis of an exemplar and thereby valuable. The apparent drawbacks of culture become reinterpreted as necessary instruments for the highest value. In other words, the sins of culture are thereby redeemed.

In section 5, Nietzsche begins his examination of the development of modern culture by asking why Wagner and a series of musical geniuses (such as Beethoven) have emerged now, at this point in history, when modernity is at such a nadir. Indeed, this 'series of great artists' is an 'event paralleled only once before, in the age of the Greeks' (281). What does it mean? Nietzsche discusses two reasons for Wagner's emergence and hence two contributions that he makes: the frustrations in modern culture about expressing genuine feeling and about developing a genuine character.

First, Nietzsche notes that 'Wagner was the first to recognize a state of distress' that modern individuals felt that in the 'civilized world *language* is diseased' (281, original emphasis). In the pre-modern world, Wagner argued in *Opera and Drama*, we used language 'to enable suffering human beings to communicate with one another about their most basic necessities of life'. However, the modern world, with the expansion of modern science and the accumulation of knowledge, has fetishised concepts. We have abstracted ourselves from our feelings and come to examine these general concepts themselves, such that 'language has everywhere become an autonomous force'. As a result of this 'madness of general concepts', we have become ever more unable to 'truly communicate [our] thoughts'. There arises 'mutual misunderstanding' through the use of these abstract terms (282). Furthermore, modern people eventually become 'slaves of words', so that we feel we must transform ourselves to serve the function of abstract concepts, rather than seeing language as serving our needs (282).

Suffering under this weight, modern culture thus embraces musicians, who can circumvent the conventions of language and express feeling directly. Their 'music is the return to nature', since 'such a return emerged in the soul of the most loving human beings' who seek an outlet for their love. Music does not represent feeling through convention, but rather expresses it directly – it is the 'purification and transformation of nature'. Music is an expression of natural feeling, as if our inner feeling were externalised, or, as Nietzsche puts it, 'nature transformed into love' (282).

Second, modern people have also begun to recognise the hollowness of their own character. Nietzsche rehearses some of the points he made in 'Utility and Liability' about the impoverished form of modern people's character. This character is all glittering surface, 'presumptuous superficiality' and 'pleasant appearance', but with no depth. Nietzsche now notices a 'gnawing dissatisfaction, laboring boredom, dishonest misery' with this condition. Modern culture has helped give rise to Wagner to unify our characters. According to Nietzsche, music 'expresses the longing for its natural sister, *gymnastics*' (283, original emphasis). That is, the experience of music does not remain at the level of mere feeling. The 'soul of music wishes to form a body for itself, that through you it seeks its path to visibility in motion, action, institution, and morality'. Indeed, Wagner himself exemplified this tendency of art, as he dramatised his music, embodying it in a story with characters on stage. The music embodied itself in a self-contained artistic unity in Wagner's works, and then expressed a further need in embodying itself in a unified character of individuals, and even in a unified 'state' based 'on music' (284).

This desire for wholeness, Nietzsche suggests, is a much more difficult contribution than the first one, as he concludes the section with a repetition of his battle metaphors and the 'avowed enemy of art', who embraces superficial surfaces and pleasure (285). For Nietzsche, his audience has to defeat the so-called 'art lover' who engages simply in the meticulous collection of 'fruitless art academies' and has abstract 'aesthetic interests' not at all connected to life (286). As Nietzsche repeats at several points in the *Observations*, the most important task for the unfashionable person is that 'he *must* nonetheless first negate in order to blaze a path for his helpful soul' (285, original emphasis).

Section 5, then, is part of Nietzsche's effort to construct a narrative of modern culture's future development. The problems of culture were necessary in order to give rise to a tremendous artist who could redeem those problems. Section 6 continues this discussion by delving further into the 'bad conscience' that modern culture has about itself (288). In modern life, we have come to celebrate above all else those who 'traffic in money' and who focus on the 'present', those, in other words, without 'spirit' [*Geist*] (287). Modern culture has grown increasingly base, interested solely in our animal desires, losing touch with what is distinctively human. Yet at the same time, our conscience stings us with its call to return to our humanity. It calls us to 'liberate' ourselves from the present. 'Wagner's art' promises just such a liberation (289).

Nietzsche calls on his audience not to regard Wagner's appearance as an 'empty, meaningless accident', because if it were so, he 'would have been crushed by the overpowering force' of modern obstacles. Rather, we should regard Wagner as the voice of our better nature, driven into our midst by a 'transfiguring and legitimizing necessity'. His art 'manifests reason, law, and purpose' for us. Instead of modern life appearing chaotic and random, finally everything appears orderly. It appears as if Wagner is the final development of a 'primordially determined nature', and his music is the 'bridge between self and nonself' of nature (290). In Wagner's music, we recognise our own errors, but errors that are incorporated into something higher and greater and thereby redeemed. His music 'resound[s]' in us because we *were least deserving of it but most in need of it* (291, original emphasis).

Nietzsche's remarks about the 'purposiveness' of nature reflect similar comments that he made in sections 6–7 of 'Schopenhauer as Educator'. These remarks, however, more clearly reveal that Nietzsche does not literally cleave to a natural teleology, but rather, in a Kantian fashion, holds that it is beneficial for us to think of nature in this way. Indeed, Nietzsche claims here that 'nature' is 'the most enigmatic thing under the sun', and he asks, 'who is capable of clearly naming the purpose for which it exists?' (290–1). We are 'able to guess that purposiveness from the manner of [nature's] evolution', but we can have no knowledge of it. We only can have the 'most blissful presentiment' [*seligsten Ahnung*] of purposiveness that derives from the exemplar's own redemptive efforts. From the 'perspective' of the exemplar 'we look back on life, then it radiates – no matter how dim and obscured it may previously have appeared' (291).

That Nietzsche adopts a Kantian rather than a Hegelian philosophy of history is important for his audience. Both Kantian and Hegelian philosophies of history posit that history is necessary for the emergence of the exemplary individual, thereby redeeming the efforts of the past. However, what makes Nietzsche's Kantian philosophy of history distinct is that it does not hold that progress towards the exemplar is in fact necessary. There may be features of modern culture that point towards the emergence of Wagner, but there are features that point away from him as well. Without the agency of human beings to help history along, Wagner could be destroyed by the hostile counter-forces to a rejuvenated culture. Far from being an unrepentant elitist, then, Nietzsche's democratic sentiments run deep. He says here that 'everyone should collaborate in [Wagner's] work' (290). If we were simply tools that the exemplar used for his own benefit, then our individual lives would hardly have any more value than an inanimate object that the exemplar uses. The exemplar, however, requires the agency of individuals around him, and so through the exertion of our freedom we can justify our existence.

7 The freedom of the audience

This section expands on the agency of the audience, because it may seem incredible to think that we can be important for the exemplar: 'the viewer who gazes upon a nature such as Wagner's must involuntarily be thrown back from time to time on himself, on his own insignificance and frailty, and he asks himself: "What does this nature want from you? Why do *you* actually exist?"' (291, original emphasis). The 'fact that he feels alienated from his own being' is an important, distinctive feature of human beings, which testifies to our capacity for freedom, to liberate ourselves from instinct and evaluate our desires. This 'observation' [*Betrachten*] involves a 'mysterious antagonism' between two parts of ourselves (291). Nietzsche's use of *Betrachten* here resonates with his use of

the term in section 1 of 'Utility and Liability', where he first introduced the contradiction at the heart of human beings. The use of
these terms in this context helps clarify the meaning of the title
of the work, *Unzeitgemässe Betrachtungen*. That is, his observations
are not just 'unfashionable' reflections on culture, but also timeless
reflections on our own nature.

Wagner's art dramatises this inner antagonism of the human
being. It does so in its very form, in the unique interplay between
music and drama in his works. The dramatic events of the works
always point towards the music to confer on them their full meaning. As Nietzsche describes it, 'everything visible in the world wants
to deepen itself and intensify its inwardness by becoming audible,
and it searches for its lost soul'. On the other hand, the music
demands embodiment in dramatic form, the characters living in
accordance with the other-worldly music: 'everything audible in
the world wants to emerge and rise up into light as a phenomenon
for the eye' (292). Or, otherwise put, in the terms discussed above,
Wagner's music dramas express the tension between our desire for
perfection and wholeness.

Nietzsche describes this tendency 'to retranslate visible motion
into soul and primal life and, on the other hand, to see the hidden
fabric of the inner world as a visual phenomenon and to give it
the semblance of a body' as the 'essence of the dithyrambic dramatist'. In this way, Wagner reflects the work of Aeschylus. Nietzsche's
use of the dithyrambic dramatist and his comparison of Wagner
and Aeschylus echo his own analysis in *The Birth of Tragedy*, written several years earlier. Importantly, however, the Dionysian and
Apollinian drives have disappeared, replaced by the drive for perfection and wholeness. Nietzsche's shift to a non-metaphysical
account of humanity and tragedy – attributed generally to his
middle and late periods – can already been seen here.

Indeed, rather than claiming that tragedy balances the Dionysian and Apollinian as he did in *The Birth of Tragedy*, he here argues
that the conflicting drives become interdependent in the work of
art. Wagner is the 'genuinely free artist', who is not constrained by
any particular didactic message or artistic genre or form. Instead,
he incorporates all forms together into an interdependent whole,
which 'mediates and conciliates between apparently separate

spheres'. Experiencing this work of art, the audience cannot latch on to a central principle for judgement, but we become 'transported beyond ourselves' and we 'no longer possess a criterion for judgments; everything governed by laws, everything fixed begins to move' (293). Within the work of art, we can engage in what Schiller called free play, tracing out the interconnections among the work's many parts. The artwork itself expresses freedom as self-determination, as the artwork is not determined by anything outside of itself, but is an interdependent, self-sufficient whole. Accordingly, the audience immersed in this art finds itself 'in free nature and in the realm of freedom'. It has transcended 'the horrible tension' of our human nature, between 'himself and the tasks that have been imposed upon him'. From this artistic perspective, 'we see . . . ourselves . . . as something sublime and meaningful' (294).

This account of Wagner's liberating artwork explains how we, the audience, can be free within it. Indeed, the promise of freedom within his art means that we 'crave and demand that [this] magician come to us', but at the same time 'we are afraid of him', because of the suffering involved in confronting our own nature (293). Nietzsche also reminds us of the redemptive character of exemplary individuals, that Wagner cares not just for his own artistic excellence, but that he also 'yearn[s] to descend out of the heights into the depths, the loving longing to return to earth, to the happiness of community'. Like the rest of us, Wagner is driven not only by the need for perfection, but also for wholeness. He seeks to '"lift up to heaven in fiery arms" all that is weak, human, and lost in order finally to find love and not just devotion, and to renounce himself utterly in love!' (295). He reveals our nature's 'most deeply hidden secrets' to us, and confers on us the 'wisdom of tragic thought' (296).

8 Wagner's life

Section 2 reintroduced the idea that, for Nietzsche, an exemplar's art and life reflect one another. Sections 4–7 proceeded to examine the significance of Wagner's art. Section 8 examines Wagner's life. It is an unusual biography in that it narrates his life in accordance with the two drives that Nietzsche thinks constitute Wagner's character. However, in examining his life in this way, Nietzsche can connect it with the tragic nature of life that he argues is central to Wagner's art.

Nietzsche divides Wagner's life into three 'stages' [*Stufen*]. In his early stage, the tyrannical 'turbulent drive' consumed him completely and his 'higher' artistic 'self' 'condescends to be of service' to this 'violent, more earthly brother' (299). As a result, he sought 'power and glory' among his contemporaries, 'influence, incomparable influence', even a 'tyrannical omnipotence toward which he was so darkly driven' (297). In his early operas – *Rienzi* and *The Flying Dutchman* – Wagner learned all the 'artistic devices' of the 'grand opera' of the time, particularly from the popular composer Giacomo Meyerbeer, all in an attempt to be known as the greatest composer in Germany (298).

The problem, Wagner quickly saw, was that his 'spectators and audience' were not 'worthy of and equal to the power of his work of art as he envisioned it' (300). He longed for greatness, but ruling over a base, philistine audience is no real power. As such, he sought a worthy audience that would reflect his greatness, and he found it in the '*poeticizing common people*' [*das dichtende Volk*] (299, original emphasis). In this 'intermediate', Romantic phase, Wagner understood the Volk to be the authentic source of humanity's creativity, the wellspring of 'myth and music' for each culture (301). By committing himself to the Volk, Wagner took the first step towards 'where the higher self is at home' (299), because he began to exert his tyrannical drive against himself, focusing his efforts not on ruling but on expressing and supporting the Volk. The outcome was love for the Volk, such that his drive for power and for love coincided.

Unfortunately, modern culture has attenuated our connection to nature, filling us with 'illusory needs' for 'luxury' (299). The disillusionment of modern culture has further led to the decline in myth, as we have seen already in 'Utility and Liability'. The old Volk-founding myths have been 'refashioned into "fairy tales"' for children (301). Finally, the artificial character of modern culture serves to 'exploit' in the 'most hardhearted and clever way' the Volk, turning 'those who are powerless ... ever more subservient, abject' (299). The Volk, already oppressed politically and economically by the elite, are further oppressed culturally, as the elite hijack culture and language and castigate the Volk as hopeless yokels on the basis of their philistine standards. In order to speak to the Volk, then, Wagner had to become a 'social revolutionary', making fiery speeches in support of the revolutions of 1848, for instance.

The challenge that Wagner faced at this stage was how to revive myth in the disillusioned modern age. His answer was to look to the 'music' that 'had survived among the poor and humble', and to embody this music in the myth of the past. Wagner's drama discovered, in Nietzsche's term, a 'middle realm between myth and music' (301). For Nietzsche, *Tannhäuser* and *Lohengrin* exemplify this middle stage, dramas about mythic heroes from medieval Germany. In retrieving these myths, Wagner does not intend his modern audience to believe in myth. Rather, he uses familiar myths to dramatise modern problems – the temptation of bodily desire and the need for redemption in *Tannhäuser*, and the problem of doubt and trust in modernity in *Lohengrin* – as voiced through the music of the Volk.

Unfortunately, Wagner was widely misunderstood – 'his work of art seemed to be a communication to the deaf and blind', and 'his "common people" a figment of the imagination'. He eventually repudiated his audience, and thus became 'a political refugee and destitute' (302). In sum, he did not find a worthy audience and so had to turn inward, 'to communicate with himself' to gain satisfaction (303). Yet doing so required that he turn his 'desire for supreme power' against itself, to 'channel' it 'completely into artistic creation'. In his art, then, he turned inward to explore 'suffering in the nature of things' (302), and produced *Tristan and Isolde*. This music drama is the 'true opus *metaphysicum* of all art' and explores the 'mystery of death in life, of unity in duality' (303). In composing this work, Wagner was influenced decisively by Schopenhauer. However, Wagner is not simply a Schopenhauerian pessimist, as demonstrated by his subsequent work, *The Meistersinger of Nuremberg*. That light-hearted work, according to Nietzsche, testifies to the 'genuinely and uniquely German cheerfulness of Luther, Beethoven, and Wagner', so that Wagner can affirm life through the 'gaze of love' and with the 'smile of the convalescent' even from the woes of modern culture (304). As such, Wagner can finally synthesise his two drives, as his drive for power masters itself in the form of love, and so his spirit of love can find its home at last.

Only once Wagner had repudiated his desire for glory did his 'friends' arrive, not the Volk but 'perhaps the kernel and first life-giving source of a true human society to be realised in a distant future' (304). With this hope, then, Wagner turned his attention to conceiving of a 'new style of execution' of his music dramas. He could not transmit them as 'signs on paper', because directors had been thoroughly unable to perform them in the transformative way that Wagner intends. Only by modelling how they should be performed himself can he show what kind of effect 'upon the human soul' his dramas promise to have (305). Thus, the 'idea of Bayreuth' – where Wagner would construct his own theatre and put on his *Ring of the Nibelungen* for the first time – helped keep that promise alive for a 'distant, merely possible, but not demon-strable future' (307). This labour caused Wagner 'a dark night of toil, worry, reflection, and grief', a self-sacrifice for the ideal of art that marks him decisively as an exemplary individual who lives the life of the 'tragic illusion' (308).

9 Wagner the artist

In section 9 Nietzsche examines the main aesthetic innovations of Wagner's art. He argues that Wagner's art is 'truly liberated', and serves as a 'cure and recovery of anyone who has thought about and suffered over *how Wagner the human being developed*' (308, original emphasis). In other words, Wagner suffered physically, psychologically and professionally throughout his life – he faced limitations all around him. However, in his art he demonstrated unparalleled freedom, a model for how human beings can liberate themselves from our given circumstances.

Nietzsche focuses on two of Wagner's aesthetic innovations – poetry and music. In his poetry, Wagner expresses himself 'in visible and palpable events', namely, through particular feelings, actions and characters. Wagner's poetry is not conceptual in nature, but rather 'mythic', 'just as the common people have always thought'. For Nietzsche, these myths could be translated into a conceptual language as the 'antithesis to the common people, the theoretical human being'. Yet in doing this, we 'would have understood nothing at all', as the particular passions of human beings can be articulated but not understood in conceptual terms (309). The only way to grasp these passions is by experiencing them through poetry, in which Wagner 'communicates his nature' to us (308). Note here that Nietzsche revisits the notion of myth not to describe it as falsifying the world – indeed it expresses truths that can be conceptually articulated – but as communicating feeling. In this way, Nietzsche is exploring a way in which myth and modernity can be combined.

Wagner's main poetic innovation, however, lies rather in the fact that he expresses poetry through music. The problem with mere 'spoken drama', that is, poetry in the form of plays, for instance, is that it needs to communicate 'emotion by means of concepts and words alone'. Poetry alone thus has to rely on a healthy, rich Volk language, a resource that Nietzsche argues is being corrupted day by day. In addition, poetry runs the 'risk' of appearing 'false and artificial' when it must ascend to the 'sublimity' of 'passion' (311). It must use elevated, forced language to express these elevated thoughts. Wagner innovates on poetry by expressing the sublime through music, so that it 'transmits the fundamental internal emotions of the drama's characters immediately to the souls of the audience' without any artificiality. By combining poetry and music, the audience's 'senses had become more spiritual and their spirit more sensual' (312). The audience enters into the interdependent, self-sufficient artistic whole of Wagner's work, in which the different parts of the system compensate for the deficiencies of the other parts.

In his music, Wagner completes Beethoven's innovation, moving music from expressing 'ethos' to 'pathos'. Prior to Beethoven, music was understood to express 'permanent human states of mind ... what the Greeks call ethos'. On this traditional view, music expresses archetypes – the masculine, the feminine, the divine. Beethoven was 'the first to let music speak a new language', that of 'pathos' (314). Instead of expressing an archetype, music captured the inner passions of unique individuals, the 'dramatic course' of our subjective lives. Nietzsche gives us an early glimpse of what he means by his later immoralism – the traditionalists 'spoke up' against this revolution 'with an attitude of morality, against the emergence of immorality' (315). The turn away from general homogenising archetypes to the diverse, inner life of individuals Nietzsche understands to be the transition from morality – living according to general rules – to immoralism – living in accordance with one's own unique rule. The problem, however, was that in Beethoven the 'succession of parts in a work became arbitrary' (315). That is, the expression of psychological states did not cohere into an overall unified story, and so possessed more depth but not the wholeness of the traditional archetypal music.

Wagner's innovation was to weave the many expressions of pathos in his music into a totality, akin to the 'great Ephesian philosopher' who conceived of the world as the 'harmony that discord produces out of itself'. First, Wagner captures in his music dramas a 'multitude of passions that run in various directions' (316). Nietzsche's point is best illustrated in Wagner's extraordinary use of leitmotifs in his music dramas – recurring melodic patterns that were used before Wagner to represent a particular person or event. Wagner also used leitmotifs to represent characters and things, but he allowed his leitmotifs to undulate, grow, transform along with the character throughout the course of the music drama. These leitmotifs, then, aimed to capture the inner life of the characters. Wagner incorporated hundreds of leitmotifs in his *Ring of the Nibelungen*. However, ultimately, these myriad leitmotifs cohere in the course of the drama into a resolved unity. Wagner reveals his artistic greatness in 'govern[ing] great relationships with the joy of the lawmaker. Subduing turbulent, resisting masses into simple rhythms, asserting one will throughout a confusing multitude of demands and desires' (317).

For Nietzsche, once again, Wagner's innovation reveals his 'freedom' as an artist. By freedom, Nietzsche means self-determination, that Wagner's artistic production was not determined by outside influences or forces, but that he 'impose[d] the most difficult laws upon himself' (317). When experiencing Wagner's music drama, the audience does not look to the external causes that brought it into being, but rather his artistic hand is 'concealed'. Instead, the work appears as a self-determined whole, in which the interdependent parts relate to one another with a 'necessary' direction and purpose.[2] This self-determined whole testifies to the 'joyous freedom' of the artist who created it, who could elevate himself beyond the causal order and create a self-determined, self-sufficient, self-enclosed system of meaning (318).

10 Wagner's influence

This section considers the lasting influence of Wagner's life and art. Nietzsche portrays Wagner as precisely the disruptive founder he has been looking for throughout the *Observations*. Wagner is an unfashionable figure, not belonging 'to this generation', and speaking 'to human beings of the future' (326). He legislates stylistic laws that govern all aspiring artists, 'subjugat[ing]' all, 'forfeiting their freedom' (318). He reveals all that is 'rotten' and 'poorly constructed' in the 'edifice of our civilization' and unsettles our order (322). Of all his contemporaries, Nietzsche judges Wagner as the best hope for transforming culture for the better. Unfortunately, the 'true plight of the artist of the future' is that he needs 'human souls as mediators to the future, public institutions as guarantors of this future, as bridges between the present and the times to come'. Philosophers, by contrast, can 'hunt down knowledge in a dark forest' and can transmit their personality in 'written records'. Artists require 'skilled people' as 'transmitters' (322). Once again, Nietzsche implicitly invokes his unfashionable audience to assist Wagner in this cultural transformation.

Wagner himself recognised that he needed to transmit the 'sacred depositum and true fruit of his existence' to 'posterity' not for selfish reasons, but because it is the 'property of humanity' (320). Wagner's own freedom would thus produce a 'freer humanity' (325). In order to achieve this 'immortality', however, he must establish those 'bridges to the future' (321). As we have seen, Nietzsche repeatedly employs the metaphor of the bridge over the stream of becoming to express the artificial nature of humanity's redemption, that we do not discover being, but create eternal forms that liberate us.

---

[2] See Ridley (2007) for an extended account of freedom along these lines.

For Nietzsche, Wagner is a distinctively modern exemplar in similar ways to the other modern exemplars we discussed, Rousseau, Goethe and Schopenhauer. He emerges from a modern fragmented age of knowledge, and somehow synthesises this into an immense whole undreamt of in the ancient world. In this section, Nietzsche highlights Wagner's synthesis of the classes that were divided in the modern age. Since 'the Renaissance', modern culture has divided the 'cultivated' from the 'uncultivated', the cosmopolitan men of letters from the nationalistic Volk (324–5). Wagner exploded this distinction, his music and poetry speaking to both classes, both expressing and elevating Volk myth. His work could 'illuminate those who are humble and poor in spirit and melt the arrogance of the learned' (325). Wagner offers the promise of unifying yet another division of modern culture, forging a genuine cultural community that all would take part in. In this way, Wagner channelled the loyalty to his nation, drawing on the fervour of the Volk, particularly in his 'Imperial March' (326). However, Nietzsche denies that Wagner was simply a nationalist (and thus implicitly denies that he himself is a nationalist). Wagner's 'generous impulse' is 'too great, the horizon of his love of humanity too expansive for his gaze to be enclosed within the boundaries of any one nation' (326). Like all exemplars of modernity, Wagner destroys the limitations of national horizons and encompasses humanity as a whole.

11 The call to the audience

Ultimately, then, Wagner's future fate lies in the untimely audience's hands. As a final inspiration to his audience, Nietzsche examines how Wagner's work is not just a reflection of his life and genius, but that it was 'written for *you*', that 'it is *our* life that Wagner placed under these stars' (330, original emphasis). Much of this section is devoted to discussing the main themes of Wagner's operas. Nietzsche then connects the characters of these operas to the unfashionable audience, arguing that at least one of the characters and their virtues – Wotan, Brünnhilde, Siegfried – must express the higher self of the audience member, drawing him or her aloft (330). If Wagner can accomplish this end for the untimely audience, Nietzsche suggests, consider what he could do for a future people. Wagner's transformation could confer on the future the 'freedom' that he himself possesses, as Nietzsche puts it in a draft of this section (393).

Most notably, in this final section Nietzsche employs the terms 'free' and 'freedom' several times, once again reinforcing the point that freedom is the final end or virtue of the exemplar. However, he also connects freedom to the transcendence of morality in a way that he has not yet in his career, a move that would increasingly characterise his philosophy of the middle and late periods. Nietzsche argues that 'being honest ... is better than losing oneself in traditional morality [*Sittlichkeit*]', and indeed that 'the free human being can be both good and evil, but that the unfree human being is a disgrace to nature and shares neither in any heavenly nor in any earthly consolation' (328). Nietzsche points ahead here to his critique of morality, yet the *Observations* nicely contextualises this critique as part of Nietzsche's overall positive project to liberate humanity.

6

The *Observations*' Influence on Nietzsche's Mature Thought

What is the significance of the *Observations* for Nietzsche's mature work? One common interpretation is that as Nietzsche matured, he came to see the book merely as a product of misguided youth (Brobjer 2004). For instance, in an 1879 letter to Paul Rée, Nietzsche states that his early works are 'only the eternal ah! And oh! Of my youth' (qtd Brobjer 2004: 307). In an 1882 letter to Elise Fincke, Nietzsche writes, 'I count these *Unfashionable Observations* as writings of youth' (qtd Jensen 2016: 160). Finally, in an 1885 draft preface to the *Observations*, he reflects that 'youth is something falsifying and deceitful', and that 'one is frightened to discover how little one saw when one sacrificed at these altars' (KSA 11.41[2]; qtd Brobjer 2004: 308).

However, as Jensen points out, to say that this book belongs to his youth does not mean that Nietzsche thinks it is 'wrong', but perhaps instead 'immature, unripe', introducing themes that he would develop further in his later works (2016: 162). Indeed, in support of this latter interpretation, Nietzsche sketches in 1885 plans for a 'new *Unfashionable Observation*' (KSA 11.41[2]; Breazeale 1998: 3), to complete the work he started. Furthermore, there is evidence that Nietzsche admired the book. When giving Lou Salomé a copy of 'Schopenhauer as Educator', he writes, 'this book contains my deepest sentiments' (qtd Breazeale 1998: 4). In *Ecce Homo*, Nietzsche writes that 'Richard Wagner' amounted to 'a vision of my future', while 'Schopenhauer as Educator' 'registers my innermost history, my *becoming*. Above all my *pledge!*' (EH 'Why I Write', 'Untimely Ones', 3, original emphasis).

There is another frequent way in which some scholars cast doubt on the significance of Nietzsche's early period – namely, to claim that he 'changed fundamental aspects of his Weltanschauung' in 1876, at the beginning of what scholars have regarded as his middle period (Brobjer 2004: 303). As Brobjer puts it, he 'exchanged his earlier enthusiasm for metaphysics, idealism, pessimism, art, and aesthetics to a position which was skeptical, free-spirited, placed science above art, and praised the Enlightenment' (2004: 303). Indeed, in late 1876, Nietzsche writes,

> To readers of my writings I want to declare unequivocally that I have abandoned the metaphysico-artistic views that essentially dominate those writings: they are pleasant but untenable. If one takes the liberty of speaking in public early one is usually obliged to contradict oneself in public soon after. (KSA 8.23[259], WEN 228)

In a notebook from early 1878, Nietzsche discusses several ways in which his views have changed – he has developed a 'dissatisfaction with tragic thinking' (KSA 8.27[34], HAH2 302) and seeks an 'antidote' to Schopenhauer's 'poisonous pessimism' (KSA 8.27[34], HAH2 305). He proclaims that he has 'had enough of the desire for illusions' (KSA 8.27[82], HAH2 310).

Nietzsche changes his attitude markedly towards Wagner, becoming even more critical of him than in his ambivalent notebook entries of 1874. Wagner is no longer the hope for the future, but on the contrary expresses the 'coarseness and the gentlest weakness, nature-drive barbarity and nervous oversensitivity, a passion for emotion out of exhaustion and a desire for exhaustion' of 'our age' (KSA 8.27[32], HAH2 302). Nietzsche admits that in 'Richard Wagner' he 'had depicted an ideal monster, but one who is perhaps capable of igniting artists'. The 'real Wagner' was 'like the bad, final impression of a copper etching on cheap paper' (KSA 8.27[44], HAH2 304).

It is clear that Nietzsche underwent a philosophical transformation that justifies distinguishing his early from his middle and late period writings. However, scholars often go too far in emphasising the break, and tend to overlook the continuities that exist in his thought, the themes and arguments from his early work that are developed later. Indeed, Nietzsche himself recognised the change and continuity in his own thought in a note from 1878. In it, he describes the overall 'plan' of his philosophy to gain 'insight into the endangerment of culture'. He begins with a recapitulation of the themes from the four *Observations*, discussing the obstacles to culture from the first half of the book and the possibilities from the second. Rather than narrating a radical break in his thought at this point, Nietzsche instead suggests that in his middle period he followed the same 'plan' but now found 'new dangers'; that, for instance, the 'metaphysical leads to contempt for the real' (KSA 8.30[166], HAH2 358–9). In other words, in his middle period Nietzsche continues his concern from the *Observations* to foster culture and freedom, but he comes to shift his understanding regarding the main obstacles to that end.

Hence, Nietzsche suggests that his early work persists in part in his later work, that there is some change but also some continuity. In his 1888 *Ecce Homo*, Nietzsche reflects that '*where* I am today . . . oh, how far from all this I still was at that time! But I *saw* the land . . . *and* the success' (EH 'Why I Write', 'Untimely Ones', 3, original emphasis). Indeed, in a draft letter from 1885, Nietzsche goes so far as to say that his *Observations* 'signify promises . . . Perhaps someone will yet discover that from *Human, All Too Human* on I have done nothing but fulfill my promises' (qtd Breazeale 1998: 7). To conclude, I will pick out a main idea from each *Observation* and show how Nietzsche sought to fulfil the 'promises' implicit in them.

Unity in 'David Strauss'

One of the main innovations of the first *Observation* is Nietzsche's famous definition of culture as the 'unity of artistic style that manifests itself throughout all the vital self-expressions of a people' (9).[1] As we saw above, Nietzsche argues that unity is good because it makes freedom as self-determination possible. The disunified culture is bad

---

[1] See Katsafanas (2016: ch. 7) for an excellent discussion of unity in Nietzsche's thought.

because its identity is determined by forces external to it. Nietzsche's example is German culture, which 'remain[s] dependent upon Paris in all matters of form' (10). German culture is not self-determining, but rather French culture shapes and rules it.

Unity becomes a guiding ideal not only for culture, but also for the individual in Nietzsche's middle and late period works. Nietzsche's famous aphorism 290 from *The Gay Science* reveals the abiding influence of the ideal of aesthetic unity sketched in 'David Strauss'. Nietzsche argues that the 'one thing' most 'needful' is to '"give style" to one's character', which involves surveying 'all the strengths and weaknesses that [one's] nature has to offer and then fit[ting] them into an artistic plan'. Thus, when 'the work is complete', we witness a 'single taste that ruled and shaped everything great and small'. Moreover, Nietzsche proceeds to justify this unity on the same grounds as in the early work, that a unified character is 'perfected under their own law', revealing autonomy. By contrast, the 'weak character' is defined as those with 'no power over themselves' (Nietzsche 2001b: 290).

In *Beyond Good and Evil*, Nietzsche bemoans our 'age of disintegration where the races are mixed together', such that a 'person will have the legacy of multiple lineages in his body'. This disunity of self and culture is bad because self and culture are determined by 'drives and value standards that fight with each other' (BGE 200). That is, self and culture do not guide and shape these determinations, but the determinations shape them. For Nietzsche, modern people respond very badly to this disunity, as they seek simply peace, the pacification of these drives and standards. They do not seek freedom, but mere animality. Better to be 'Alcibiades and Caesar' who inherit these 'powerful and irreconcilable drives' and seek to master them under a unified will (BGE 200). Indeed, several aphorisms later Nietzsche defines 'greatness' as 'unity in multiplicity', an individual's self-determined whole out of the 'very scope and variety of humanity' (BGE 212).

The value of history in 'Utility and Liability'

Several scholars have identified important continuities between Nietzsche's 'Utility and Liability' essay and his mature thought.

Breazeale (1998) and Nehamas (2006) both find in Nietzsche's view of 'critical history' a precursor to the later genealogical project. Critical history, like genealogy, uncovers the contingent and accidental origins of a feature of culture taken to be natural or necessary. As Breazeale points out, there are many examples of this crucial history, from *The Genealogy of Morality* through *Twilight of the Idols* and finally *The Antichrist* (1998: 70–1). Jensen points out that Nietzsche's epistemological reflections on history – that all historical narratives are products of particular cultures – prefigure his later perspectivism in important ways (2016: 163–7).

I focus here on the value of historical knowledge for Nietzsche. Brobjer has argued that Nietzsche 'ignored and criticized his second *Untimely Meditation* on history', and that his 'view and use of history after 1876 is of much greater use, interest, and relevance' (2004: 321–2). In particular, Brobjer argues that in 'Utility and Liability', Nietzsche denigrated historical knowledge, while in his later period he came to regard 'historical sense or sensibility and knowledge of history as important, even necessary' (2004: 317). However, a closer reading of 'Utility and Liability' reveals continuity rather than change on this point.

Indeed, 'Utility and Liability' emphasises the deleterious cultural consequences of an obsession with historical knowledge. As Brobjer himself recognises, Nietzsche continued throughout his career to be concerned with 'historical illness' (2004: 315–16). However, what Brobjer misses about 'Utility and Liability' is that Nietzsche is attuned both to the necessity and the benefits of historical knowledge. As we discussed above, 'Utility and Liability' considers the modern revolution a fait accompli – it is impossible to turn back the clock and close our historical horizons again and wilfully embrace illusion. More importantly, Nietzsche also recognises the value of modern historical knowledge, which liberates exemplars from their historical horizons. For instance, the virtue of 'justice', the 'truthful person' with the 'unconditional will to be just', is only possible now in the modern age on the basis of the modern explosion of historical horizons (122–3). Modern historical knowledge makes possible the 'most venerable exemplar of the human species' as the 'most noble kernel of the so-called urge to truth' (123–4). With this historical consciousness, we can 'set our goal higher and farther' than the ancients (141). Furthermore, the modern exemplar engages in a 'loving immersion in the empirical data', but does not endlessly accumulate such data. Instead, the exemplar ascends to a suprahistorical perspective to achieve wisdom about the 'given types' in all cultures (128). Finally, we should not do away with scholars of history. On the contrary, 'we should recognize them as necessary apprentices and journeymen in the service of their master' (130).

We can find these three related themes – the liberation of the exemplar, the nature of the historical consciousness and the role of the historical scholar – persisting into Nietzsche's mature thought. First, Nietzsche portrays the modern exemplar as categorically distinct from pre-modern individuals in virtue of the modern achievement of transcending all historical horizons. In *Thus Spoke Zarathustra*, for instance, Zarathustra states that at first, 'peoples were creators' and horizons were closed, just as Nietzsche had claimed in 'Utility and Liability'. Yet with the development of modernity, 'individuals' became the creators – 'Verily, the individual himself is still the most recent creation' (Nietzsche 1966: 59). Just as Nietzsche had portrayed the just individual as issuing the 'Last Judgment' for all humanity (123), so too does Zarathustra claim that 'humanity still has no goal', and the task of setting that goal belongs to the individual (Nietzsche 1966: 60).

Second, Nietzsche's mature discussions of the historical sense, far from departing from 'Utility and Liability', build on his account of the suprahistorical perspective. In *Beyond Good and Evil*, he defines the 'historical sense' as the 'ability quickly to guess the rank order of the valuations that a people, a society, an individual has lived by, the "divinatory instinct" for the connections between these valuations, for the relationship between the authority of values and the authority of effective forces' (BGE 224). What Nietzsche describes here as historical sense is not historical knowledge, or the accumulation of facts about a culture. Rather, it is akin to his view of 'wisdom', that is, an understanding of the relationship of the parts of a culture to the whole. Indeed, Nietzsche describes the wisdom of the suprahistorical thinker as the ability to 'illuminate the entire history of peoples and individuals from the inside, clairvoyantly divining the primordial meaning of the different hieroglyphs' (94).

In his late work, the historical sense is a 'divinatory instinct [*divinatorische Instinkt*]' for the relationship between whole and parts in a culture; in his early work, the suprahistorical perspective allows one to 'divine' [*erraten*] the fundamental principle of a culture from the inside, that is, from its many parts. For this reason, Nietzsche does not denigrate historical knowledge in 'Utility and Liability', but seeks to reinterpret its task as contributing to historical wisdom. In his late period work, Nietzsche is still after the same thing.

Third, in *Beyond Good and Evil*, as in 'Utility and Liability', Nietzsche castigates the 'objective spirits' and scholars of the day. However, he argues in both works that these individuals can be a 'tool' in 'the hands of someone more powerful' (BGE 207). The scholar can serve the purposes of achieving historical wisdom. Indeed, the mature Nietzsche builds upon this account by developing an account of the 'philosophical laborers' who systematise the valuations of a culture and serve the creative activity of the philosopher. Yet it is important to recognise that already in 'Utility and Liability', Nietzsche was not anti-science or anti-history, but sought to reinterpret the purpose of these activities towards the higher end of culture.

Exemplarity in 'Schopenhauer as Educator'

Breazeale has discussed three enduring themes from 'Schopenhauer as Educator' – the nature of the philosopher, the nature of the self and 'education as liberation' (1998: 17). These are important points, though I will focus instead on Nietzsche's central concept of the exemplar. The exemplar, in Nietzsche's view, exemplifies the distinctive excellence of humanity by embodying freedom as self-determination, legislating a table of values for a people, thereby redeeming humanity. Nietzsche's later work builds on each of these points in its portrayal of the higher man. Indeed, after completing book 1 of *Zarathustra*, in a letter 1883 to Peter Gast, Nietzsche states, 'It is curious: I wrote the commentary prior to the text! Everything was already promised in "Schopenhauer as Educator". But there was still a long way to go from *Human, All Too Human* to the "Übermensch"' (qtd Breazeale 1998: 7). He explicitly traces the origin of the *Übermensch* back to 'Schopenhauer as Educator'.

Nietzsche's famous portrait of the 'sovereign individual' from *The Genealogy of Morality* provides the best illustration of freedom as self-determination in the exemplar. The sovereign individual is 'like only to itself, having freed itself from the morality of custom', and so is an 'autonomous, supra-ethical individual'. He determines his own will, and so gives to himself his own 'standard of value'. This 'rare freedom and power over himself and his destiny' has 'penetrated him to the depths and become an instinct, his dominant instinct' that drives him (GM 2.2). That is, the sovereign individual is not determined by natural instinct or social pressure, but by a law that he has given to himself and internalised into his character. This notion of freedom is expressed already in the first section of 'Schopenhauer as Educator'.

The exemplar legislates a law for himself, but he also gives the law to a people. Already in section 3 of 'Schopenhauer as Educator', Nietzsche envisions the philosophical exemplars as the 'legislators of the measure, mint, and the weight of things' (193). Nietzsche would continue to conceive of the philosopher in this way, including in his famous discussion of the 'true philosophers' in *Beyond Good and Evil*, who are '*commanders and legislators*: they say "That is how it *should* be!" they are the ones who first determine the "where to?" and "what for?" of people' (BGE 211, original emphasis). Indeed, he argues later in *Beyond Good and Evil* that the life of the exemplar provides the 'meaning and highest justification [*Rechtfertigung*]' of the 'kingdom or community' that the exemplar helps create (BGE 258). Nietzsche's discussion of the *Rechtfertigung* of existence is rather ambiguously developed in this later text. The *Observations* provides great insight in its lengthy treatment of the problem of the value of existence, and how exemplars justify it.

However, the exemplar does not craft a community for his own personal interest, sacrificing others for his will, as is still the impression of many Nietzsche readers. Earlier in *Beyond Good and Evil*, Nietzsche describes the philosopher as having the 'most comprehensive responsibility, whose conscience bears the weight of the overall development of humanity' (BGE 61). The aim of the exemplar is to redeem humanity, not subject it to his will. We see this theme's first development in section 4 of 'Schopenhauer as Educator', and it becomes an enduring theme across his corpus.

For instance, in Zarathustra's speech 'On Redemption', he speaks of the task of the exemplar to 'redeem those who lived in the past', and he does so by reinterpreting 'it was' into 'thus I willed it', that is, by incorporating the suffering of the past as a necessary part of his own personality (Nietzsche 1966: 139).

Self-tyranny in 'Richard Wagner'

Several commentators have recognised in 'Richard Wagner' an embryonic concept of the will to power. In Wagner, Nietzsche states, 'there rages the rapid current of a violent will that seeks out, as it were, all paths, crevices, and ravines to bring itself to light and that desires power' (264). In my view, 'Richard Wagner' also anticipates the self-reflexive character of the will to power that becomes crucial to Nietzsche's mature period view of categorising and evaluating different expressions of the will to power. As we saw above, in sections 2 and 8 of 'Richard Wagner', Nietzsche argues that Wagner's drive for power does not find satisfaction in dominating the external world, and only achieves satisfaction through turning the drive for power against itself. In so doing, Wagner's drive for power unites with his free, creative spirit of love.

One of the enduring criticisms of Nietzsche's will to power is that it does not incorporate a normative perspective on higher and lower states of the soul, but rather reduces human excellence to quantitative degrees of power (Rosen 1989). Indeed, Nietzsche sometimes states that 'life itself is essentially a process of appropriating, injuring, overpowering the alien and the weaker, oppressing, being harsh, imposing your own form, incorporating, and at least, the very least, exploiting' (BGE 259). The will to power hence licenses brutal barbarism of all sorts, and does not allow us to distinguish between, say, the genius of Goethe and of Genghis Khan.

However, this criticism overlooks Nietzsche's reflections on the self-reflexive character of the will to power introduced already in 'Richard Wagner'. In his later period works, as Richardson (2004) has shown, Nietzsche conceives of higher stages of the will to power in how an agent exercises power over himself. In *Beyond Good and Evil*, for instance, Nietzsche argues that philosophy itself is a form of 'self-tyranny', which 'creates the world in its own image'. On this view, the philosopher does not dominate others physically, but dominates the desire to dominate others by offering a higher ideal or purpose for life. This higher ideal or purpose then dominates the minds of others, and so philosophy becomes the 'most spiritual will to power' (BGE 9). Indeed, Nietzsche is even clearer in the case of the 'saint', who exercises 'self-conquest' and thus expresses a 'strength of will' that all of us can 'recognize and honor', our 'own strength and pleasure in domination' (BGE 51).

Throughout his mature period, Nietzsche offers an account of why the spiritualisation or self-sublimation of the will to power generates a higher form of excellence in humanity. The blond beasts of *The Genealogy of Morality* are simple, superficial creatures, whereas slaves had to turn their will to power against themselves and thereby deepen their souls. Thus 'man first became an *interesting animal* on the foundation of this *essentially dangerous* form of human existence … and that the human soul became *deep* in the higher sense and turned evil for the first time' (GM.1.6, original emphasis). The 'history of mankind would be far too stupid a thing if it had not had the intellect [*Geist*] of the powerless injected into it' (GM.1.7). Slave morality ultimately defeated the noble morality of the ancients, because physical power is inherently limited, while the power of spirit can be universal. Spirit can dominate the body by reinterpreting it as evil or unclean. In this way, the spiritual norms of a people can master nature's instincts. For Nietzsche, however, the will to power must take a third, self-reflexive step, in which the individual exercises mastery over these spiritual norms and engages in individual self-determination (Richardson 2004: ch. 2, sections 3–4). These three steps are already prefigured in 'Richard Wagner', section 8.

Unfashionable Observations is a significant work of philosophy in its own right and also important for the light it can shed on Nietzsche's mature views. Indeed, as I have argued, readers are advised not simply to read the 'greatest hit' from this work – the 'Utility and Liability' essay – because a full understanding of each part of the book can only be obtained through a study of the whole. My hope is that this book has helped guide the reader through the parts to an understanding of the whole.

Glossary of Key Terms

Culture [*Kultur*]: the type of spiritual community that Nietzsche seeks to promote in the *Observations*, given the decline of religion in the modern age. A culture consists in a 'unity of artistic style that manifests itself throughout all the vital self-expressions of a people' (9). Its final aim is '*to foster the production of philosophers, artists, and saints within us and around us*' (213, original emphasis). The modern age, especially in Germany, manifestly fails to achieve culture in Nietzsche's view, producing instead a fragmented society that aims at satisfying the material aims of the state or the market.

Cultivated philistine [*Bildungsphilister*]: the chattering classes of Nietzsche's day. Public intellectuals, journalists and scholars who understand themselves to be cultured or educated, yet who have in Nietzsche's view an exceedingly shallow understanding and appreciation of genuine culture.

Cultivation [*Bildung*]: an important term that Nietzsche inherits from classical German thought, especially Goethe. Cultivation describes a comprehensive process of moral and intellectual development towards genuine culture. Nietzsche argues that modern people have 'no real cultivation, but rather only a kind of knowledge about cultivation' (110).

Education [*Erziehung*]: Nietzsche uses *Erziehung* rather than *Bildung* when describing his own view of moral and intellectual development. For Nietzsche, education involves a process of drawing out and up [*er-ziehen*] rather than of formation [*bilden*]. Education, above all, consists in 'liberation, removal of all weeds, rubble, and vermin' from one's self-development (175).

Exemplar [*Exemplar*]: a term that Nietzsche appropriates from Kant's *Critique of Judgment*. It refers to an individual who develops a novel way of life, lives this life with excellence, and founds or shapes culture based on his novel way of life and excellent embodiment of it. The exemplar expresses freedom as self-determination, and is the ultimate end of culture, for Nietzsche.

Freedom [*Freiheit*]: Nietzsche employs freedom in two senses: first, in a negative sense, freedom means liberation from the obstacles to self-development, especially the state, society and the market – the philosophical genius, Nietzsche says, needs 'freedom and nothing but freedom' from political interference in order to flourish (241). Second, in a positive sense, freedom means the capacity to 'live according to our own standards and laws' (173), a form of self-determination in accordance with 'the fundamental law of your authentic self' (174).

History [*Historie/Geschichte*]: Nietzsche uses two distinct German terms that translate 'history'. *Geschichte* is the more common word for history, and it refers in Nietzsche's text to the events of history, as when, for instance, he speaks of the 'history of [one's] city' becoming one's 'own history' (103). *Historie* refers to the reflection on, and study of, *Geschichte*. Above all, Nietzsche uses the term to describe the scientific study of history common in his day, though he also discusses three types of *Historie* (monumental, antiquarian and critical) from the pre-modern era.

Humanity [*Menschheit*]: humanity for Nietzsche represents a basic normative standard, which contrasts with 'animality' [*Tierheit*] (210). What is distinctive to humanity is that we can live in accordance with self-given laws or principles, while the animal is pushed and prodded by its instincts. Humanity also refers to the overall *telos* of the species as a whole, its achievement of freedom out of a purely animalistic origin. For instance, Nietzsche contrasts his view of humanity's end with Hegel's – 'the goal of humanity cannot possibly be found in its end stage, but only in its highest specimens [*Exemplaren*]' (151).

Idealism [*Idealismus*]: Kant's Transcendental Idealism holds that the standards of truth and the good are not derived from the world, but rather from the categories and laws legislated by our own reason or subjectivity. Nietzsche draws on this 'idealism' and the 'extreme relativity of all knowledge and reason' to support his own ethical idealism (35). According to Nietzsche's idealism, the normative standard for the good life does not come from the world outside us, but from a self-generated law that we give to ourselves.

Life [*Leben*]: Nietzsche's term to capture the formal nature and end of biological things. He describes it as 'that dark, driving, insatiable power that lusts after itself' (106). All living things experience desire, an expression of incompleteness, and all life strives for wholeness. The striving of all living things for wholeness entangles them in a struggle for existence. Nietzsche at first measures history according to how well it promotes life, which has led some scholars to identify life as his fundamental normative standard. I disagree, arguing instead that human beings can liberate themselves from the drives of life, which introduces a higher normative standard.

Shaping power [*Plastische Kraft*]: an important precursor to Nietzsche's mature period notion of the 'will to power'. The shaping power is that capacity of all living things to transform the external world in their own image. For most biological creatures, the shaping power is exerted by 'incorporating' or consuming the external world. We human beings can use our shaping power at a higher level to 'incorporate' the external world into a value system of our own making (90).

Guide to Further Reading on the *Observations*

Keith Ansell-Pearson, 'Holding on to the Sublime': an analysis of each essay, focusing on the general theme of the sublime.

Shilo Brooks, *Nietzsche's Culture War*: a comprehensive examination of the work as a whole that attends to the political and cultural context for Nietzsche's text.

Jeffrey Church, *Nietzsche's Culture of Humanity*: a reconstruction of Nietzsche's early period argument as a whole, including *The Birth of Tragedy*, 'On Truth and Lies in an Extra-Moral Sense', and other works, focusing on the ideal of culture.

James Conant, 'Nietzsche's Perfectionism': an important Kantian and even egalitarian reading of 'Schopenhauer as Educator'.

Christian Emden, *Friedrich Nietzsche and the Politics of History*: a helpful examination of the political context for and influences on Nietzsche's early view of history.

Anthony Jensen, *An Interpretation of Nietzsche's 'On the Uses and Disadvantage of History for Life'*: a rigorous philological analysis of 'Utility and Liability', as well as an insightful philosophical examination of the work, focusing on its epistemological elements.

Katrin Meyer, *Ästhetik der Historie*: a thorough treatment and reconstruction of 'Utility and Liability', with attention to the aesthetic nature of history.

Richard Schacht, 'Nietzsche's First Manifesto': a useful overview of the main concerns and argument of 'Schopenhauer as Educator', in Schacht 1995.

Quentin P. Taylor, *Republic of Genius*: a reconstruction of Nietzsche's early period argument as a whole, focusing on the themes of nature, spirit, the Greeks and the state.

Bernard Yack, *The Longing for Total Revolution*: a discussion of the early Nietzsche in the context of the post-Kantian philosophical tradition that 'longs for total revolution'.

Catherine Zuckert, 'Nature, History and the Self': an illuminating close reading of 'Utility and Liability' and 'Schopenhauer as Educator' that focuses on Nietzsche's critique of modernity.

Bibliography

Acampora, Christa Davis. 2006. 'On Sovereignty and Overhumanity: Why It Matters How We Read Nietzsche's *Genealogy* II:2', in *Nietzsche's On the Genealogy of Morals: Critical Essays*, ed. Christa Davis Acampora. Lanham, MD: Rowman & Littlefield, 147–62.

Ansell-Pearson, Keith. 2013. 'Holding on to the Sublime: On Nietzsche's Early Unfashionable Project', in *The Oxford Handbook to Nietzsche*, ed. Ken Gemes and John Richardson. Oxford: Oxford University Press, 226–51.

Appel, Fredrick. 1999. *Nietzsche contra Democracy*. Cambridge, MA: Cambridge University Press.

Arrowsmith, William, ed. 1990. *Nietzsche's Unmodern Observations*. New Haven, CT: Yale University Press.

Bambach, Charles R. 1990. 'History and Ontology: A Reading of Nietzsche's Second "Untimely Meditation"', *Philosophy Today*, 34.3: 259–72.

Beiser, Frederick. 2011. *The German Historicist Tradition*. Oxford: Oxford University Press.

— 2014. *The Genesis of Neo-Kantianism, 1796–1880*. Oxford: Oxford University Press.

— 2016. *Weltschmerz: Pessimism in German Philosophy, 1860–1900*. Oxford: Oxford University Press.

Bergmann, Peter. 1987. *Nietzsche, 'The Last Antipolitical German'*. Bloomington: Indiana University Press.

Berkowitz, Peter. 1995. *Nietzsche: The Ethics of an Immoralist*. Cambridge, MA: Harvard University Press.

Bernstein, J. M., ed. 2003. *Classic and Romantic German Aesthetics*. Cambridge: Cambridge University Press.

Blue, Daniel. 2016. *The Making of Friedrich Nietzsche: The Quest for Identity, 1844–1869.* Cambridge: Cambridge University Press.

Borchmeyer, Dieter. 1996. 'Nietzsches zweite "Unzeitgemässe Betrachtung" und die Ästhetik der Postmoderne', in *'Vom Nutzen und Nachteil der Historie für das Leben': Nietzsche und die Erinnerung in der Moderne*, ed. Dieter Borchmeyer. Frankfurt: Suhrkamp, 196–217.

Breazeale, Daniel, 1998. 'Becoming Who One Is: Notes on "Schopenhauer as Educator"', *New Nietzsche Studies*, 2.3/4: 1–25.

—— 2000. 'Nietzsche, Critical History, and "Das Pathos der Richtertum"', *Revue Internationale de Philosophie*, 54.211: 57–76.

Brobjer, Thomas H. 2004. 'Nietzsche's View of the Value of Historical Studies and Methods', *Journal of the History of Ideas*, 65.2: 301–22.

—— 2008. *Nietzsche's Philosophical Context: An Intellectual Biography.* Urbana: University of Illinois Press.

Brooks, Shilo. 2018. *Nietzsche's Culture War: The Unity of the Untimely Meditations.* Basingstoke: Palgrave Macmillan.

Cavell, Stanley. 1990. *Conditions Handsome and Unhandsome: The Constitution of Emersonian Perfectionism.* The Carus Lectures, 1988. Chicago: University of Chicago Press.

Church, Jeffrey. 2015a. *Nietzsche's Culture of Humanity: Beyond Aristocracy and Democracy in the Early Period.* Cambridge: Cambridge University Press.

—— 2015b. 'The Aesthetic Justification of Existence: Nietzsche on the Beauty of Exemplary Lives', *Journal of Nietzsche Studies*, 46.3: 289–307.

—— 2016. 'Nietzsche's Early Ethical Idealism', *Journal of Nietzsche Studies*, 47.1: 81–100.

Clark, Maudemarie. 1990. *Nietzsche on Truth and Philosophy.* New York: Cambridge University Press.

—— 1999. 'Nietzsche's Antidemocratic Rhetoric', *Southern Journal of Philosophy*, 37.51: 119–41.

Conant, James. 2001. 'Nietzsche's Perfectionism: A Reading of Schopenhauer as Educator', in *Nietzsche's Postmoralism*, ed. Richard Schacht. Cambridge, MA: Cambridge University Press, 181–256.

Crawford, Claudia. 1988. *The Beginnings of Nietzsche's Theory of Language*. Berlin: Walter de Gruyter.

Dannhauser, Werner. 1990. 'Introduction to "History in the Service and Disservice of Life"', in Friedrich Nietzsche, *Unmodern Observations*, ed. William Arrowsmith. New Haven, CT: Yale University Press, 75–86.

Detwiler, Bruce. 1990. *Nietzsche and the Politics of Aristocratic Radicalism*. Chicago: University of Chicago Press.

Emden, Christian. 2005. *Nietzsche on Language, Consciousness, and the Body*. Urbana: University of Illinois Press.

— 2008. *Friedrich Nietzsche and the Politics of History*. Cambridge: Cambridge University Press.

— 2014. *Nietzsche's Naturalism: Philosophy and the Life Sciences in the Nineteenth Century*. Cambridge: Cambridge University Press.

Foucault, Michel. 1984. 'Nietzsche, Genealogy, History', in *The Foucault Reader*, ed. Paul Rabinow. New York: Pantheon Books, 76–100.

Franco, Paul. 2011. *Nietzsche's Enlightenment: The Free-Spirit Trilogy of the Middle Period*. Chicago: University of Chicago Press.

Gemes, Ken, and Simon May, eds. 2009. *Nietzsche on Freedom and Autonomy*. Oxford: Oxford University Press.

Gerhardt, Volker. 1988. 'Leben und Geschichte: Menschliches Handeln und historischer Sinn in Nietzsches zweiter "Unzeitgemässer Betrachtung"', in *Pathos und Distanz: Studien zur Philosophie Friedrich Nietzsches*. Stuttgart: Philipp Reclam, 133–62.

Gray, Richard. 1995. 'Translator's Afterword', in Friedrich Nietzsche, *Unfashionable Observations*, trans. Richard T. Gray. Stanford: Stanford University Press, 395–413.

Green, Michael Steven. 2002. *Nietzsche and the Transcendental Tradition*. Champaign: University of Illinois Press.

Habermas, Jürgen. 1993. 'The Entry into Postmodernity: Nietzsche as a Turning Point', in *Postmodernism: A Reader*, ed. Thomas Docherty. New York: Harvester, 51–61.

Hartmann, Eduard von. 1931. *Philosophy of the Unconscious: Speculative Results according to the Inductive Method of Physical Science*, trans. William Chatterton Coupland. New York: Harcourt, Brace.

Havas, Randall. 2000. 'Nietzsche's Idealism', *Journal of Nietzsche Studies*, 20: 90–9.

Hayman, Ronald. 1980. *Nietzsche: A Critical Life*. Harmondsworth: Penguin.

Hegel, G. W. F. 1991a. *The Philosophy of Right*, trans. H. B. Nisbet. Cambridge: Cambridge University Press.

— 1991b. *The Encyclopedia Logic*, trans. T. F. Geraets, W. A. Suchting and H. S. Harris. Indianapolis: Hackett Publishing.

Heidegger, Martin. 2016. *Interpretation of Nietzsche's Second Untimely Meditation*, trans. Ullrich Haase and Mark Sinclair. Bloomington: Indiana University Press.

Hill, R. Kevin. 2003. *Nietzsche's Critiques: The Kantian Foundations of his Thought*. New York: Oxford University Press.

Hollingdale, R. J. 1999. *Nietzsche: The Man and His Philosophy*. Cambridge: Cambridge University Press.

Hübner, Kurt. 1996. 'Vom theoretischen Nachteil und praktischen Nutzen der Historie: Unzeitgemässes über Nietzsches unzeitgemässe Betrachtungen', in *'Vom Nutzen und Nachteil der Historie für das Leben': Nietzsche und die Erinnerung in der Moderne*, ed. Dieter Borchmeyer. Frankfurt: Suhrkamp, 28–47.

Hurka, Thomas. 2007. 'Nietzsche: Perfectionist', in *Nietzsche and Morality*, ed. Brian Leiter and Neil Sinhababu. New York: Oxford University Press, 9–31.

Hussein, Nadeem. 2004. 'Nietzsche's Positivism', *European Journal of Philosophy*, 12.3: 326–68.

— 2007. 'Honest Illusion: Valuing for Nietzsche's Free Spirits', in *Nietzsche and Morality*, ed. Brian Leiter and Neil Sinhababu. New York: Oxford University Press, 157–91.

Janaway, Christopher. 2006. 'Nietzsche on Free Will, Autonomy and the Sovereign Individual', *Aristotelian Society Supplementary Volume*, 80.1: 339–57.

Jenkins, Scott. 2014. 'Nietzsche's Use of Monumental History', *Journal of Nietzsche Studies*, 45.2: 169–81.

Jensen, Anthony. 2013. *Nietzsche's Philosophy of History*. Cambridge: Cambridge University Press.

— 2016. *An Interpretation of Nietzsche's On the Uses and Disadvantage of History for Life*. New York: Routledge.

Johnson, Dirk R. 2001. 'Nietzsche's Early Darwinism: the "David Strauss" Essay', *Nietzsche-Studien*, 30: 62–79.

Kant, Immanuel. 1996. *Practical Philosophy*. Cambridge: Cambridge University Press.

— 2000. *Critique of the Power of Judgment*, trans. Paul Guyer and Eric Matthews. Cambridge: Cambridge University Press.

— 2007. *Anthropology, History, and Education*. Cambridge: Cambridge University Press.

Katsafanas, Paul. 2016. *The Nietzschean Self*. Oxford: Oxford University Press.

Kaufmann, Walter. 1978. *Nietzsche: Philosopher, Psychologist, Antichrist*. Princeton: Princeton University Press.

Köhnke, Klaus Christian. 1991. *The Rise of Neo-Kantianism: German Academic Philosophy Between Idealism and Positivism*, trans. R. J. Hollingdale. Cambridge: Cambridge University Press.

Lacoue-Labarthe, Philippe. 1990. 'History and Mimesis', in *Looking After Nietzsche*, ed. Laurence A. Rickels. New York: SUNY Press, 209–32.

Lampert, Laurence. 1993. *Nietzsche and Modern Times: A Study of Bacon, Descartes, and Nietzsche*. New Haven, CT: Yale University Press.

Large, Duncan. 2012. 'Untimely Meditations', in *A Companion to Friedrich Nietzsche: Life and Works*, ed. Paul Bishop. Rochester, NY: Camden House, 86–108.

Leiter, Brian. 2010. 'Who is the "Sovereign Individual"? Nietzsche on Freedom', in *The Cambridge Critical Guide to Nietzsche's On the Genealogy of Morality*, ed. Simon May. Cambridge: Cambridge University Press, 101–19.

— 2013. 'Nietzsche's Naturalism Reconsidered', in *The Oxford Handbook of Nietzsche*, ed. John Richardson and Ken Gemes. Oxford: Oxford University Press, 576–98.

Lemm, Vanessa. 2007. 'Is Nietzsche a Perfectionist? Rawls, Cavell, and the Politics of Culture in Nietzsche's "Schopenhauer as Educator"', *Journal of Nietzsche Studies*, 34.34: 5–27.

— 2010. 'History, Life, and Justice in Friedrich Nietzsche's *Vom Nutzen und Nachteil der Historie für das Leben*', *The New Centennial Review*, 10.3: 167–88.

— 2013. 'Nietzsche, Einverleibung, and the Politics of Immunity', *International Journal of Philosophical Studies*, 21.1: 3–19.

Magnus, Bernd, and Kathleen Higgins. 1996. 'Nietzsche's Works and Their Themes', in *The Cambridge Companion to Nietzsche*, ed. Bernd Magnus and Kathleen Higgins. Cambridge: Cambridge University Press, 21–70.

Martin, Nicholas. 1996. *Nietzsche and Schiller: Untimely Aesthetics*. New York: Oxford University Press.

Meyer, Katrin. 1998. *Ästhetik der Historie: Friedrich Nietzsches 'Vom Nutzen und Nachteil der Historie für das Leben'*. Würtzburg: Königshausen & Neumann.

Moore, Gregory. 2002. *Nietzsche, Biology, and Metaphor*. New York: Cambridge University Press.

Nehamas, Alexander. 2006. 'The Genealogy of Genealogy: Interpretation in Nietzsche's Second Untimely Meditation and in On the Genealogy of Morals', in *Nietzsche's On the Genealogy of Morals: Critical Essays*, ed. Christa Davis Acampora. Lanham, MD: Rowman & Littlefield, 57–66.

Niemeyer, Christian. 2009. 'Vom Nutzen und Nachteil der Historie für das Leben', in *Nietzsche-Lexikon*, ed. Christian Niemeyer. Darmstadt: Wissenschaftliche Buchgesellschaft, 50–6.

Nietzsche, Friedrich. 1962. *Philosophy in the Tragic Age of the Greeks*, trans. Marianne Cowan. Washington, DC: Regnery Publishing.

— 1966. *Thus Spoke Zarathustra*, trans. Walter Kaufmann. Harmondsworth: Penguin.

— 1986. *Sämtliche Briefe*, ed. Giorgio Colli and Mazzino Montinari. Berlin: Walter de Gruyter.

— 1990. *Unmodern Observations*, ed. William Arrowsmith. New Haven, CT: Yale University Press.

— 1994. *On the Genealogy of Morality*, trans. Carol Diethe. Cambridge: Cambridge University Press.

— 1995a. *Unfashionable Observations*, trans. Richard T. Gray. Stanford: Stanford University Press.

— 1995b. *Unpublished Writings from the Period of Unfashionable Observations*, trans. Richard T. Gray. Stanford: Stanford University Press.

— 1999a. *The Birth of Tragedy*, trans. Ronald Speirs. Cambridge: Cambridge University Press.

— 1999b. *Kritische Studienausgabe*, ed. Giorgio Colli and Mazzino Montinari. Berlin: Walter de Gruyter.

— 2001a. *The Pre-Platonic Philosophers*, trans. Greg Whitlock. Urbana: University of Illinois Press.

— 2001b. *The Gay Science*, trans. Josefine Nauckhoff. Cambridge: Cambridge University Press.

— 2002. *Beyond Good and Evil*, trans. Judith Norman. Cambridge: Cambridge University Press.

— 2004. *On the Future of Our Educational Institutions*, trans. Michael W. Grenke. South Bend, IN: St. Augustine's Press.

— 2005. *The Anti-Christ, Ecce Homo, Twilight of the Idols, and Other Writings*, trans. Judith Norman. Cambridge: Cambridge University Press.

— 2009. *Writings from the Early Notebooks*, trans. Ladislaus Löb. Cambridge: Cambridge University Press.

— 2013. *Human, All Too Human II*, trans. Gary Handwerk. Stanford: Stanford University Press.

Nietzsche Research Group, ed. 2004. *Nietzsche-Wörterbuch, Band 1: Abbreviatur-einfach*. Berlin: Walter de Gruyter.

Norton, Robert. 2007. 'The Myth of the Counter-Enlightenment', *Journal of the History of Ideas*, 68.4: 635–58.

Ottmann, Henning. 1999. *Philosophie und Politik bei Nietzsche*. Berlin: Walter de Gruyter.

— ed. 2000. *Nietzsche-Handbuch: Leben–Werk–Wirkung*. Stuttgart: Metzler.

Pinkard, Terry. 2002. *German Philosophy, 1760–1860: The Legacy of Idealism*. Cambridge: Cambridge University Press.

Pletsch, Carl. 1991. *Young Nietzsche: Becoming a Genius*. New York: The Free Press.

Reich, Hauke. 2012. *Rezensionen und Reaktionen Zu Nietzsches Werken: 1872–1889*. Berlin: Walter de Gruyter.

Richardson, John. 2004. *Nietzsche's New Darwinism*. Oxford: Oxford University Press.

Ridley, Aaron. 2007. 'Nietzsche on Art and Freedom', *European Journal of Philosophy*, 15.2: 204–24.

Rosen, Stanley. 1989. *The Ancients and the Moderns: Rethinking Modernity*. New Haven, CT: Yale University Press.

Rousseau, Jean-Jacques. 2012. *The Major Political Writings of Jean-Jacques Rousseau*, trans. John T. Scott. Chicago: University of Chicago Press.

Safranski, Rüdiger. 2002. *Nietzsche: A Philosophical Biography*, trans. Shelley Frisch. New York: W. W. Norton.

Salaquarda, Jörg. 1984. 'Studien zur Zweiten Unzeitgemässen Betrachtung', *Nietzsche-Studien*, 13.1: 1–45.

Schaberg, William H. 1995. *The Nietzsche Canon: A Publication History and Bibliography*. Chicago: University of Chicago Press.

Schacht, Richard. 1995. *Making Sense of Nietzsche: Reflections Timely and Untimely*. Urbana: University of Illinois Press.

Scheibenberger, Sarah. 2016. *Kommentar zu Nietzsches Ueber Wahrheit und Lüge im aussermoralischen Sinne*. Berlin: Walter de Gruyter.

Schiller, Friedrich. 2003. 'Kallias or Concerning Beauty: Letters to Gottfried Körner', in *Classic and Romantic German Aesthetics*, ed. J. M. Bernstein. Cambridge: Cambridge University Press, 145–84.

— 2004. *On the Aesthetic Education of Man*, trans. Reginald Snell. New York: Dover Publications.

Schopenhauer, Arthur. 2009. *The Two Fundamental Problems of Ethics*, trans. Christopher Janaway. Cambridge: Cambridge University Press.

— 2014. *Parerga and Paralipomena: Short Philosophical Essays*, trans. Sabine Roehr and Christopher Janaway. Cambridge: Cambridge University Press.

Shaw, Tamsin. 2007. *Nietzsche's Political Skepticism*. Princeton: Princeton University Press.

Smith, Gregory Bruce. 1996. *Nietzsche, Heidegger, and the Transition to Postmodernity*. Chicago: University of Chicago Press.

Smith, Steven B. 1989. *Hegel's Critique of Liberalism: Rights in Context*. Chicago: University of Chicago Press.

— 2016. *Modernity and Its Discontents: Making and Unmaking the Bourgeois from Machiavelli to Bellow*. New Haven, CT: Yale University Press.

Solomon, Robert C. 1998. 'A More Severe Morality: Nietzsche's Affirmative Ethics', in *Nietzsche: Critical Assessments*, vol. 3: *On Morality*, ed. Daniel Conway and Peter Groff. New York: Routledge, 321–39.

Stack, George J. 1983. *Lange and Nietzsche*. Berlin: Walter de Gruyter.

— 1993. *Nietzsche & Emerson: An Elective Affinity*. Athens: Ohio University Press.

Strauss, David F. 1997. *The Old Faith and the New*, trans. Mathilde Blind. Amherst, NY: Prometheus Books.

Strauss, Leo. 1964. *The City and Man*. Chicago: University of Chicago Press.

Taylor, Quentin P. 1997. *Republic of Genius: A Reconstruction of Nietzsche's Early Thought*. Rochester, NY: University of Rochester Press.

Yack, Bernard. 1992. *The Longing for Total Revolution: Philosophic Sources of Social Discontent from Rousseau to Marx and Nietzsche*. Chicago: University of Chicago Press.

Young, Julian. 2006. *Nietzsche's Philosophy of Religion*. Cambridge: Cambridge University Press.

— 2010. *Friedrich Nietzsche: A Philosophical Biography*. Cambridge: Cambridge University Press.

— ed. 2014. *Individual and Community in Nietzsche's Philosophy*. Cambridge: Cambridge University Press.

Zuckert, Catherine. 1976. 'Nature, History and the Self: Friedrich Nietzsche's Untimely Considerations', *Nietzsche-Studien*, 5.1: 55–82.

Index

great justice, semblance of justice
    and, 100–4
great thinker, 137
greatness, 79–81, 108
    of individual, 84, 166
    nature and, 165–6
    the Greeks, 9, 99
    culture of, 69
    Nietzsche as student of, 59–60
    polis, 27, 87
    on value, of existence, 154

habit, of antiquarianism, 87–8
happiness
    active life and, 78–9
    of animals, 63–4
    in humanity, 119, 161–2
    knowledge of, 66
    modern scientific knowledge
        and, 118–19
Hartmann, Eduard von, 117–21
health, of cultures, 69
heaven, 38–42
Hegel, G. W. F., 60, 103, 118,
    209–10
    on Greek polis, 87
    philosophy, of history, 114–15
    Philosophy of Right by, 34
Hegelian idolatry, 114–16
Heidegger, Martin, 55
the Hellenic, 210–11
Heraclitus, 66
hero worship, 176
heroism, 167
heuristic, of nature, 189
historical age, 58–60, 81–2
historical cultivation, 112, 114
historical education, 128
historical existence, 88
historical individual, 74–5
historical justice, 109

historical knowledge, 58–9, 70,
    96–7, 123, 127
historical life, 84–5
historical memory, 64–7
historical perspective, 75–8, 86–7
historicism, 34, 76
history, 241
    ancient approaches to, 104
    culture and, 55
    diversity of human aspirations
        in, 49
    end of, 113–15, 118, 121
    exemplar and, 76, 159–60
    explanatory nature of, 64
    faith and, 113
    fictitious, 83
    as flux, 66, 80
    German, 32–3
    Hegel on, 114–15
    human beings in, 58, 62–3
    individual in, 85, 116
    laws of, 66
    modern scientific approach
        to, 77
    monumental-critical, 107–8
    normative nature of, 64
    of philosophy, 98–9
    philosophy of, 111–16, 120
    pre-modern, 77, 100
    reason in, 43
    of science, 74, 87–8, 93
    in service of life, 73
    transition from ancient to
        modern, 92–6
    types of, 77, 92, 160
    value of, 58, 233–6
    Wagner on, 209–10
    see also antiquarian history;
        critical history; monumental
        history; new history; the
        suprahistorical